ELEMENTARY SCHOOL SOCIAL STUDIES
FOR TODAY'S CHILDREN

EXPLORATION SERIES IN
EDUCATION Under the Advisory Editorship of JOHN GUY FOWLKES

ELEMENTARY SCHOOL SOCIAL STUDIES FOR TODAY'S CHILDREN

JOHN E. ORD
BRIGHAM YOUNG UNIVERSITY

HARPER & ROW
PUBLISHERS   New York   Evanston   San Francisco   London

CONTENTS

REFACE

Over the past decade there has been a ferment in the social studies that has resulted in many notable developments, alterations, and improvements of the entire curricular pattern for instruction in elementary social studies. Today there are many guidelines as to the future direction these advances may take. Increased emphasis is being placed on the skills of inquiry and problem solving, on inductive approaches to learning, and on creativity. Individualization of instruction in the social studies has now become a reality, with effective means available for its accomplishments.

The central purposes of this book are to (1) identify the major approaches, trends, and developments in the social studies; (2) provide both preservice and in-service teachers with more modern methods of teaching the social studies, particularly to help each child achieve his fullest potential in the social studies through individualization of instruction; and (3) suggest numerous ways in which teachers may help each boy and girl grow to maturity as a more responsible, sensitive citizen of our great nation.

In the first chapter the goals of the social studies are identified, and the contribution of each separate social science discipline to elementary school social studies is described. In Chapter 2 traditional approaches to teaching the social studies are discussed and newer trends and developments are identified. Chapters 3 and 4 contain a discussion of modern teaching strategies, including the unit approach to teaching the social studies and methods of constructing individualized units of work. Chapter 5 is devoted to a discussion of maps and globes and to specific methods of instruction at both the primary and upper-grade levels of the elementary school. Chapter 6 contains a discussion of educational materials and media and identifies both the "hardware" and "software" available for more effective teaching of the social studies today. Chapter 7 deals with methods for more effective teaching of current affairs and controversial issues. Chapter 8 is concerned with a discussion of the important ingredients of citizenship education and international understanding. The final chapter is concerned with methods of effective evaluation of learning in the social studies. The Appendixes serve as additional sources of information and as guides for further study and exploration.

I am deeply indebted to many people who have directly influenced this work. Above all, I dedicate this book to my wife, Faun, who has provided moral and technical support. As an outstanding elementary school teacher, she has supplied many suggestions from a "practitioner's" point of view. I owe a great deal to other elementary school teachers who have so generously permitted me to observe their work in the classroom. Special thanks is given to elementary teachers in the Ogden City Schools and in Alpine School District who participated in social study workshops and contributed many ideas and units of work.

Finally, I am indebted to the many students, both undergraduate and graduate, from whom I have learned much and to my colleagues in the College of Education at Brigham Young University for their important contributions to my thinking.

J.E.O.

**ELEMENTARY SCHOOL SOCIAL STUDIES
FOR TODAY'S CHILDREN**

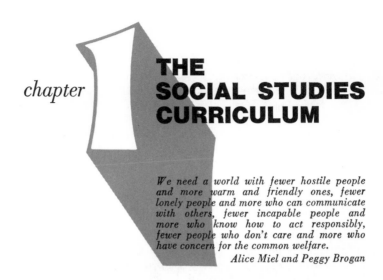

chapter

THE SOCIAL STUDIES CURRICULUM

We need a world with fewer hostile people and more warm and friendly ones, fewer lonely people and more who can communicate with others, fewer incapable people and more who know how to act responsibly, fewer people who don't care and more who have concern for the common welfare.

Alice Miel and Peggy Brogan

The forces of change are more wide-spread and more insistent today than ever before and are effecting change at an ever-increasing rate. The vast changes taking place in society are bringing with them many complex problems that challenge the ability of our political, economic, and social institutions to adapt and grow to meet the changing needs of our society. The capacity to bring the knowledge of the social sciences to bear effectively upon these problems will be of critical importance to the freedom and future well-being of our country. As yet the adaptations in the social studies have not been entirely satisfactory. Although much progress has been made, a serious lag still exists between what the social studies now teach and what might be accomplished if the new knowledge now available in the social science disciplines were utilized to best advantage.

THE IMPORTANCE OF THE SOCIAL STUDIES

Only recently has it been widely recognized that the magnitude of the social and technological changes occurring and the increases in knowledge required to meet them necessitate new approaches to learning at every level of education and in all areas of the curriculum. Over a decade ago the new mathematics, science, and foreign languages began to change traditional classroom practices radically. Already a newer math, drawn up in the summer of 1963 at Cambridge, Massachusetts, by some of the country's leading mathematicians and mathematics users, has marked the beginning of what might be termed a "second revolution" in mathematics.

The social studies come comparatively late to the contemporary curricular reform movement. It is ironic that the social studies, the area most vitally and directly concerned with some of the world's most pressing problems—war, the population explosion, race relations, environmental pollution, elimination of poverty, control of crime, civil rights—should be one of the last segments of the curriculum to come under careful and systematic review.

Obviously, children on the elementary school level cannot grasp the full magnitude and complexities of such pressing social problems. However, social studies can introduce the child to these problems at his own maturity level and can help equip him with the skills, abilities, values, and sensitivities that will help him later on to find rational solutions to the unsolved problems and to new ones that may arise.

Today it is a must that people learn to understand and live with each other in respect and harmony. Through modern means of transportation and communication the world has now become "a little neighborhood." Thus, the need has never been greater for improved friendship and tolerance toward all people everywhere. Inasmuch as social studies is the area of the curriculum with a major focus on human relations and social understanding, it has assumed a place of greater importance than ever before. Clearly, the more we can make the accumulated experiences of mankind, as represented by the social sciences, available to students, the greater our hopes for the future.

In addition to their focus on current social problems, the social studies are important because they contain a body of knowledge, ideas, and methods of inquiry which can challenge the creative and intellectual abilities of our better students—the results of which can improve the way of living of all mankind.

In summary, social studies are important because they may become the means of helping us accomplish the following major tasks:

> 1 To develop a larger number of creative social scientists to redress the imbalance between technically trained man power and trained social scientists
>
> 2 To develop a generation capable of social innovations and institutional remodeling to meet the demands of our changing world
>
> 3 To help children and youth adjust to a changing world and uncertain future by a greater emphasis on creativity, discovery, inquiry, and autonomous thinking in the social studies
>
> 4 To work toward the ideal of education for every citizen of this country to the limit of his capacity
>
> 5 To learn how to use the great advances of science and technology for the good of man and a democratic way of life
>
> 6 To become better able to understand our own selves and how to live peacefully with others here at home as well as in international relations—promoting man's humanity to man
>
> 7 To help American values and ideals continue to survive by opposing "hate" campaigns and ruthlessness in the world with a spirit of brotherhood toward all mankind and with a respect for the law.

THE SOCIAL STUDIES DEFINED

The term "social studies" is a comparatively recent one, which came into general usage only slightly more than fifty years ago. Prior to that time the part of the elementary school curriculum now called the social studies was traditionally designated and taught as separate subjects. The Massachusetts Bay Law enacted in 1642 decreed that all children should be taught "to read and understand the principles of religion and the capital laws of the country." Within the next century, history and geography joined the early "civics" and became part of the curriculum for students at all levels.

Among the earliest elementary school geography texts published in this country was Jedidiah Morse's *Geography Made Easy,* published in 1784. Although no formal history texts had been published at that time, stories from history were prevalent in many of the early readers. Much of the historical material included in early reading texts was developed by Noah Webster. It was hoped that such materials would develop in children a love of country and an appreciation of their great heritage of freedom.

During the first half of the nineteenth century, laws were passed requiring the teaching of civics, geography, and history in the public schools. The other social sciences now commonly included in the elementary school curriculum, such as economics, sociology, and anthropology, came comparatively late upon the school scene. Although they had their academic origins in the late 1800s and early 1900s, it was not until some two or three decades later that knowledge and interest in these fields increased to the point that they became firmly entrenched in the school curriculum.

Teaching methods were dictated to some extent by the organization of the textbook. The text materials used in elementary schools prior to the progressive movement in education consisted primarily of isolated facts to be memorized. In most instances learning activities were organized in the form of questions and answers. The practice of teaching the social sciences separately, with little functional relationship to one another, lasted well into the second decade of the twentieth century.

Although mention of the term "social studies" was made in educational literature as early as 1905, it was not used generally by educators until 1916 when the Social Studies Committee of the Commission of the Reorganization of Secondary Education, appointed by the National Education Association in 1914, published and gave official sanction to its use. With the formation of the National Council for the Social Studies in 1921, and with the expression's consistent use in professional literature, it became widely accepted at both the secondary and elementary levels of education to describe a broad area of study dealing with integrated content drawn from the separate social sciences.

People generally have many misconceptions regarding the meaning of *social studies.* There is a surprising lack of agreement even among educators. To the subject-matter specialist the term might suggest something less than the intellectual rigor that they would deem desirable and imply that a loss of basic information occurs when the content of their special field loses its identity under the broad label of the social studies. Some view it as a designation that is too vague and that should have long ago been discarded.

Parents often hold the notion that the term relates only to teaching children to socialize, and view it as being more "social" than "study." Others say that the blending together of several subjects produces a hodgepodge which results in little learning and that we should return to the teaching of good old history and geography.

What, then, are the social studies? Is the expression singular or plural? How is it differentiated from "social sciences," "social education," and "social living"? Has the term "social studies" outlived its usefulness? At this point, it is important that some clear distinctions be made.

The social studies program is the vehicle through which the schools direct the children's interaction with their social heritage and provide the background for effective participation in a democratic society. The following definition is illustrative:

> The social studies help young people to understand American Citizenship. The social studies, like the social sciences, are concerned primarily with human relationships. The term "social studies" designates that portion of the curriculum which deals specifically with man in his dynamic relation to his social and physical environments. The social studies are concerned with a knowledge of how man is influenced by his environment, how he in turn uses and alters his environment to satisfy individual and group needs, how customs and institutions have emerged, how man is attempting to solve current problems, and how he draws upon his experience to plan for the future.[1]

Common to any definition of the social studies is the fact that *they focus primarily on the study of one or more aspects of man's relationships with his fellow man or on human relationships.* They have to do much with people, their historical backgrounds, how they solve their problems of getting along together in different kinds of groups, and how they become constructive participants in them. A hermit is an example of one whose apparent concerns would be farthest removed from the central concerns of the social studies inasmuch as he feels no need for any social relationships with his fellow men, and he seems to care but little, if at all, for the welfare of mankind.

A social study is an inquiry focused on socially significant problems, concepts, questions, or theories that provides opportunity for children to formulate questions and to seek answers to them through careful scrutiny and research. The term "social studies" merely refers to more than one social study. It most emphatically does not refer to a particular kind of organization or approach. It is a label that is applied to programs of a single-subject type as well as to those of the unified (fused) variety. There are many who believe that for the elementary pupil some type of interdisciplinary (fused) arrangement is best. These and other approaches to the social studies will be discussed in more detail in a later chapter.

It is important to distinguish clearly between the social studies and those inquiries in the elementary school that do not focus primarily upon human relationships, such as mathematics and the physical sciences. There are few,

[1] "Report of the State Central Committee on Social Studies to the California State Curriculum Commission" (Sacramento: State Department of Education, 1961), p. 5.

if any, subjects that are devoid of social implications or content, but only in the social studies is the content as well as the purpose social. Although mathematics is an essential part of many other domains of knowledge, a person engaged in its study cannot be said to be engaged in a social study, because the main focus of concern is on numbers and procedures. The focus of concern, therefore, becomes of critical importance in distinguishing a social study from other kinds of inquiries. For example, a problem dealing with the present-day social upheavals resulting from racial problems is social in nature. A person attempting to find basic causes and possible solutions for the unrest is involved in a social study. A person attempting to develop a new, harmless chemical to be used in riot control for the dispersal of unruly crowds of people would be working mainly in the area of the physical sciences. Although both studies were prompted by a common problem, that of social unrest, and although both persons involved in the solutions to them may have been most sensitive to the human welfare, in each case different kinds of subject-matter background, knowledge, and skills were required for them to be successful in their individual tasks.

THE SOCIAL SCIENCES—THEIR RELATIONSHIPS TO THE SOCIAL STUDIES

Knowledge may be classified into four major divisions: mathematics, the natural sciences, the social sciences, and the humanities. The natural sciences include the physical and life sciences. The humanities include literature, languages, art, music, and philosophy. The social sciences include such disciplines as history, human geography, sociology, and political science. History may be placed in either the social sciences or the humanities, but curriculum workers generally have included it in the social sciences. Geography may be placed in either the physical sciences or the social sciences, depending on its emphasis. Human geography, however, is properly classified as a social science.

The social sciences, therefore, embrace those fields of scholarly inquiry that deal primarily with human relationships or the human social condition. As such, they provide the major source of concepts for the elementary school social studies program. At one time history, civics, and geography were the areas most commonly emphasized in elementary school social studies. Currently, however, concepts from virtually every social science field are included in the program. This is quite a change from what has been taught in the past in social studies. Such broader and more meaningful programs that include understanding from previously neglected social science areas were long overdue in the elementary school curriculum. Those social science disciplines making the most direct contributions to the elementary social studies curriculum are history, geography, political science, sociology, economics, and anthropology.

Contributions of History to the Social Studies

The dictionary defines history as "the branch of knowledge that records and explains past events." Written accounts of past events always incorporate the notion of interpretation. Thus, history is considered both narrative and inter-pretive.

Another important aspect of history is that of validity. In reading written history the question must be raised as to whether what is read is interpreted accurately, whether the "facts" are correct, and whether the relationships established are sound. A complete meaning of the word "history" is summed up by Haskins as follows:

> Let us say that history, the study of the evolution of human society, investigates, records, and interprets for the present events of social significance. Thus, history is event, record, and process.[2]

Historical Method / Because the historian deals with events and conditions in the past, he is faced constantly with knowledge that the events he studies can never be known directly—only by the records that happen to remain of these events. He feels an obligation to deal with the records accurately, fully, and objectively. A historian needs a question or a problem as a starting point. Without a question a researcher would not know what kind of evidence to collect. Once the question is defined, he proceeds by interpreting evidence. He will gather and examine as much pertinent evidence as he can find. Evidence consists of any remains from the past—written records, documents, oral traditions, buildings, paintings, and relics of all kinds. The range of such sources is virtually endless. As an adjunct to collecting evidence, he will attempt to determine the authenticity of his data. Historical accounts are always subject to the limitations of the historian's ability to analyze his findings accurately. The evidence may then be placed in categories for purposes of organization and classification. New questions will arise from the data which may open up new areas of research or raise other questions. The significance that the historian attaches to past events is never static—history is being rewritten constantly. Views change as new evidence becomes available.

The complete process of historical research may be identified as a mode of inquiry. It would seem that if we are to prepare children to live intelligently in tomorrow's world, we must introduce them to the structure or the fundamental ideas of all the major social science disciplines and provide them with the skills of inquiry of the historian and the social scientist.

History in the Elementary School / History has been a part of elementary programs in this country for nearly two hundred years. Prior to the turn of the present century, history in school mainly consisted of memorization of past events. For many pupils history has meant only names, dates, places, battles, and other facts that had to be memorized. There is little wonder that in the past there has been much pupil dislike for the study of history.

Obviously, much of the fault lies in the manner in which history has been taught. Historical events are inherently interesting. If approached by the methods the historian employs, a historical study can catch the imagination

---

[2] Ralph W. Haskins, "History," in *The Social Sciences: Foundations of the Social Studies,* eds. John U. Michaelis and A. Montgomery Johnston (Boston: Allyn & Bacon, 1965), p. 27.

and interest of students. Some students may thus develop lifelong interest in the study of history. Of course elementary school pupils are not being prepared to become historians, but there is much in the historical method that can be useful to anyone who would gain an understanding of the past. Knowing something about the methods of the historian can help children gain a better understanding and appreciation of historical accounts, a greater respect for objectivity in recording human events, and a better knowledge of the reasons why history is reinterpreted as new evidence becomes available.

Pupils can apply on an elementary level some of the historian's methods of study to their own studies of the local community, state, or nation. They can examine firsthand some of the traces of events, including both primary and secondary source materials, that are related to the area of study. For example, they can visit libraries, museums, newspaper offices, historical sites, and older members of the community to obtain firsthand information. Through research on a problem they can verify events and validate the accuracy of an historical account. Assembling evidence and coming to possible solutions based on objective data may be a first step for elementary pupils leading to analytical and reflective thinking about social issues and events.

Children see many evidences of history all around them. They ask numerous questions about it. They ask questions about when their father and mother were children; they see relics of a past era, look at monuments and historic markers, collect coins, view television programs of past eras, and read biographies and stories that are historically oriented. In school a social study will have historical elements and concepts associated with it whether based on history per se or on one of the other social science disciplines. Thus history provides the time dimension to most studies in which children engage.

The teaching of historical material to young children in the primary grades must take into account important limits set by maturational factors in the understanding of time concepts. In viewing the past, children tend to telescope time. For example, as a third-grade teacher was discussing with the class the tragic assassination of President Kennedy, a child asked, "Did you feel sad, too, when Lincoln was shot?" The process of helping children obtain accurate time concepts is a gradual one extending over a period of several years. The young child in the primary grades is concerned mainly with the here and now. Therefore, the development of time concepts should begin with the study of events close to his personal experiences. The bearing of the past upon the present should be made clear.

Although children in the primary grades have already gained a wide variety of understandings about the past, a formal study focused on an extended period of history is more appropriate for intermediate and upper-grade pupils. On the primary level, studies of historical periods are usually of brief duration, with little attempt made to probe the depths. For elementary school children, holidays and special events provide an ideal setting for the study of historical ideas. Discussions and other activities in connection with such observances as Washington's and Lincoln's birthdays, Flag Day, Columbus Day, and Veterans Day are of particular value if based on accurate historical fact. These kinds of observances can do much to acquaint the child with his rich cultural heritage and help him grow in his appreciation of it.

History continues to occupy a position of importance in the elementary school. It is true that there are many forms of history too advanced to have meaning for elementary pupils. But history has many aspects which can be approached in meaningful ways by children. History is all around children; therefore, they enter school with some concepts, though incomplete, about the past. If the teacher recognizes this fact, much more can be done earlier in the school experiences of the child to extend his understanding of historical concepts.

Contributions of Geography to the Social Studies

The teaching of geography in the elementary schools of the nation can be traced back to a period of time immediately following the American Revolution, when the first textbooks in geography were published. During the nineteenth century, geography was taught as a separate subject, and the emphasis of study was upon the physical environment and place location. Children were taught the size and shape of major countries, the location of principal cities, rivers, and mountains, and the names of the major products of each country studied. This traditional pattern of teaching geography persisted well into the twentieth century. By the early 1920s the interdisciplinary approach to teaching the social studies was generally accepted by the more progressive school systems throughout the nation. This approach provided for the integration of subject matter in which basic ideas from each of the social science disciplines were functionally related for more effective and meaningful learning. It was held, and rightly so, that "integrating" material from related disciplines in the study of a topic or problem could broaden the subject offerings without a corresponding loss in depth and understanding. For example, many felt that one need not lose the distinctive method of geographical reasoning merely because geographic ideas were taught in relation to historical facts and reasoning.

Unfortunately, early attempts at integrating knowledge from the various social sciences were not always successful, and in many cases, this resulted in a gradual lessening of emphasis upon geographic understandings. In some schools, the teaching of geography became incidental in nature and was all but lost. By World War II, the need for trained geographers became acute. It soon became evident that the school had failed to provide students an adequate foundation of knowledge in this important area of study. It is not surprising, therefore, that the past quarter of a century has been marked by an increasing interest in providing improved instruction in geography at all levels of the school curriculum.

Methods of Inquiry in Geography **/** As previously noted, geography is a discipline recognized by its methods of investigation as well as by its subject matter. However, its real uniqueness lies in the manner in which it approaches the study of geographical phenomena. Each of the social science disciplines has to some extent its own methods of research, its own methods of collecting, comparing, and presenting data. The possibility of having elementary pupils learn a mode of inquiry and practice some of the methods used by scholars in the various disciplines is a new and exciting concept in teaching elementary school social studies. The purpose is not to develop miniature social scientists but rather to help pupils develop the abilities to think geographically or historically, and so on, in approaching problems.

Geographic inquiry is recognized by its point of view and by its methods of investigation. To the geographer, these are known as the *regional concept* or the *regional method.* The concept of region has brought a new unity to the field of geography. Geographers see the regional method as an approach to selecting and studying areal distinctions: the uniqueness of areas and variations from place to place in physical and cultural environments. Anything which is irregularly distributed over the earth's surface is of concern to geographers, for it is through studying the uneven distribution of resources over the face of the earth and their relationships to the human condition that the geographer seeks to create meaning and significance.

Briefly, the steps involved in an objective study of geographic phenomena include the identification of the purpose of the study, determining the dimensions of the region to be analyzed in terms of stated purposes, collecting, recording, analyzing, and communicating data through the use of various analytical techniques and tools common to the field of geography. Gopsill describes the geographer's method of inquiry as follows:

1 To observe or to seek information

2 To record what has been found

3 To reason about these observations and to draw relevant conclusions from them.[3]

As the historian, the geographer collects objective data from a variety of sources. But whereas the historian organizes ideas in relation to time, geographers organize subject matter spatially. When the geographer selects a specific region or area for study, he begins collecting information about it from many sources. Much of his information comes from firsthand observations, descriptive reports of places, statistical tables, charts, maps, and photographs.

The geographer relies most heavily upon the firsthand observation and study of an area for data concerning it. To study a landscape in the open is the most effective way to learn geography because it is through this means that one may obtain the most accurate descriptions of land forms. The geographer, therefore, spends a good portion of his time in the field mapping and taking notes. Maps are important tools of the geographer, and he must be an expert in cartographic or map-making skills. He uses a number of different kinds of map projections to record his observations, to study relationships, and to communicate some of his findings. The information he records on maps is later combined with that collected by aerial photographs and by other means for further analysis and study. Figure 1 outlines the geographic method of investigation.

Elementary school children can be introduced to geographic concepts and can learn to think geographically in the early grades.[4] Simple geographic

---

[3] G. H. Gopsill, *The Teaching of Geography* (New York: St. Martin's Press, 1958), p. 18.
[4] See Chapter 5 for a more detailed discussion of the central concepts of geography and teaching map and globe skills to children.

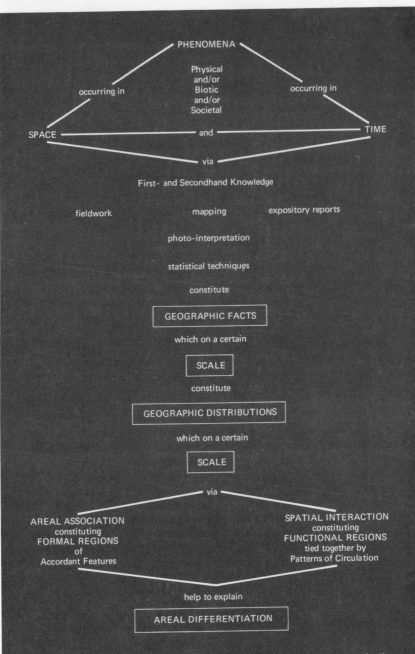

1 Fundamental Ideas of Geography / From *Concepts and Structure in the New Social Science Curricula,* edited by Irving Morrissett. Copyright © 1967 by Holt, Rinehart and Winston, Inc. Reproduced by permission of Holt, Rinehart and Winston, Inc.

problems can be introduced in the elementary grades which will require that children use the basic research methods of geographic inquiry. For example, children can be engaged in a regional study which will require that they consult a variety of specialized sources for information and data concerning it. They may go into the field on a study trip to obtain firsthand information, and they may learn to use various geographic tools such as maps and globes in analyzing data. The process of identifying associated phenomena and drawing conclusions and inferences from these associations is the essence of learning to think geographically.

Contributions of Economics to the Social Studies

For many years economics has been taught on a limited basis in the elementary schools. Although called by many different names, economic concepts have been present in the curriculum. For example, in the expanding-environment approach to the social studies, children have studied such basic human activities of mankind as "producing, exchanging, and consuming," which represent a study of economic ideas. But there is widespread agreement among educators that there is need today for improved programs and teaching in this vital area, particularly on the elementary level. Someone has said that our general lack of understanding of economic knowledge is the ninth wonder of the world.

In the increasingly complex society in which we live, the need for improved economic understanding has been the subject of discussion in business, financial, and government circles. Ernest O. Melby, former dean of the New York University School of Education, stated:

> Democracy will live if it works and it will die if it does not work. Moreover, regardless of what democracy may do in the cultural and human relations area, if it fails on the economic front, it will most certainly go down in defeat. If, then, we are interested in the survival of our way of life, there is no kind of education more important than that which seeks to make the average American intelligent about our economic system and effective as a citizen in relation to it.

Economics is concerned with the study of the way in which societies produce, distribute, exchange, and consume goods and services to meet human needs and wants. All people, from the time they get up in the morning until they go to bed at night, are engaged in a number of decisions and problems related to economic matters. Children are naturally motivated to learn economic concepts because of the close relationship of these principles to their daily lives. Children's experiences touch on every one of the social sciences but are particularly rich in elements of economic importance. The child and his family face a constant succession of economic problems. What should they buy at the grocery store? Who should get the next pair of shoes? Should the family spend or save? And is it important to give up this to get that? This kind of knowledge is important in the child's world and will continue to be so all his adult life.

Thousands of teen-agers join the part-time work force each year. Even elementary school-age children are making money by delivering newspapers, mowing lawns, and helping with various tasks around the home. Thus young people are an important force in the market for foods, beverages, clothing, cosmetics, recreation, and transportation. Producers of goods and services strive to please this market with advertising campaigns geared to the interests of young people. It is of critical importance, therefore, that the youth of our country gain an understanding of some of the basic principles of economics. There seems to be almost a complete lack of understanding or a serious economic illiteracy among our population about economic principles associated with credit buying, money and banking, insurance, and the stock market. Many American families face serious financial problems because their credit has enabled them to buy beyond what they can afford. Our schools are turning out a well-educated generation of Americans with high earning powers. Yet many of our high school and college graduates have never had a course in economics.

Economic Inquiry in Elementary Classrooms / Although everyone is enmeshed in economic decisions in his daily life, those decisions do not necessarily lead to an understanding of the fundamental ideas in economics. To have economic understanding means that one has acquired certain "ways of thinking" about economic problems and has developed the ability to deal with economic problems in an organized scientific way. Economics is a social science that seeks to define and analyze a problem by scientific methods and then to determine, as far as possible, the consequences of following a given line of action. As in the study of geographic or historical problems, economic inquiry requires skill in problem-solving and in analytical thinking. The development of these skills requires a long process of conditioning and experience in using them. This development should begin in kindergarten and grade 1 of the primary grades.

Through games, dramatization, discussion, and other learning experiences children can be introduced to the fundamental idea relationships of economic knowledge during their earliest school years. As they proceed into the upper grades, teachers can help relate their increasingly sophisticated experiences to this fundamental knowledge. Children in the elementary school can become aware of many basic economic relationships. Among the most important of these are:

> 1 The scarcity concept. Every society faces a conflict between unlimited wants and limited resources. People want more than they can have. Human wants, desires, and demands for goods and services always exceed the resources available to meet those demands. Fulfillment is determined by preference, income, and price.
>
> 2 The specialization of labor. Division of labor eases the conflict but makes people more dependent upon each other for products.
>
> 3 Interdependence makes trading necessary. This requires a market. To facilitate trade, men have developed monetary sys-

tems and methods of transportation. Also, rules or laws have been enacted to help regulate trade in an orderly fashion.

4 The development of methods for deciding what to produce, how much to produce, how to produce, and who will receive what is produced.

5 The development of the market as a means of bringing producers and consumers together, resulting in decisions as to what and how much to produce.

6 The modification of the market by the government to promote economic growth, stability, security, freedom, and justice (see Figure 2).

These fundamental idea relationships of economics are basic to any study in this area in that they provide a framework of knowledge around which instruction on all grade levels is organized. There are a variety of sources available to the teacher, which may help in identifying the more specific content drawn from these fundamental understandings.[5]

Following this pattern of organization, some of the basic principles of economics can be introduced in an elementary way to children at the beginning of their school experiences. The same fundamental ideas will be revisited in more complex forms at later stages in the educational program. Presenting the fundamentals of economics in this manner will provide children with a much more meaningful and usable kind of knowledge than that which may be obtained from a program based on a somewhat random selection of economic concepts to be taught at various grade levels.

Contributions of Anthropology to the Social Studies

Anthropology has been defined as "the science of man and his works." It is concerned directly with the study of the relationships between man and culture (see Figure 3). The major concerns of the social scientists working in the area of anthropology are outlined by Servey as follows:

> As an area of study, anthropology is a social science which rigorously attempts to define man realistically and scientifically. The social scientists working in the area of anthropology strive to learn how man has come to be what he is as a species. They study the structure of the institutions developed by man as reflected in his artifacts, his behaviors, his beliefs, and values. The more they can learn of his institutions, the more clearly they can define men as reflected in his culture. At times they seek to know why culture is the way it is, to know its significant innovations and their sources. Are the innovations crystallized expressions of the unique culture, or are they borrowed from neighboring or visiting cultures? Anthropologists have no concern for what man should be, only for what he is. To discover this, they observe and record carefully, interview perceptively, and examine in detail artifacts obtained in many ways. The purpose of their investigation is to construct a mirror that accurately reflects man so that he may recognize

[5] See "New Developments in Economics" discussed in Chapter 2.

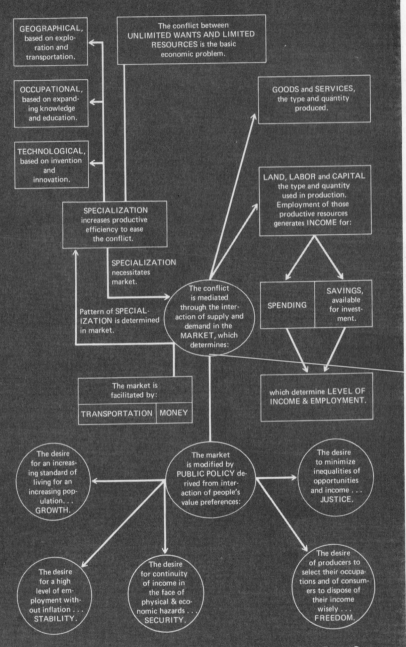

2 Fundamental Idea Relationships of Economic Knowledge / From *Concepts and Structure in the New Social Science Curricula*, edited by Irving Morrissett. Copyright © 1967 by Holt, Rinehart and Winston, Inc. Reproduced by permission of Holt, Rinehart and Winston, Inc.

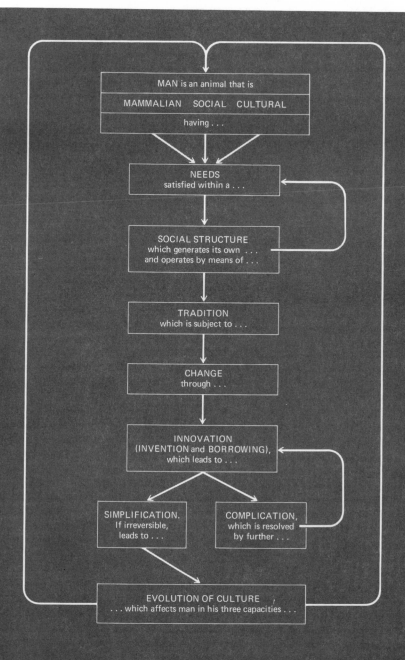

MAN is an animal that is

MAMMALIAN   SOCIAL   CULTURAL

having . . .

NEEDS
satisfied within a . . .

SOCIAL STRUCTURE
which generates its own . . .
and operates by means of . . .

TRADITION
which is subject to . . .

CHANGE
through . . .

INNOVATION
(INVENTION and BORROWING),
which leads to . . .

SIMPLIFICATION.
If irreversible,
leads to . . .

COMPLICATION,
which is resolved
by further . . .

EVOLUTION OF CULTURE
. . . which affects man in his three capacities . . .

and know himself wherever he may be. When man can understand himself in terms of his culture, the members of his own
culture cannot be alien to him, nor can the members of any
other culture.[6]

Anthropology has had a minor place in the social studies during the past,
but today some of the most stimulating new programs are oriented to developing anthropological concepts. Some time ago Spindler pointed out the importance of anthropology in the elementary curriculum as follows:

Anthropology—a subject until now studied mainly in colleges
. . . can make an important contribution to the social-studies
curriculums of elementary and secondary schools. . . .

Teachers may at first find it difficult to use anthropological
knowledge in their teaching, and many have trouble acquiring
the needed new materials. But the pioneering effort will be
worth the struggle. Our children will be the winners when well-
informed teachers are able to offer them learning opportunities
in social studies enriched by the contributions from anthropology.[7]

Contributions of Political Science to the Social Studies

The scope of political science is broad and complex in nature; therefore, no
simple definition of it can be given. Its direct concerns are with the study of
political systems. Political science is a field of inquiry in which social scientists seek to extend man's knowledge about how to establish and maintain
public authority in political systems both complex and simple. A major area
of investigation is concerned with gaining an understanding of the relationships between the governors and the governed. In a highly complex society,
these relationships cover a wide range of problems and issues. In collecting
and analyzing data political scientists employ a wide variety of objective
methods. These consist mainly of historical analysis, observation of behavior,
interviews, and statistical analysis.

According to Jarolimek, for purposes of the elementary school curriculum
political science is concerned with the study of government, political processes, and political decision-making.[8] In the past, on the elementary level,
many of the fundamental ideas of political science have been neglected in
instructional programs (see Figure 4). Traditionally, a course in civics has
been taught in the upper grades, generally on the ninth-grade level, with the
main emphasis upon a description of the legislative, judicial, and executive
branches of government.

Research by Easton and Hess has shown that children's attitudes toward
and concept of government are formed fairly early in life with the truly
formative years being between the ages of 3 and 13.[9] Not only do the child's

[6] Richard E. Servey, *Social-Studies Instruction in the Elementary School* (San Francisco:
Chandler, 1967), pp. 48–49.
[7] George Spindler, "Anthropology in the Social Studies Curriculum," *NEA Journal* 47: 626–627,
December 1958.
[8] John Jarolimek, *Social Studies in Elementary Education* (New York: Macmillan, 1967), p. 361.
[9] David Easton and Robert Hess, "The Child's Political World," *Midwest Journal of Political
Science* 6: 229–246, 1962.

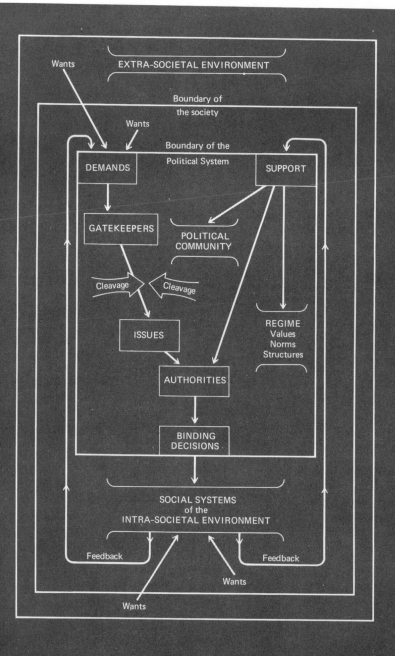

Wants

EXTRA-SOCIETAL ENVIRONMENT

Boundary of
the society

Wants

Boundary of the
Political System

DEMANDS

SUPPORT

GATEKEEPERS

POLITICAL
COMMUNITY

Cleavage   Cleavage

ISSUES

REGIME
Values
Norms
Structures

AUTHORITIES

BINDING
DECISIONS

SOCIAL SYSTEMS
of the
INTRA-SOCIETAL ENVIRONMENT

Feedback

Feedback

Wants

Wants

4 A Systems Analysis of Political Life / From *Concepts and Structure in the New Social Science Curricula,* edited by Irving Morrissett. Copyright © 1967 by Holt, Rinehart and Winston, Inc. Reproduced by permission of Holt, Rinehart and Winston, Inc.

attitudes and concepts about government begin to take form before the elementary school years, but by the time he reaches high school age his basic political orientations are well established. The evidence indicates that little change in these orientations is likely to occur during the high school years. In other words political learning begins earlier than has often been recognized, and the task is to expand upon this early learning and give it a firm basis before inadequacies become solidly entrenched. It seems that during the years that the child is in the elementary school, he is relatively flexible in his political outlook—making these years the extremely critical ones for instruction in the fundamentals of governmental process.

As it relates to the elementary school, political science is basically a social science dealing with government in a democracy. The complete scope of the program on the elementary level includes three basic dimensions. First, helping children practice the ways of democracy in the classroom. Civic literacy and social concern are coupled with certain skills, habits, attitudes, appreciations, and understandings necessary for participation in constructive social life by actual living in a social situation in a classroom that is itself a democracy. When confronted by challenging problems, children develop independence, grow in power to meet situations, and learn to choose wisely, to think and act responsibly, to cooperate, to respect the rights of others, to be tolerant, to challenge dubious and unsupported statements, and to acquire the other characteristics essential to effective citizenship in a democratic society. Second, providing opportunities for children to understand the meaning behind democratic symbols and ceremonies by taking part in the rituals of our democratic society. Third, helping children develop concepts and understandings about the processes and institutions of government at the local, state, national, and international levels.

In the primary grades, pupils learn many social science ideas indirectly or in relation to other ideas. For example, through a study of the roles of the various members of the family, the child may learn that the forces which keep the family together are similar to those important to the larger society. In the later grades, social science ideas are learned both directly and indirectly. At this level more can be done in direct teaching of the manner in which our system of government functions.

Contributions of Sociology to the Social Studies

Sociology is a science concerned with the study of man's group behavior. It is a study which focuses upon social groups, their internal forms, and the processes that tend to maintain or change these forms of organization. More specifically, the special concerns of sociology are with social organization, why and how groups form, how different kinds of groups function, subcultures, social classes, and the relations between various groups in society, as indicated in Figure 5.

Sociology contributes a significant amount of content to the elementary school social studies program. This is particularly true in the primary grades, where the focus of study has traditionally been on the structure and role of some of the basic institutions of our society: the family, the school, and

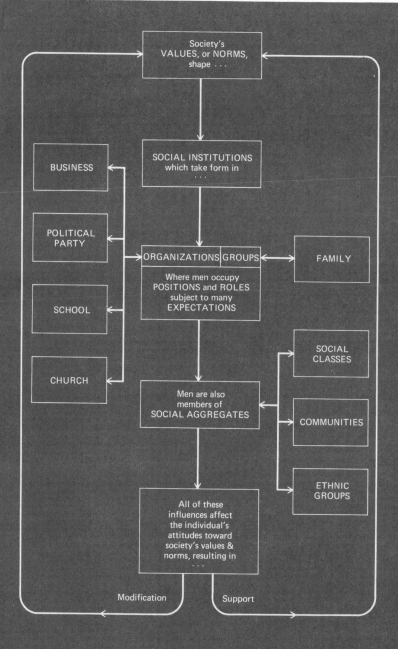

Society's
VALUES, or NORMS,
shape . . .

SOCIAL INSTITUTIONS
which take form in
. . .

BUSINESS

POLITICAL
PARTY

SCHOOL

CHURCH

ORGANIZATIONS GROUPS
Where men occupy
POSITIONS and ROLES
subject to many
EXPECTATIONS

FAMILY

Men are also
members of
SOCIAL AGGREGATES

SOCIAL
CLASSES

COMMUNITIES

ETHNIC
GROUPS

All of these
influences affect
the individual's
attitudes toward
society's values &
norms, resulting in
. . .

Modification   Support

5 Fundamental Ideas of Sociology / From *Concepts and Structure in the New Social Science Curricula,* edited by Irving Morrissett. Copyright © 1967 by Holt, Rinehart and Winston, Inc. Reproduced by permission of Holt, Rinehart and Winston, Inc.

neighborhood and community workers. Through the study of various institutions and communities of men, pupils can acquire basic learning about social interdependence. Thus the foundations can be laid in the primary grades for the later study of group influences upon the individual's attitudes toward society's values and norms, which ultimately determine the direction of social reforms.

In recent years there has been a major reshaping of the well-established disciplines and substantial growth in the newer ones. Important contributions to the social studies curriculum are now coming from fields of study such as social psychology, philosophy, jurisprudence, and ethics. Although these fields provide little of the basic content to be studied by elementary pupils, they contribute richly in a supportive sense to the overall program. Social psychology is directly concerned with the effects of group life on the behavior of the individual. Social psychologists have contributed much to our knowledge of group processes and how teachers can work most effectively with children in group projects. Understanding of the effects of group pressure on individual behavior, attitudes, and values also has many implications for social studies methodology.

The basic concern of philosophy is the search for truth. Much work in the social studies deals with values, questions regarding right and wrong of events, acceptable means of attaining goals, and understanding differences between statements of fact and opinion.

Too, other fields of inquiry outside the social sciences, the natural sciences and the humanities, make significant contributions to the social studies. These bring within the range of the elementary school new opportunities for broader curricula in the social studies, which will help children build a more effective framework of basic ideas about human behavior and the nature of our complex world.

SOCIAL EDUCATION

The social studies should not be thought of as synonymous with social education. Social education is broader in scope than social studies in that it relates to the total interpersonal social life of the child. It has to do with the social learnings a child acquires at school, at home, and in the various groups with which he is associated. Obviously the social studies program alone cannot carry the entire load of social education. Each subject taught during the day must make some contribution to the development of positive social learnings. Beyond this, such learning requires the cooperation of the home, community, and social groups within the community to which the child belongs to be successful. The complete process of socialization is beyond the scope of the elementary social studies program.

OBJECTIVES OF THE SOCIAL STUDIES

Objectives represent the goals that are to be achieved through the curriculum, and they should be in harmony with the philosophy of the school and with the values and ideals of the culture in which the school operates. All school practices and learning experiences should flow into the general objectives, as a tributary stream flows into a river, and contribute effectively to the accomplishment of major outcomes. Often social study guides are developed with no consistent connection between general objectives, lesson objectives, and the learning activities.

In the worldwide ideological conflict the United States of America stands as a leader of nations seeking to maintain and extend freedom to all people of the world. The perpetuation of freedom in the world and in our own country depends in great measure on the success of society in educating its members in the underlying values, loyalties, and principles of a free society based on a democratic way of life. The schools have been charged with the specific responsibility to teach the ways of democracy to each new generation and to become laboratories where children can practice democracy in a meaningful way. Because of the nature of its subject matter, the social studies program has been most directly concerned with the accomplishment of this lofty aim. The knowledge, loyalties, and behavior essential to the perpetuation of our democratic society cannot be inherited—in every case they must be learned. Each child must learn for himself the behaviors and understandings necessary for effective participation in a democratic society; they cannot be just handed to him as if on a platter. It is a somewhat frightening fact that we always stand within one generation of losing our democratic way of life or seeing it erode away. This underlines the importance of the role of the social studies in a democratic society. The social studies, unlike the more neutral social science disciplines which select data without regard to personal value commitments, must serve the utilitarian purposes to which the school or the community subscribes.

It is generally agreed that the most inclusive aim of the social studies is to help young people learn the ways of democratic citizens and to work for the continued improvement of conditions within the society in which they live. There remains, however, considerable difference of opinion among educators as to what constitutes the "good citizen" and what approaches to teaching citizenship are best. The most unsophisticated advocates of "citizenship" education have insisted that the whole social studies program must be oriented toward developing good and responsible citizens, even to the extent of selecting only that content which will inculcate allegiance to the values of democracy. More intelligent proponents of this important aim would hold a much different view of the requirements of citizenship education. They would view the development of a good citizen as a much more complex task than that of transforming education into indoctrination and would insist on a social studies curriculum addressed to multiple objectives—all of which would effectively contribute to the ultimate development of a democratic citizen or the goals of a democratic society.

No two authorities state social studies objectives in exactly the same way. Most agree, however, that the objectives can be classified under four general headings: (1) gaining knowledge and understandings that describe and explain human society, (2) developing intellectual curiosity and critical thinking, (3) acquiring social values and attitudes, and (4) developing social study skills.

Gaining Knowledge and Understanding

At long last a sensible balance is being achieved in the social studies between content to be learned and the processes of learning. Prior to the 1920s there was an overemphasis on the memorization of specific, unrelated factual detail, with almost complete disregard for the development of understanding and meaning, intellectual inquiry, or objectives other than content achievement. The progressive education movement, which came into ascendancy in the 1920s and early 1930s, was essentially a rebellion against this meaningless and sterile kind of learning. This movement introduced a new approach to learning that placed greater emphasis on the processes of learning and on the child as an individual. This new emphasis in its extreme form, however, minimized somewhat the importance of basic subject-matter content and produced a curriculum that was to some extent defective in the quality of content.

In recent years scholars and educators have worked together to identify basic concepts from the social sciences that would provide the subject-matter emphasis for the elementary school social studies. Thus, an emphasis on content has returned, but it is important in planning social studies objectives that the right kind of balance be maintained between content, process, and the nature of the learner.

If students are to acquire the needed knowledge and understandings for effective living in the complex society of today, which includes an understanding of many cultures in the world, it is necessary during their elementary school experience to introduce a wide range of concepts not only from history and geography but also from anthropology, economics, and the other fields of the social sciences. Although mastery of content is one of the important outcomes of learning, knowledge for its own sake cannot be considered a proper educational goal. To be of value, knowledge requires application to life and utilization in constructive lines of behavior. The ability of a person to make wise decisions is directly based upon the knowledge he possesses.

It is not always easy to identify precisely the kinds of knowledge a child must acquire to become an effective citizen. Nevertheless, the following general objectives related to knowledge and understanding are important for the social studies:

1 A basic understanding of the cultural history, geographical, political, economic, and social factors of greatest importance to the child's own society

2 A basic understanding of the major world cultures and culture areas selected to represent varying beliefs and practices and different stages of development

3 A basic understanding of the growing interdependence of individuals, groups, and peoples of the world

4 A basic understanding of economic resources both natural and human and how to make the most intelligent use of the natural environment

5 A basic understanding of the role of home, school, church, government, and other social institutions in human affairs

6 An understanding and knowledge of a basic social studies vocabulary.

Developing Intellectual Curiosity and Critical Thinking

A second important objective of the social studies is the development of a spirit of inquiry and more effective ways of thinking. The importance of developing individuals capable of critical thinking scarcely needs to be emphasized. In a complex technological society such as ours in which changes are taking place at a rapid rate, the accomplishment of this objective in the schools takes on new importance. Educators have long been in agreement that children need to learn how to think; however, this objective has not been implemented as effectively as it might have been, because so little has been known about the nature of the developmental sequence in thinking. The ability to think critically cannot be taught all at once; it is a long-range goal requiring some continuity at each grade level and within each subject-matter area.

Developing independent thinking requires many different processes, including those of observing, questioning, experimenting, interpreting, investigating, searching, calculating, and applying. Recently a considerable amount of research has been done relative to the improvement of thought processes. Hilda Taba[10] worked with teachers and children in Contra Costa, California, where she was interested in whether training could make it possible to develop logical thought operations at an earlier age. To achieve this objective an analysis was made of the various tasks involved in thinking. Three different tasks were identified, namely:

> 1 Concept formation, or the ways in which students can interrelate and organize discrete bits of information to develop abstract concepts (e.g., the concepts of cultural change, of interdependence, and of standard of living)
>
> 2 Inductive development of generalizations, or the ways in which students interpret data and make inferences that go beyond what is given directly in the data
>
> 3 Application of principles, or the ways in which students use acquired knowledge—facts and generalizations—to explain new phenomena, to make predictions, and to formulate hypotheses.

These tasks provide a developmental sequence in thinking and become increasingly abstract. A teaching strategy was developed for moving pupils to the higher levels of thinking. Certain ideas evolved from this study that seem important if teachers are to be effective in developing independent thinking. Some of these are as follows:

> The "seeking" functions of teaching assume a greater importance than those of "giving." This reverses the usual role of the teacher.
>
> The role of questions becomes crucial. The type of questions asked by the teacher limits or releases the mental operations performed, the points to be explored, and the modes of thought students learn.
>
> Some pupils require a great deal more concrete information before being able to move to the next level of thinking.

[10] Hilda Taba, *Teacher's Handbook for Elementary Social Studies* (Reading, Mass.: Addison-Wesley, 1966), p. 9.

Thus the teacher must time his questions used in the lifting of thought levels according to his diagnosis of the "readiness" of his class to move up to the next level of thinking.

Attempts to lift thought levels prematurely may result in either confusion or regression.

The teacher must understand the structure and sequence of the thinking process and have a thorough understanding of the content being taught.

Opportunities for learning experiences or questions are needed on each level of the processes to establish firm thinking at this level. This is a different type of learning from "instantaneous" learning, such as memorizing a historical date.

It would seem that slow learners can achieve a higher level of formal thought provided they can examine a greater number of concrete instances than are now provided by most teachers.

Open-ended but focused questions are needed. Open-ended questions set a focus and allow the students to respond in terms of their own perceptions.

It would appear that students can be trained in the stages of thought at an earlier age than previously supposed possible.[11]

Closely related research on developing thinking is that of Suchman,[12] who devised an inquiry development program designed to stimulate and sustain inquiry by students in elementary classrooms in developing their skill in the pursuit of new understanding and meaning through the process of inquiry. A chief purpose of Suchman's inquiry training is to make children more autonomous learners by developing skills in questioning, thinking, verifying, and applying knowledge. The teacher plays a key role in this process. The teacher must create a free environment which allows the learner to pursue new meaning and new understanding in his own way, to construct theories and explanations in his own terms, and to progress at a rate that satisfies the learner. In total, the teacher's role is to (1) stimulate and challenge the students to think, (2) insure freedom of operation, (3) provide support for inquiry, (4) diagnose difficulties and help students overcome them, and (5) identify and use the "teachable moments" when new organizers can be introduced most effectively.

The task of helping youth grow in their ability to think rationally, of course, cannot be limited to the learning experiences provided by the social studies or any one subject-matter area. To be completely effective it will require a form of integration or pooling of forces for this development in all subject-matter areas no matter how diverse the content of these subjects.

In this category of general objectives it is important that the teacher help children develop the following kinds of attitudes and abilities:

1 An interest in and acquaintance with the methods of inquiry used by social scientists in their respective fields

2 A commitment to doubting, questioning, and reconstruction

3 A desire to utilize the scientific method

4 An understanding of the purpose and procedures of inquiry—developing a mode of inquiry or involvement process whereby students "learn how to learn."

Acquiring Social Values and Attitudes

The area of social values and attitudes is of the greatest concern to those who are oriented to a social-living approach to the social studies or to an approach that places greatest emphasis upon the social development of the child and upon learning the ways of a democratic society.

A body of research evidence indicates that the value systems of students develop early in life. The values children learn at home, in their peer groups, and in church before they begin school, and then in the elementary grades have the greatest effect in guiding their future behavior. By the time students reach high school and college age their value systems are quite firmly established. After this time, values change slowly, and it becomes increasingly more difficult to effect the desired changes. The elementary school, therefore, and particularly teachers of the social studies, can be a positive influence in modifying and changing hostile, undemocratic, and antisocial attitudes of children.

In the past the school curriculum has stressed fact-finding to the exclusion of the study and development of values. Often only meager learning experiences have been provided by which values might be learned. This has produced a dangerous pseudo-neutrality toward such critical issues as minority relations, racial problems, and patriotism, which face our society today. In all too many cases, it has been hoped that proper attitudes and values would emerge as a by-product of obtaining the knowledge objectives. It is little wonder, then, that we have not been as effective in this area of teaching as we might have been.

The classification of objectives in the affective domain is made easier by distinguishing the different kinds of values with which this objective concerns itself. Getzels[13] has identified two different kinds: those representing the democratic creed in American society, which he calls the "sacred values," and those that he calls the "secular values," which guide daily conduct in our society and shape American character.

The following objectives stem directly from the basic tenets of American democracy and are representative of the "sacred values" of greatest concern to the social studies:

1 An abiding faith in our democratic beliefs—the free agency of man, the dignity and worth of the individual, justice, the right to assemble, freedom of religion, government by the citizenry, and other basic values

2 A willingness to sacrifice for these concerns or principles

3 Open-mindedness and respect for the opinions of others

[13] J. W. Getzels, "The Acquisition of Values in School and Society," in *The High School in the New Era*, eds. F. S. Chase and H. A. Anderson (Chicago: University of Chicago Press, 1958), p. 146.

4 A responsiveness to democratic values which motivate a person to action in ways that are conducive to the welfare of society and to human progress.

Some of the "secular values" of greatest concern to the social studies are those related to individual development, sensitivities, and feelings such as:

1 Developing self-confidence, independence, and individuality

2 Developing respect for work and a willingness to carry tasks through to successful completion

3 Extending sensitivities to cultural differences of others

4 Learning to respond emphatically in social situations

5 Developing a willingness to help others and to work with others for desirable group goals.

Developing Social Study Skills

The last category of objectives in the social studies emphasizes the development of the skills and tools of study. Social studies instruction is ideally suited to the development of many of these skills. Others are shared with other parts of the school program and can be developed throughout the school day in many different kinds of learning situations. To become most effective, skills should be utilized in practical situations where the teacher requires work from students in which specific skills are woven into the whole task. Skills tend to level off at whatever level of quality the student is permitted to display in his performances on a day-to-day basis. The following skills and abilities are of major importance:

1 Gathering facts, organizing and interpreting information objectively; knowing what facts are needed, how to put them together effectively, and how to apply them to the problem

2 Following specific directions

3 Planning, working at, and completing tasks

4 Working independently

5 Reading skills essential to effective research

6 Library skills utilized in research

7 Use of reference books and materials

8 Effective writing skills
   a) Taking meaningful class notes
   b) Outlining material effectively
   c) Writing meaningful reports

9 Interpreting graphic materials such as maps, globes, charts, graphs, cartoons, and time lines

10 Organizing and presenting social studies materials—making outlines and presenting effective oral and written reports

11 Becoming an independent seeker of truth

12 Learning to participate effectively in a group—perceiving the different roles in a group, assuming the role of leader or follower as needed to carry out group plans, using parliamentary procedures effectively, and learning effective means of evaluating group progress.

The twentieth century has so far been a period of great achievement and technological advancement; but it has brought with it conflict, stress, and many complex problems. We have facing us such crucial problems as the world struggle in the cold war; danger of atomic weapons in the hands of irresponsible leaders; problems of how to direct the great advances of science and technology toward humane ends; and conflicts related to getting along with others in a shrinking, interdependent world.

Will the objectives of the new social studies prepare children to meet effectively the problems which have become their legacy in the last half of the twentieth century? Admittedly, this is a different question to answer because of the uncertain nature of the future. We are living in an era of profound and rapid social, economic, and technological change. This makes predictions of conditions to which the rising generation must adapt far more difficult than ever before in the history of our country. Formerly, changes came about slowly and were counted in terms of generations. Today, however, profound changes are taking place every few years and are constantly accelerating. One does not know what kind of world children presently enrolled in the elementary school will live in after the turn of the century. Even predictions of conditions during the next decade would be hazardous at best. Nevertheless, the objectives of the social studies can be shaped to give children the best possible preparation for an uncertain future. Such preparation will require a change of emphasis from facts set out in advance to be learned to the development of concepts, skills of acquiring information, appropriate attitudes, critical thinking, and creative talents. Inasmuch as 6-year olds will assume roles as responsible citizens twenty years from now, it is possible that what is done now in the schools, more especially in well-planned social study programs, may make a significant difference to the future welfare of mankind. Clearly, the more effectively we can utilize the accumulated experiences of mankind as represented in the social sciences, the greater our chances for an educated citizenry capable of protecting the democratic way of life and extending the benefits of democracy to all.

Recent technological advances have changed and are changing the way in which man lives. However, while great scientific advances emancipate men in many ways which would enable them to live more fully and freely, they do not automatically ennoble life. For example, a great advance such as nuclear fission can bring mankind to a new age of well-being or can be used as a destructive force causing a great holocaust. Every time new power is put into our hands there is a change in what we *can* do, out of which emerges questions pertaining to what we *ought* to do. Each step in human advance introduces new problems and perils along with the benefits. We owe it to generations yet unborn to leave an inhabitable world. But as yet we have not done well in learning how to control and use the advances of science. Man's greatest challenge since the beginning of recorded history still remains how to get along with others—the area in which he has failed most. Hence the need for effective social study programs on the elementary level that achieve all the objectives set forth.

Time may prove to be the most critical factor in our attempt to preserve freedom. In our own country problems of race and public order are becoming increasingly serious issues. People are becoming polarized and may well let hate become the ruling force. If we are to oppose the swift advance of catastrophe, we must strive in all haste with all our energies and resources to inculcate in children and youth now in our schools loyalty to the values of a free society.

PROBLEMS IN THE DEVELOPMENT OF A SOUND SOCIAL STUDIES CURRICULUM

To be most effective, today's social studies curriculum must cope with many problems. Among the most significant ones are (1) the extended scope of social studies objectives, (2) the explosion of knowledge, (3) the obsolescence of descriptive knowledge, and (4) the range of individual differences and abilities within the classroom.

The Extended Scope of Objectives

The scope of the new social studies has been broadened to provide a greater emphasis upon objectives other than the mastery of subject-matter content. In the past it was assumed that the mastery of knowledge would somehow automatically develop autonomous or creative minds. We can no longer assume this to be the case. The extension of objectives beyond the acquisition of knowledge requires well-organized learning experiences geared specifically to the kind of objective sought. The learning experiences, and not the content as such, become of major importance in the achievement of all objectives other than the mastery of knowledge. However, as yet we have not been as effective in developing adequate learning experiences for the development of creativity, reasoning skills, attitudes, and values as we have for cognitive objectives. Partly, this has been due to the fact that these kinds of objectives cannot be acquired all at once, but require continued practice in many different contexts for their development.

The Explosion of Knowledge

The explosion of knowledge presents a formidable task in selecting what to teach in the social studies. Since the birth of Christ it is estimated that the first doubling of knowledge occurred in 1750, the second in 1900, the third in 1950, and the fourth in 1960. In all likelihood the next doubling of knowledge will be accomplished in less than a decade of time.

The explosion of knowledge has brought a vast array of new ideas to an already overcrowded social studies curriculum. Often, new additions to the curriculum have been in the form of increased masses of facts or bits of information which have only served to aggravate the problem of content coverage. If we are to encompass more than just the residue from the advance of knowledge, we must take a new look at what kind of knowledge is most durable and valuable. Learning masses of facts, many of which will be proven false and most of which will soon be forgotten, cannot equip a child adequately for the future.

Much dead wood in the form of obsolete knowledge can be eliminated from the social studies curriculum. A new selection of content should be made which focuses upon concepts, the basic structure of social science disciplines, and upon skills of inquiry. The ability to use a mode of inquiry should help children become self-propelling learners and thus better prepared to cope with the explosion of knowledge.

The Obsolescence of Descriptive Knowledge

In traditional assign-recite-test programs, major stress is placed upon the retention of specific, and often isolated, facts. This kind of learning, focused as it is upon factual knowledge, is inefficient because much of what is learned is difficult to retain, even if it were useful. Secondly, many of the facts learned change rapidly and soon become outdated. For example, much of the factual material covered in the social studies, such as population statistics or production figures, change constantly. It is a waste of school time, therefore, to dwell on bits of information or to cover a wide range of specific facts in hope of permanent retention. Rather, it would be more productive if the emphasis were on a selectivity of facts related to the development and understanding of a given concept or principle.

The Range of Individual Differences and Abilities

Research findings of the past fifty years have greatly increased our understanding of the growth and development characteristics of children. Among these findings have been those demonstrating the wide range of individual differences that exist among learners in the typical classroom—differences that can be found in all aspects of development. Each child is unique and differs from all other individuals not only in physical characteristics and social and emotional development, but in experiential background, intelligence, and interests. Any attempt, therefore, at developing a uniform social studies curriculum that all children must acquire at the same speed and depth of understanding is futile. Obviously, what is needed is a more flexible curriculum designed to facilitate the optimum development of all pupils, the desired goal, by providing some means for the individualization of instruction and for the use of a greater range of knowledge.

Modern teaching in the social studies is not possible unless the teacher understands the nature of the learners and their patterns of growth. Most teacher-training institutions require the preservice teacher to take a number of courses designed to help him gain a substantial knowledge of the psychological and physiological characteristics of the learner. Too, many good books are available that present this important information, and every teacher should be acquainted with them.

As previously stated, the goals of the social studies should be consistent with both what is required by our society and what is possible for growing children. In many instances, we have underestimated the abilities of children in our modern world. Bruner's idea that "any subject can be taught effectively in some intellectually honest form to any child at any stage of development" has received wide acceptance.[14] If this hypothesis is true, then the traditional readiness concept of deferment of instruction until children mature must be rejected in favor of this new principle. This means that pupils can be introduced to the basic structure of a discipline as early as desired, and that as our ability to devise more meaningful learning experiences increases, children will be able to grasp meanings that we now consider too difficult for them.

In summary, if the new social studies curriculum is to meet the needs of children in the latter part of the twentieth century, it must be designed to take into account expanding content, be applicable to pupils having a greater range of abilities, build a more sophisticated understanding of the world, and develop better skills in human relations.

QUESTIONS AND ACTIVITIES

1 / List at least three reasons why effective teaching of the social studies is so important in today's world.

2 / Differentiate the terms: social studies, social sciences, and social education.

3 / What are some of the major objectives elementary school social studies should accomplish in each of the following domains: cognitive, affective, and psychomotor?

4 / .Obtain a number of different curriculum guides in the social studies. Make a comparison of objectives, noting similarities and differences.

SELECTED REFERENCES

Amidon, E., and Hunter, Elizabeth. *Improving Teaching.* New York: Holt, Rinehart & Winston, 1966. Chap. 3.

Bloom, Benjamin S. *Taxonomy of Educational Objectives: Cognitive Domain.* Third edition. New York: McKay, 1956.

Bruner, Jerome S. *The Process of Education.* Cambridge, Mass.: Harvard University Press, 1961.

California State Department of Education. *Social Studies Framework for the Public Schools of California.* Sacramento, 1962.

Clements, H. Millard; Fielder, William R.; and Tabachnick, B. Robert. *Social Study: Inquiry in Elementary Classrooms.* Indianapolis, Ind.: Bobbs-Merrill, 1966. Chap. 1.

Fenton, Edwin. *The New Social Studies.* New York: Holt, Rinehart & Winston, 1967. Chap. 2.

Fraser, Dorothy McClure, and McCutchen, Samuel P. (eds.). "Social Studies in Transition: Guidelines for Change." Curriculum Series Number Twelve. Washington, D.C.: National Council for the Social Studies, 1965.

[14] Jerome S. Bruner, *The Process of Education* (Cambridge: Harvard University Press, 1961), p. 33.

Gallagher, James J., and Aschner, Mary Jane. "A Preliminary Report on Analyses of Classroom Interaction." *The Merrill-Palmer Quarterly of Behavior and Development.* Vol. 9, No. 3, 1963.

Getzels, J. W. "The Acquisition of Values in School and Society." In *The High School in the New Era.* F. S. Chase and H. A. Anderson (eds.). Chicago: University of Chicago Press, 1958. P. 146.

Goodlad, John I., et al. *The Changing School Curriculum.* The Fund for the Advancement of Education, 1966.

Guilford, J. P. "The Structure of Intellect." *Psychological Bulletin* 53 (4): 267–293, July 1956.

Jarolimek, John. *Social Studies in Elementary Education.* Third edition. New York: Macmillan, 1967. Chap. 1.

Krathwohl, David R.; Bloom, Benjamin S.; and Masia, Bertram S. *Taxonomy of Educational Objectives: Affective Domain.* New York: McKay, 1964.

Lee, John R., and McLendon, Jonathon C. (eds.). *Readings on Elementary Social Studies—Prologue to Change.* Boston: Allyn & Bacon, 1965. Part A.

Michaelis, John U., and Johnston, A. Montgomery. *The Social Sciences: Foundations of the Social Studies.* Boston: Allyn & Bacon, 1965.

Quillen, James, and Hanna, LaVone A. *Education for Social Competence.* Revised edition. Glenview, Ill.: Scott, Foresman, 1961. Chap. 1.

Ragan, William B., and McAulay, John D. *Social Studies for Today's Children.* New York: Appleton-Century-Crofts, 1964. Chap. 1.

Taba, Hilda. *Teacher's Handbook for Elementary Social Studies.* Reading, Mass.: Addison-Wesley, 1966.

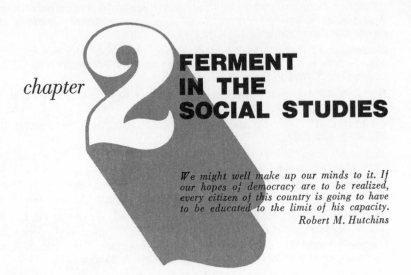

FERMENT IN THE SOCIAL STUDIES

We might well make up our minds to it. If our hopes of democracy are to be realized, every citizen of this country is going to have to be educated to the limit of his capacity.

Robert M. Hutchins

One cannot understand why the social studies have assumed their present dimensions in the elementary school curriculum without looking at their beginnings. Nor can one speculate intelligently upon possible future directions in this area without a knowledge of past developments, particularly over the last half century.

TYPES OF APPROACHES TO THE SOCIAL STUDIES

Over the years many different approaches have been recognized as successful ones for teaching social concepts to young children. The very nature of our decentralized educational system has fostered this kind of development. Diversity in planning is desirable in a democratic country that seeks to educate all children to the level of their ability and to provide for a wide variety of needs. We have prospered nationally in the social studies by diversity. It is almost certain that any effort to plan in terms of a uniform national curriculum or to create a single "ideal" approach to the social studies would fail in the face of strong differences of opinion among leading educators in this area as to just what the curriculum should be.

As noted, today one may find a wide variety of successful approaches to teaching the social studies. However, for purposes of this discussion, four major ones are identified and summarized:

1 The separate-subjects approach
2 The unified or interdisciplinary approach
3 The expanding-environment approach
4 The life-situations or social-living approach.

Each of the above approaches has played a prominent role in the past development of the social studies. Although some have gained greater acceptance among educators than others, all are currently found in use in the schools. It is not uncommon, however, for the teacher to use a combination of approaches, or to use two entirely different ones during a given school year. Wide variation in teaching practices is the rule; therefore, many programs cannot be categorized neatly into just one of the main approaches—there is much overlapping. Nevertheless, the approaches selected for attention are basic to an understanding of past procedures of organizing content, selecting instructional materials, and providing learning experiences in the social studies. Presently, a number of new approaches to teaching the social studies are gaining prominence. These will be discussed in some detail later in this chapter.

The Separate-Subjects Approach

The separate-subjects approach traditionally organized the social studies program into the separate subjects of history, civics, and geography. The general practice was to teach each subject separately with little functional relationship to one another. This pattern of teaching the social studies stemmed from the earliest days of free public education in this country and remained in ascendancy well into the second decade of the present century. Since this time the traditional dominance of history, civics, and geography has been reduced as materials and content from other social sciences have been introduced into the elementary social studies curriculum.

In a separate-subjects approach the content for instruction is selected mainly from the three basic social sciences and is based upon what the authorities or "society" deems to be important for children to learn. Topics to be studied are set out in advance, and each is considered separate from others. The historical approach to a topic is chronological in nature, with considerable emphasis upon the symbolical learning of names, places, dates, and events. Geography is presented mainly in descriptive or place locational terms.

The textbook plays an important role in this type of pattern in that it organizes the content into a sequential order that all children are required to follow in a lockstep fashion from cover to cover. Separate texts are provided in each subject-matter area. The success of this method is usually determined by assessing how well the pupil can assimilate the material covered in the text and repeat it back to his instructor.

Although today some elementary schools still organize and teach the social studies according to subjects, the increasing popularity of newer and more productive approaches is evident.

Criticisms of the Separate-Subjects Approach **/** There have been many negative criticisms of the separate-subjects approach. Among these criticisms are the following:

1. Segregation of subject-matter content into various disciplines taught in isolation from each other is highly inappropriate for children in the primary

grades. It is held that primary school children do not have the background of experience or the concepts and thought processes necessary to deal with the separate subjects which represent an "adult" arrangement of subject matter. It is held that adaptations of this approach may be more appropriate for use on the junior and senior high levels.

2. The single-subject approach does not present a realistic picture of peoples' ways of living. A culture cannot be explained adequately or accurately in terms of a single discipline such as history or geography.

3. The separate-subjects approach overemphasizes rote learning, the kind of learning that crammed the mind of youth with miscellaneous and isolated bits of information but did not give him a grasp of ideas or stimulate his thinking.

4. The subject-centered approach does not develop the skills essential for independent thinking, nor does it provide for the development of a critical attitude toward generalizations about human behavior.

5. The separate-subjects approach violates several sound principles underlying effective education. It tends to treat children as though they were all exactly alike, each needing the same dosage of material.

The Unified Approach

Traditional schooling came under severe attack shortly after the turn of the present century with the rise of the progressive education movement in America. Earlier statements of principle by William James, John Dewey, Francis W. Parker, and others influenced the rapid development of this movement and the widespread experimentation with the "new education." Much of Dewey's philosophy was translated into actual classroom practice by William Heard Kilpatrick of Teachers' College, Columbia University. Kilpatrick, an educational theorist, had far greater practical influence on the development of the child-centered curriculum in the classroom than did his mentor, John Dewey. Most of the research and literature during this period supported the "new" education. Virtually everything found in traditional settings suffered under the criticisms of the progressive educationalists.

Toward the close of the second decade of this century, rigid subject-matter lines began to break down and become more flexible. Widespread recognition of the fact that maintaining separate-subject lines was inappropriate for working meaningfully with primary grade children led to early attempts at unification of the social sciences. It was at this time that the "unified approach" based on a fusion or integration of the social sciences had its beginnings. The earliest attempts at unification resulted in an integration of history and geography. As knowledge in other social science fields increased, content from these areas was included along with history and geography, although to a more limited extent. Under this broad arrangement of the social studies, significant ideas from several disciplines are brought to bear on the study of a given topic. The terms "fused" and "unified" are applied to programs that are interdisciplinary in nature. Figure 6 represents a

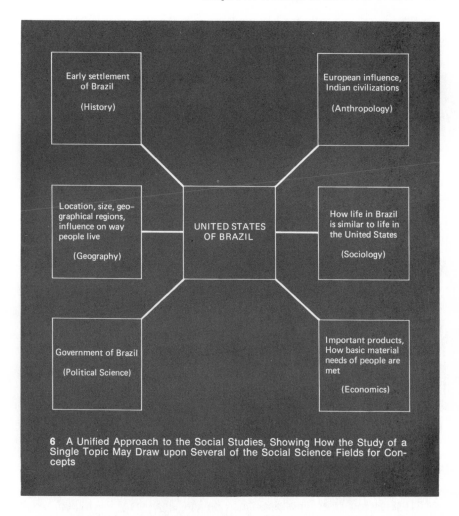

6 A Unified Approach to the Social Studies, Showing How the Study of a Single Topic May Draw upon Several of the Social Science Fields for Concepts

unified approach to the social studies and shows how the various social science disciplines might contribute to a broad topic.

This pattern is found commonly in schools where a broad-fields curriculum is in use. In this curriculum pattern, one of the fields typically set up embraces the social studies, and learnings from many of the social sciences might be included for study during the same class period.

In some cases the major focus might be on a single discipline, as would be the case in the study of a special unit on geography or economics. Nevertheless, other social sciences become an integral part of the program as they relate to the basic geographic or economic understandings covered in the special unit.

Many believe that a correlated-subjects approach to the social studies is best for elementary school pupils. This pattern introduces the children to the basic concepts and structure of many social science disciplines and provides them with a general background of information prior to any later specialization in a given field.

In this approach, as in the separate-subjects approach, content to be learned is set out in advance. Generally, a multiple-basal text provides a basic guide and establishes the scope and sequence of the content to be learned. Carefully prepared guidebooks to accompany the basic text are available to the teacher. They provide a teaching plan for the most effective use of the text and contain many useful suggestions for teaching the basic content. Although many well-written social study texts are multidisciplinary in nature, integration of subject matter may be accomplished without the domination of the textbook. For example, the teacher may develop a unit of work which uses a wide variety of learning experiences to convey the subject matter to the learners. This approach involves the use of many different kinds of audiovisual materials, teaching aids, supplementary texts, and reference books. The basic text becomes one tool among many as a source of information.

Regardless of the approach used, the teacher remains the key factor in the success of any program. It is safe to say that good teachers, even under a separate-subjects plan of organization, have always found ways to meaningfully integrate subject matter from related disciplines. Experience has shown that good teaching or poor teaching can take place under many different kinds of arrangement. The organizational format may be less important to good teaching than the quality of the learning experiences that are employed.

Criticisms of the Unified Approach **/** Although the unified approach is dominant in elementary classrooms today, it has come under a number of criticisms. They may be listed as follows:

1. Subject-matter specialists feel that a significant loss occurs when the content of their special field loses its identity under the broad label of social studies.

2. The blending of several disciplines on the elementary level produces a hodgepodge that results in little learning.

3. It is impossible to obtain from combined courses results which are as good as those obtained from separate subject-matter approaches when measured in terms of pupil achievement in subject-matter content and social study skills.

4. The unified approach, much like separate subject-matter approaches, is based on content set out in advance to be learned. Such an approach places little emphasis upon present life situations, current problems, problem-solving, and the development of creativity.

5. It is also held by some educators that the unified approach to the social studies is characterized by uniformity of learning tasks and that problems and issues are often selected for study with relatively little regard for children's understanding or interest.

The Expanding-Environment Approach

Largely because of its logical sequence of themes beginning with the family and moving outward to study of the larger communities of men, and because the major themes ensure a continuity of learning from grade to grade, the expanding-environment or widening-horizons principle has, within the last thirty years, gained widespread acceptance on the elementary level throughout the country.[1] The popularity of this approach has been made evident by the fact that many textbook publishers have geared the content of elementary school social study texts to the scope and sequence of this approach.

The scope of the program refers to the "what" or "breadth" of learning experiences and is defined in terms of the "basic human activities" of mankind. Throughout the ages there have been certain social activities or functions basic to human living in an organized society. These basic aspects of living, common to all cultures, have been carried on in a variety of ways and effectiveness under different environmental conditions and different levels of civilization. They are listed as follows:

1 Producing, exchanging, distributing, and consuming goods and services

2 Transporting people, goods, and services

3 Communicating information, ideals, and feelings

4 Providing education

5 Providing recreation

6 Protecting and conserving life, health, property, and resources

7 Organizing and governing

8 Expressing and satisfying aesthetic and spiritual needs

9 Creating new tools, technics, and institutions.[2]

Sequence has to do with the "when" or "order" in which various learning experiences are to take place. The principle of sequence development which has been used in the expanding-environment approach is that of "widening horizons" based on a system of expanding communities beginning with the "family community." This principle has been deemed to be "psychologically correct" as it begins with a study of the "here and now," things close to the child or within his experiential background, and as he gains in understanding and maturity moves outward to a study of people and places more removed from him in time and space.

The complete approach is outlined in some detail by Paul R. Hanna as follows:

> In the elementary schools, by following the wholistic and co-ordinated approach to the study of men living in societies, we design our program as follows: The sequence of themes or emphases is drawn from the fact that each of us lives within

---

[1] The rationale for this approach has been developed by Paul R. Hanna of Stanford University. Early experiments with the approach were conducted in the Virginia Study in 1934, and in the Santa Barbara Study, completed in 1940.
[2] Paul R. Hanna et al., *Geography in the Teaching of Social Studies* (Boston: Houghton Mifflin, 1966), p. 83.

a system or set of expanding communities that starts with the oldest, smallest, and most crucial community—the family in the center of the concentric circles—and progresses outward in ever widening bands through the child's neighborhood community; the child's local communities of city, county, and/or metropolis; the state community; the regions-of-states community; and the national community. The set of communities—family to nation—is a highly interdependent system: e.g. the problems and possible solutions of the family groups are always colored by the larger communities of which the family is the smallest but core group. Even the national community reaches inward through all of the intervening bands of lesser communities to influence the life of the family group. . . .

The logic of the expanding-communities-of-men design suggests that each larger component community be studied in sequence by the child. In the first grade, the child might start his study of the system with emphasis on his own family and his own school. As he studies each of these communities, he learns what phases of life are properly the concern of himself as a member of these small intimate groups. He also learns that families need to join families to provide, through neighborhood apparatuses, fire protection, food and clothing, schools, etc. Consequently, the child moves naturally to the third emphasis in the sequential structure—the neighborhood community which exists to provide services not available to families or to the school in isolation.

This particular social studies design may assign the study of the neighborhood to the second grade. However, the grade assignment of the community to be emphasized is relatively unimportant; following the sequence from the lesser community to the next larger is the governing principle here. . . .

Over this set of expanding communities of men, we now lay a grid of clusters of human activities. Universally, men in groups have in the past, do now, and no doubt will continue to carry on basic human activities, here catalogued under nine headings: protecting and conserving life and resources; producing, exchanging, and consuming goods and services; transporting goods and people; communication facts, ideas, and feelings; providing education; providing recreation; organizing and governing; expressing aesthetic and spiritual impulses; and creating new tools, technics, and institutions. Note the similarity of the names given these clusters and the names used to designate social science disciplines: "producing, exchanging, and consuming" might as well be labeled economics; "organizing and governing" could be replaced by the term political science.

The point to stress here is that the grid of basic human activities (essentially the regrouping of the content of the social science disciplines) is laid over each of the expanding communities of men: the child studies the ways men in groups carry out the several basic human activities and then another, this structure encourages the wholistic approach to the community being studied. All the interlocking social science disciplines are seen as part of the seamless web that we experience in living in family or state or nation.

Possible emphases beyond the United States national community. But our suggested design for the elementary school social studies is, to this point in our statement, incomplete. We have yet to complete our particular logic of expanding communities of men beyond the national community. Modern science and technology made obsolete the once defensible notion that the nation is the ultimate boundary of the system of expanding communities of men. We know today that nations cannot exist as islands: some multinational values, institutions, laws, and customs are even now appearing, while others wait for the birth time when men shall find it desirable and possible to welcome larger-than-national communities.

What we face today is a new set of *emerging* communities of nations that are increasingly important to the survival of the lesser national communities. These larger-than-national communities can be identified and assigned sequentially to school grades in some such pattern as this: [See Figure 7.]

Emphasis

8 / U.S. and Inter-American Community
9 / U.S. and Atlantic Community
   (There is logic to support a reversal of Emphases 8 and 9 on the grounds that the Atlantic Community is of greater significance to us.)
10 / U.S. and Pacific Community
11 / U.S. and World Community

Let it be re-stressed that the sequential order of the emphases is more important than the assigning of the study of a given community to a particular grade. One school district or state might telescope and assign both the national and the Inter-American communities to grade five; the Atlantic, the Pacific, and the world communities to grade six. Or another district might stretch the design through grade seven, or grade eight, or even grade nine, depending upon the decisions to be made in the remaining grades of the secondary school.

Several strategies of this design should be noted here. When the child moves beyond his national community, he is now focusing on the need for multinational solutions. The social studies program need not take each and every one of the more than 20 nations in the emerging Inter-American community for detailed study. The child should begin to observe the nearly half-billion people living on the American continents, working together through multinational action to create private and public solutions to their common problems. The U.S.–Canadian joint efforts could be studied realistically. The Alliance for Progress could be examined as one possible approach to the concern all of us have for economic, social, and political de-

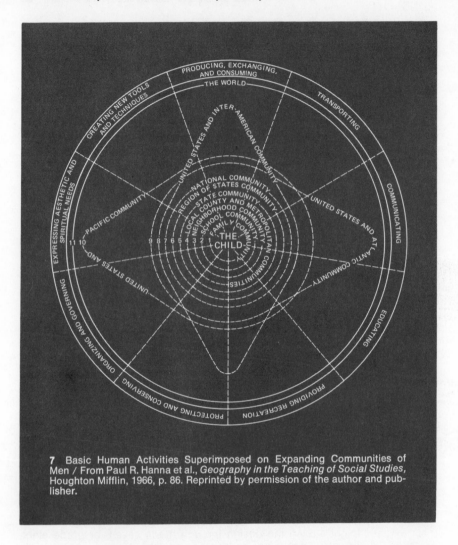

7 Basic Human Activities Superimposed on Expanding Communities of Men / From Paul R. Hanna et al., *Geography in the Teaching of Social Studies,* Houghton Mifflin, 1966, p. 86. Reprinted by permission of the author and publisher.

velopment of our neighbors to the south. Attention would be given to the nature of power and international policy as well as to cultural comparisons. The history we have in common in the Americas of ten thousand years of Indian culture, 300 years of European colonization, and 100 years of struggle for freedom and independence is probably of greater use to our youth than a detailed study of the history of any single neighbor nation. The design calls for the larger and more universal pictures of emerging multinational communities.[3]

It should be noted that this plan stresses the basic principle that the sequence of expanding communities should be followed in a logical order from

[3] Paul R. Hanna, "Revising the Social Studies: What Is Needed?," *Social Education* 27: 190–195, April 1963. Reprinted by permission.

"the lesser community to the next larger one." However, the complete set of communities—family to world—is considered a highly interdependent system. Although children are expected to follow a definite *sequence* of expanding communities, boundary lines between them are not considered to be hard and fast. That is, it was never intended that children be restricted narrowly to a study of a given community on any grade level without reference to others or without expanding their horizons beyond the immediate environment. For example, children studying the immediate family would have ample opportunity to compare ways in which the family meets its basic needs for food and shelter with those of other families in more distant countries of the world under different environmental conditions. Major themes have been suggested only as *areas of emphasis* for given grade levels, not the total program, and have always provided opportunity for children to compare, explore, and cut across wider communities in their studies. Figure 8 is illustrative.

The "unit method" is often used as an organizational pattern for the various themes or problems studied in this approach. The following titles are typical of the kinds of units studied. "The Family," "Community Helpers," "Westward Movement," "Transportation," and "Communication." When this method is used, frequently the major topic, theme, or problem selected becomes the "core" around which other subject-matter content is meaningfully integrated. For example, doing research and making reports on a given topic in the social studies involves the functional use of the language-arts skills of reading, writing, speaking, and listening. Other subject-matter areas such as physical education, music, art, and literature are integrated meaningfully with the social study as children learn folk dances, sing songs, draw murals, and read supplementary materials related to the unit of work. Thus, the social studies are ideally suited to serve as an integrating center of the curriculum where there are many opportunities for children to use fundamental skills from other subject-matter areas in functional situations.

Criticisms of the Expanding-Environment Approach **/** The expanding-environment approach to designing the social studies curriculum has recently come under severe attack. The major criticisms may be summarized as follows:

1. The grade-level themes or sequence has been criticized by some for becoming too inflexible and restrictive for modern-day youth. That is, among other things, it is reasoned that because children today watch television and travel more widely than ever before, they can move out of the small circle of the home, school, and neighborhood to a study of people and places more remote from them earlier in their school experience. In many cases young children spend valuable school time studying things they already know a great deal about, such as the work of firemen and policemen. Maximum learning cannot take place where children are so restricted.

2. Defining scope according to the basic human activities of mankind discourages the utilization of current issues and problems important for today's world and for future survival.

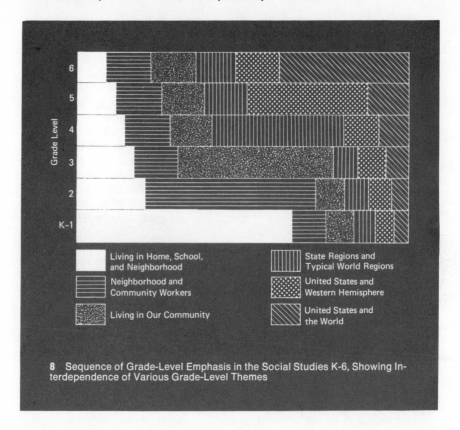

8   Sequence of Grade-Level Emphasis in the Social Studies K-6, Showing Interdependence of Various Grade-Level Themes

3. Since the first three grades all deal with aspects of the community, there is a considerable amount of repetition of content in these early years.

4. Under this framework, content to be learned is often set out far in advance. Topics become outdated rapidly and therefore, in many cases, are unsuitable to meet the emerging needs of society.

5. Part of the danger in this framework lies in the temptation to accept it as the only thread and to ignore the fact that this particular approach is often too age-grade oriented. For example, the family has value as a focus of study for more than the first years a child is in school. It is a false notion that once family content has been looked at in the first grade it need never be reviewed again.

The Life-Situations or Social-Living Approach

The life-situations approach developed by Stratemeyer et al.[4] departs markedly from the conventional subject organization in that it looks to the growth and development of the child and to significant life situations encountered by

[4] Florence B. Stratemeyer et al., *Developing a Curriculum for Modern Living*, Second edition revised (New York: Teachers College, Columbia University, 1957).

children in everyday living to develop a design for the social studies. The sequence is usually determined by proceeding from the understanding of the immediate experience to a wider understanding and to action. The emphasis is on the "here" and "now"—the present needs of the child. The notion is that grade-by-grade sequence cannot be predetermined but that the sequence develops as the learner matures and meets recurring life situations in new experiences.

The scope of the program is defined in terms of the emerging personal-social problems of childhood. It is held that vital learning experiences are to be found in the persistent life situations, personal-social problems, encountered by children at different stages of life from infancy to maturity. These situations are classified under the following main headings:

A. Situations Calling for Growth in Individual Capacities
   1. Health
   2. Intellectual Power
   3. Responsibility for Moral Choices
B. Situations Calling for Growth in Social Participation
   1. Person-to-Person Relationships
   2. Group Membership
   3. Intergroup Relationships
C. Situations Calling for Growth in Ability to Deal with Environmental Factors and Forces
   1. Natural Phenomena
   2. Technological Resources
   3. Economic, Social, and Political Structures and Forces

Although this approach has identified specific life situations as a unifying scheme around which to group learning experiences, Stratemeyer and her associates point out that:

> . . . The persistent life situations . . . listed are in no sense a basis for fixed curriculum units; nor are they the only ones at which a school faculty might arrive. Normally every area, and practically every persistent situation within that area, will be faced in some form at each grade level. . . . The intensity of study of a specific life situation, as well as the way in which it will be approached, depends on the needs of the particular pupil group. The . . . list should never be used to prescribe the order in which learners should face these persistent life situations or the grade levels at which they should be focal.[5]

This program, then, places heavy emphasis upon the personal-social problems of children and upon problems and issues which "persist" from day to day in our society. It is held that the social studies curriculum should be based upon real problems proposed by children. Since the needs and interests of children differ from group to group, topics for study cannot be outlined in advance. Often, many problems arise spontaneously that can be used to develop important social studies concepts. For example, if the community is considering the fluoridation of water, this may begin a new social study in the classroom. As the crisis develops in the Middle East, places formerly unheard of become familiar to children. Often problems of interpersonal

[5] Ibid., p. 115.

relationships arise on the playground or in the classroom over behavior interpreted as slighting or insulting. These situations may provide opportunity for children to study and learn how to be more considerate of others. It is the responsibility of the teacher to help children develop socially useful meanings through these studies. He must also determine which problems are beyond the developmental level of children and which ones lack the significance to warrant further study.

Adherents of this point of view hold that the child who learns to recognize and solve problems that arise in his limited environment will be better equipped to solve the more complex problems that will face him as an adult citizen.

Criticisms of the Life-Situations or Social-Living Approach / This approach to social learning has come under severe attack. This opposition may be due partly to the fact that this scheme of learning represents a somewhat radical departure from more conventional programs. The following criticisms are among those most commonly mentioned:

1. A program based entirely upon the study of pupil-initiated problems will neglect many important areas of knowledge. While it is true that children are highly motivated to investigate problems close to their immediate interests, many important areas of knowledge included in preplanned units should be studied by pupils whether or not they themselves initiate the study. A program based solely upon child-initiated problems may omit much valid and significant content which society deems to be essential for all children.

2. The program has failed to provide a sequence of learning experiences from grade to grade. This has been left to the teachers to develop for themselves. Teachers generally do not have the confidence, preparation, and training necessary to devise the needed continuity of learning experiences from the centers of interests suggested. As a result, there are huge gaps in the learning experiences of children from year to year.

3. This approach, based mainly on problems of social living, is not looked upon by some as a complete social studies program in and of itself but only as a supplemental aspect dealing with immediate concerns of children which could well be included along with the organized content categories of more traditional programs.

The preceding approaches represent those which have been most widely used by teachers of elementary school social studies over the past years. Although sharp differences between these approaches in teaching were noted, in actual practice it would be difficult to find any of these followed without any variations or adaptations to local needs. Today a variety of different plans for the social studies curriculum is being presented. Many of the newer programs on the horizon seem to offer much promise for the future.

RECENT DEVELOPMENTS IN THE SOCIAL STUDIES

Interest in the revision and improvement of social studies curricula is clearly increasing at all levels—from national agencies and organizations such as the United States Office of Education and the National Council for the Social

Studies to the state level and local school systems. During the past decade there has been a ferment in the social studies which has resulted in many notable developments, alterations, and improvements of the entire curricular pattern for instruction in elementary social studies and has offered many guidelines as to the future directions these advances may take.

Some educators have felt that the curricular-reform movement under way in the social studies is not revolutionary in nature but is instead an "evolutionary progression of ideas." A semantic disagreement over naming what is happening in the social studies in no way invalidates the fact that something is occurring. Differences between the social studies programs of a decade ago and those of the present are discernible. The reasons for this upheaval are varied and interrelated. Some of them are as follows:

1 The effects of curriculum change in other fields, particularly in the areas of science and mathematics

2 Recent social changes in our society and a general agreement among educators that existing programs are not adequate to prepare children for the future

3 The "explosion of knowledge" in many fields, including the social sciences

4 A renewed concern with the "structure" of the various social science disciplines

5 New knowledge about the way in which children learn, demanding new approaches to acquiring content and new teaching materials

6 An increase in funds from private foundations and the government available for research, drawing scholars in the social science disciplines, college professors of education, school administrators, and teachers into the task of curricular reform.

Goodlad points out that "more new projects are now appearing each year in the social sciences than in any other division of knowledge."[6] These proposals are mainly coming from centers operating under Project Social Studies and from a smaller number of privately financed projects.[7]

The United States Office of Education initially launched the venture to develop improved curricula in the social studies throughout the nation with Project Social Studies, which began in 1962 with funds from its Cooperative Research Program under Public Law 83-151. Under this program, a number of curriculum-study centers in the field of social studies were established throughout the country. The purposes of these centers were:

1 To redefine the nature and aims of the social studies and curricula at various levels

2 To develop instructional methods and materials that will achieve specific aims

3 To experiment with, evaluate, and revise new instructional methods and materials

[6] John I. Goodlad, *The Changing School Curriculum* (New York: Fund for the Advancement of Education, 1966), p. 56.
[7] For a complete listing of projects, see John U. Michaelis and A. Montgomery Johnston (eds.), "A Review of New Curriculum Developments and Projects," in *The Social Sciences: Foundations of the Social Studies* (Boston: Allyn & Bacon, 1965), pp. 275–305.

4 To disseminate information about the most promising methods and materials to interested individuals and groups.

Project Social Studies is providing a careful and systematic review of the social studies under the leadership of outstanding scholars. Results of this research are already reaching out and influencing present instruction in the social studies.

The movement to improve and upgrade the social studies was well received by educators because of general dissatisfaction with existing programs. Efforts to improve the social studies became contagious and widespread as information regarding new developments began to be disseminated to the schools. School systems in all parts of the country began to devise and experiment with new programs based on this new information. The result has been an unparalleled "revolution" in the social studies. Learned societies and privately financed research associations have joined in the effort by sponsoring and developing new programs.

It is important, therefore, that attention be directed to the nature of these recent changes, the influence of these developments upon current efforts to strengthen existing programs, and the emerging trends which stem from these efforts. An attempt has been made to identify some of the most promising new developments under each major social science discipline, beginning with history. Obviously, all that is new in elementary school social studies cannot be surveyed in one brief chapter. Therefore, a somewhat arbitrary selection has been made of the new projects to be included in this discussion.

New Developments in History

History has had a prominent place in the social studies program down through the years. Local history, state and regional history, early American history, and world history are included in the elementary social studies curriculum in many school systems today. It is common practice to provide instruction in these areas, excepting local history, on the junior and senior high levels also.

In the current curriculum-reform movement, history has not received the same intensity of study as have some of the newer fields of the social sciences. Nevertheless, the examination of the role of history and the teaching of it has been an important part of some of the current curriculum projects. In some instances the central emphasis of the project has not been on history specifically. But combined with other social science disciplines, historical elements have added greatly to the strength of programs. Too, it is with the aid of other social science disciplines that historical phenomena are explained most meaningfully.

Among the new developments in social studies projects are the study of American society in grades 5 through 12;[8] the development of major social science concepts in grades 5, 8, and 11;[9] and "postholing" in important eras

[8] Jonathon C. McLendon, *New Approaches to and Materials for a Sequential Curriculum on American Society for Grades Five to Twelve* (Syracuse: Department of Education, Syracuse Univ., 1963).
[9] Roy A. Price, director, *Identification of Major Concepts from the Social Sciences* (Syracuse: Department of Education, Syracuse Univ., 1963).

in history.[10] In an attempt to gain greater depth in the understanding of our nation's history, back-to-back American history courses which will "posthole" in important issues or crucial eras are being planned. Postholing provides for the study in depth of a given era or of a representative country as a segment of a culture region. From a depth study of a country, comparisons and generalizations are then made that relate to the basic human activities of all countries or peoples within a given culture region. For example a study of the Middle East has traditionally consisted of a cursory study of each separate country, with the entire area being covered in one or two brief social study periods. The concept of postholing would, in place of such cursory coverage, provide for a depth study of one representative country of the Moslem world, such as Saudi Arabia. After "postholing" in Saudi Arabia, brief comparisons would then be made with other predominantly Moslem countries in this region, such as Egypt, Syria, and Lebanon.

History is included with other social sciences in a comprehensive project that embraces kindergarten through grade 14 and is focused on key concepts, generalizations, and methods of inquiry.[11]

Another plan for the social studies curriculum has been developed by the Educational Research Council of Greater Cleveland under the direction of Raymond English. Although this program deals with history as part of other social sciences in the program of instruction, it may be appropriately included at this point. This plan departs widely from the more traditional expanding-environment approach in that children are introduced to a study of people and places more remote from them earlier in their school experiences. Topics such as "Children in Many Lands" and "Explorers and Discoverers" are introduced as early as kindergarten and the first grade. Among the new developments of the program has been the preparation of primary reading materials on famous people.[12]

Concepts and Inquiry / The Educational Research Council Social Science Program has been adopted by Allyn & Bacon as a basic social studies program. The program interweaves concepts inherent in history, political science, economics, geography, sociology and anthropology, philosophy, religion, and psychology. History and geography are used as the laboratory in which the other disciplines are examined and tested. All materials have been classroom tested on a large scale, both in the participating schools of the Educational Research Council and in other schools that have purchased the experimental editions of the pupil books and teacher materials. The principles of the program are outlined as follows:

> *Concepts and Inquiry: The Educational Research Council Social Science Program,* developed and tested as the Greater Cleveland Social Science Program, was inaugurated in February 1961 in accordance with the recommendations of the Educa-

[10] See *New Dimensions: New Directions Social Studies in Kentucky* (Office of Curriculum Development, Bureau of Instruction, Kentucky Department of Education, 1967).
[11] Edith West, director, *Social Studies Curriculum Guides and Materials for Grades K–14* (Minneapolis: Department of Education, Univ. of Minnesota, 1963).
[12] *Greater Cleveland Social Science Program* (Cleveland: Educational Research Council, 1964). (Rockefeller Building, Cleveland, Ohio 44113.)

tional Research Council Advisory Committee of Superintendents of participating schools. Consultants and teachers studied existing social science materials and developed a rationale and plan for an improved program. The principles of this program were and remain as follows:

First: Social science, like any other serious subject, comprises *a body of knowledge to which all citizens should be exposed* in the course of their school years.

Second: That body of knowledge is contained and classified in certain *disciplines:* political science, economics, anthropology, sociology, history, geography, and certain aspects of philosophy and psychology; the social science program should therefore pay constant attention to all these disciplines.

Third: Since the most important aspects of social science are *conceptual,* emphasis in education should be on concepts, skills, methods, and structure—not merely on rote learning or memorization of facts.

Fourth: The conceptual approach, being designed to enable the student to investigate, understand, and make decisions when faced with many combinations of facts, must be used in conjunction with *inquiry and problem-solving* techniques.

Fifth: In order to provide each student with adequate opportunity of exposure to the disciplines and their concepts and methods, the social science program should be *planned, sequential, and cumulative,* from kindergarten through grade twelve; the prevailing pattern of haphazard and uncoordinated courses in social studies must be discarded.

Sixth: Social science in the school must be concerned with *values, both universal and culturally relative;* this concern is shared by all subject-matter fields and their teachers, but the teacher of social science should pay critical attention to the values that govern men's behavior, and, in particular, those that govern behavior in our own society.

Seventh: The special contribution of social science education is to provide students with a basis on which to form *prudent judgments* throughout their lives, that is, to apply their value system realistically and effectively.[13]

Since the program is sequential and cumulative, its materials are arranged by grade levels. However, since abilities and speeds of learning vary, the pupil materials are not labeled according to grades: They can be used in nongraded schools or can be individually paced. The sequence of the program is as follows:

Kindergarten

1 Learning About the World

2 Children in Other Lands (He learns about children living in four different countries of the world: Japan, Mexico, England, and American Samoa)

First Grade

1 Our Country

2 Explorers and Discoverers

[13] See *Concepts and Inquiry: The Educational Research Council Social Science Program* (Boston: Allyn & Bacon, 1969), 25 pp.

Second Grade

1 Communities at Home and Abroad (Our Community, The Aborigines of Central Australia, The Eskimos of Northern Alaska)

2 American Communities (Historical Community [Williamsburg, Virginia], Military Community [Fort Bragg, North Carolina], Apple-growing Community [Yakima, Washington], Forest-products Community [Crossett, Arkansas], Steel-making Community [Pittsburgh, Pennsylvania], Rural Community [Webster City, Iowa])

Third Grade

1 The Making of Anglo-America

2 The Metropolitan Community

Fourth Grade

1 The Story of Agriculture

2 The Story of Industry

3 India: A Society in Transition (Enrichment Textbook and Teachers' Guide)

Fifth Grade

1 The Human Adventure: Ancient Civilization

2 The Human Adventure: Four World Views (China, India, Israel, and Greece)

3 The Human Adventure: The Classical World of Greece and Rome

4 The Human Adventure: Medieval Civilization

5 The Middle East (Enrichment Textbook and Teachers' Guide)

Sixth Grade

1 The Human Adventure: The Coming of Modern Age

2 The Human Adventure: New World and Eurasian Cultures

3 The Human Adventure: Nation-States and Revolutions

4 The Human Adventure: The Coming of World Civilization

5 Latin America (Enrichment Textbook and Teachers' Guide)

The publishing schedule of Allyn & Bacon for the materials of the *Concepts and Inquiry* program for the elementary school is: K–3, 1970 and 4–6, 1971.

There can be little doubt that this program has set high standards of boldness and imagination. It has demonstrated clearly that in the social studies we need not cling to the indefensible proposition that, ipso facto, things further away from a child in time and space will be more difficult for him to understand. Further experimentation and evaluation, however, may be needed to thoroughly test the effectiveness of the new social study reading materials developed in the program for primary grade children.

Another program by Clements, Fielder, and Tabachnick[14] presents a plan

---

[14] H. Millard Clements, William R. Fielder, and B. Robert Tabachnick, *Social Study: Inquiry in Elementary Classrooms* (Indianapolis, Ind.: Bobbs-Merrill, 1966), pp. 153–260.

for the social studies curriculum based on an inquiry approach. Topics are suggested for inquiry in four categories of social study: (1) The Now and Here (Some People Live Nearby), (2) The Now and There (Some People Live Far Away), (3) The Then and Here (The History of Here), and (4) The Then and There (The History of the Far Away).

Some provision is made for children to study in each of the four areas every year and at every grade level. Considerable importance is placed upon helping children develop the skills of inquiry of the historian, particularly in a study of The Then and There, where opportunity is provided for pupils to learn about yesterday's peoples and events in their own locality. This approach to the social studies provides more flexibility in selecting content for study than do more traditional approaches. It is maintained that when a teacher has a wide choice of content selection, and when a program is not too tightly structured, the teacher can be more effective. This approach places much of the responsibility for maintaining a balanced social studies curriculum upon the teacher.

New Developments in Geography

Modern geography, like history, must utilize knowledge from other fields of the natural sciences and from the social sciences to be complete. Therefore, no new projects deal exclusively with geography in elementary schools. Several projects, however, have included the basic understanding from geography along with those from the other social science disciplines.[15] Much of the new emphasis has been on identifying the fundamental ideas or key concepts of geography that represent its basic structure. Also some attention has been given to identifying the methods of research that characterize geographic inquiry.

In the early 1950s a series of studies under the direction of Paul R. Hanna at Stanford University were undertaken in an attempt to identify generalizations for the social studies curriculum drawn systematically from the frontier thinking of scholars in each of the social science disciplines.[16] These studies represent the most comprehensive effort to date on the selection of updated understandings from the social sciences for use in curriculum-building in the school.

The most extensive statewide effort at devising a plan for the social studies based on generalizations drawn from the various social science disciplines is the California Framework.[17] Scholars in each of the various social science disciplines were asked to contribute what they deemed to be the most important and crucial ideas from their discipline. Through a series of meetings by educators, these ideas were placed in a sequence for teaching. When refined there was a total of 157 important generalizations from all areas.

A major curriculum project conducted by the National Council for Geo-

[15] See studies cited in footnotes 8, 9, and 10.
[16] The first of these studies was Douglass' *Interrelationships Between Man and the Natural Environment for Use in the Geographic Strand of the Social Studies Curriculum* (Stanford University, unpublished doctoral dissertation, 1954). This was followed by a series of several dissertations which sought generalizations from the other social sciences.
[17] *Social Studies Framework for the Public Schools of California*, prepared by the State Curriculum Commission, California State Department of Education (June 1962), 109 pp. See Appendix for a list of major generalizations included in this framework.

graphic Education stresses the unity of physical and cultural geography and identifies nine basic concepts that are essential to a balanced program:

> 1 *Globalism:* the shape of the earth and its relationship to certain physical conditions; how the shape of the earth relates to man's activities
>
> 2 *The round earth on flat paper:* mapping the earth; map uses; interpretation of maps
>
> 3 *The life layer:* land, water, and air and their impact upon human regions
>
> 4 *Areal distinctions, differences, likenesses:* the uniqueness of areas; variations from place to place in physical and cultural environment
>
> 5 *The region:* the understanding of how regions are defined
>
> 6 *Resources culturally defined:* resources defined in terms of use; resources within a cultural context and a given level of cultural development
>
> 7 *Man the chooser:* man as a decision-making creature; economic implications of the choices made by man
>
> 8 *Spatial interaction:* interrelationships among places on the earth involving both human and nonhuman elements
>
> 9 *Perpetual transformation:* conditions on earth are in a constant dynamic state; human and nonhuman elements are in a constant state of change.[18]

A new development in the social studies which holds great promise for the future is that which has been worked out over the past few years by a team of social scientists who have attempted to outline the structure or fundamental ideas of various social sciences. The fundamental ideas of each discipline are introduced to the child in the primary grades and are taught with increasing depth and complexity, in a spiral development, as the child progresses from grade to grade. The basic structure of geography has been worked out by Peter Greco of Syracuse University. The fundamental ideas shown in Figure 1 are outlined below:

> 1 Every geographic area is affected by physical, biotic, and societal forces.
>
> 2 The impact of these forces on a geographic area creates similarities among areas. These similar areas are called uniform regions. They are static in character.
>
> 3 The similarities among different areas have been brought about through different combinations of physical, biotic, and societal forces.
>
> 4 An area may be kept together through a pattern of circulation binding the area to a central place. This area is called a nodal region, held together by functional relationships. The nodal region is dynamic in character.
>
> 5 Uniform and nodal regions are often related to each other through gravitation to the same central place.[19]

[18] Wilhelmina Hill (ed.), *Curriculum Guide for Geographic Education* (Normal, Illinois: National Council for Geographic Education, Illinois State Normal University, 1964), pp. 9–27.
[19] Lawrence Senesh, "Organizing a Curriculum Around Social Science Concepts," in *Concepts and Structure in the New Social Science Curricula,* ed. Irving Morrissett (New York: Holt, Rinehart & Winston, 1967), pp. 35–36.

It is held that these fundamental ideas of geography can be related meaningfully to the experiences of children. Since all social science disciplines are necessary to explain social phenomena, the fundamental ideas of all the disciplines would be introduced in the elementary school curriculum. The same fundamental ideas which are introduced at the beginning of the child's school experience would be revisited on higher levels of understanding as the child progressed through school. This would require an "orchestration" of the social studies curriculum in which units would be constructed to give emphasis to the different areas of the social sciences. In some units economics may play the solo role while the other social sciences play the accompaniment, and vice-versa. This would not only provide for meaningful integration of subject matter, but would assure that each child would have some acquaintance with the fundamental ideas from each of the basic social sciences on the elementary level. This kind of organization of subject matter would insure a meaningful sequence of learning, guided by the basic structure of knowledge in each discipline.

New Developments in Economics

In recent years economic education for elementary pupils has received more attention and has been promoted with more enthusiasm than perhaps has any other area of the social studies. A considerable number of new projects dealing specifically with economics in the elementary school are now under way. Some of those which seem to be in the vanguard of the new developments in this area have been selected for discussion purposes.

The Joint Council on Economic Education, organized in 1948, has developed the most extensive curriculum materials in economics that are available today for use in the schools. In cooperation with state and local councils on economic education, the Joint Council has developed a large number of teaching units, teacher source materials, and other teaching aids. The Joint Council on Economic Education has published a valuable *Teacher's Guide to Economic Education,* which classifies important economic concepts by grade levels and contains suggestions for classroom practice.[20] The Council continually encourages the better teaching of basic economic understanding throughout the elementary schools of the nation. They are presently in the process of developing a sequential program in economic education entitled "The Developmental Economic Education Program" (DEEP). Begun in 1964 by the Council, this program encourages curriculum renovation in local districts and provides the means for such development in the area of economics for certain pilot schools.

A notable project which has been particularly influential in stimulating interest in economic education in elementary schools is Senesh's "Our Working World" economic program planned for grades K–12. Dr. Senesh, widely recognized economist and professor of economic education at Purdue Uni-

---

[20] See Joint Council on Economic Education, *Teacher's Guide to Economic Education, Part I,* "Economic Ideas and Concepts"; *Part II,* "Suggestions for Grade Placement and Development of Economic Ideas and Concepts." (New York: Joint Council on Economic Education, 1964). Materials may be obtained for a small charge by writing the Joint Council on Economic Education, 2 West 46th Street, New York, N.Y. 10036. M. L. Frankel, director.

versity, developed some materials for "Our Working World" in the classrooms of the Elkhart, Indiana, public schools as part of an experiment in economic education financed by the Carnegie Corporation of New York and other sources of private support. The Elkhart project was begun in the fall of 1959, and more than 2000 primary grade students participated in the program during a four-year period prior to its publication by Science Research Associates. Materials are being prepared for a K–12 program. Presently the program through grade 3 has been published.

The child is taught to recognize fundamental economic concepts, to distinguish between these concepts, and to understand how they interact with one another. The program acknowledges the broad experience of an elementary school child and helps him to develop a sound understanding of how the world around him operates and the important part he, as an individual, can play in it. Therefore, the other social sciences, such as anthropology, geography, history, sociology, and political science, become an integral part of the program as they relate to the basic economic understandings.

In "Our Working World" story materials and activities have been planned around situations familiar to an elementary school child, beginning with economic concepts related to the child's life at home and expanding to the neighborhood, city, and larger communities of men. In this manner the whole set of basic economic ideas gains wider depth as the child's experience increases. This approach begins with the fundamental concepts of economics and teaches them with increasing depth and complexity as the children climb the academic ladder from grade to grade. Called by the author "the organic curriculum," this approach stresses the interrelationships of ideas determined by the basic structure of economics as opposed to the idea of concepts presented atomistically between grade 1 and grade 12. It is hoped that by the end of their school careers children will possess the analytical qualities needed to participate actively and intelligently in a dynamic society. The grade-level themes for the primary grades are as follows:

> Grade 1. Families at Work
> Work Inside the Home
> Work Outside the Home
>
> Grade 2. Neighbors at Work
> What Is a Neighborhood?
> Types of Neighborhoods
> Institutions Guided by Prices and Profit
> Institutions Guided by General Welfare
> Dynamics of the Neighborhood
> School: Threshold to the World
>
> Grade 3. Cities at Work

This program has demonstrated that elementary and fundamental principles of economics can be taught effectively to children even as early as the primary grades if appropriate teaching materials are developed. Instruction in this area need not be deferred until high school or college as has been the practice in the past. There is agreement among economists and educators that the lack of economic literacy on the part of Americans in our increasingly complex society is a costly weakness this nation can no longer afford.

A second project based upon a fundamental structure of economics is the Elementary School Economics Program developed at the University of Chicago, Department of Industrial Relations, and directed by William D. Rader. The project focused on an economic program for the intermediate grades. Six units have been developed for use in grades 4 and 5 that are organized around basic economic understandings. The first two units deal with the scarcity concept—how scarcity affects all individuals in our society, how nations make choices of what and how to produce, and why all choices cannot be satisfied. Units three through six are centered on how Americans deal with the problem of scarcity. Included in these units are understandings related to our exchange system, the impact of consumer choices on our economic life, why people save money, and the relationships among wants, work, and money.

New Developments in Anthropology

A pioneering effort in anthropology for the elementary grades (1 through 7) was approved at the University of Georgia under Project Social Studies. This project was initiated to prepare "instructional materials logically organized according to the discipline of anthropology."[21] "The Concept of Culture" is the topic selected for grades 1 and 4. The first-grade unit develops three ethnographies—American, Kazak, and Arunta. The point of departure is the American culture compared with that of the Arunta and Kazak. These two cultures were selected because they are so little known that neither teacher nor pupil would approach the study with stereotypes. The first-grade unit covers the following seven topics:

1 How We Study People
2 Housing
3 Material Culture
4 Earning a Living
5 The Family
6 The Community
7 Religion.

The fourth-grade unit covers these topics:

1 How We Study People
2 Concept of Culture
3 Cultural Universals and Cultural Variations
4 Enculturation
5 Culture Dynamics.

The instructional units were developed by two groups of cooperating teachers with the expert help of project leaders. One group of teachers received systematic instruction in anthropology prior to teaching the units. Suitability of materials for more widespread use in the schools will be checked by comparing the achievement of pupils taught by "trained" teachers with

[21] Wilfred C. Bailey and Marion J. Rice, *Development of a Sequential Curriculum in Anthropology for Grades 1–7* (Athens: University of Georgia, 1964).

that of pupils taught by "untrained" teachers. Results of the findings will undoubtedly throw a much-needed light on the kind of anthropological concepts that can be taught to elementary children and how teachers can prepare to do this most effectively.

Another significant project in this area is that of Educational Services, Incorporated (ESI) under the direction of Jerome Bruner, director of the Center for Cognitive Studies at Harvard University, and Program Co-Directors Elting E. Morison of M.I.T. and Franklin K. Patterson of Tufts University. The content for the course of study is man: his nature as a species, the forces that shaped and continue to shape his humanity. According to Bruner three questions recur throughout:

> What is human about human beings?
> How did they get that way?
> How can they be made more so?[22]

In pursuit of the answers, five great humanizing forces are explored: "tool-making," "language," "social organization," "the management of man's prolonged childhood" and "man's urge to explain." A complete K–12 series of units was produced. The elementary project was essentially a study of the prehistory of man, with units based upon significant turning points in human history until approximately 2500 B.C., when urban life emerged and the urban-rural setting, in which most of conventional Western history has taken place, was complete. The sequence of units is as follows: I. The Netsilik Eskimo, II. Aborigines and Bushmen, III. Evolution, IV. The Origins of Husbandry, V. The Origins of Urban Life, and VI. The Origins of the Western Tradition.

The first unit is concerned with the Netsilik Eskimo of Pelly Bay, Canada. The basic idea developed is the relationship between man and his environment, relating by analogy to the long period of human existence during which men were hunters and gatherers of food. The second unit, based mainly on film footages, studies two hunting and gathering societies inhabiting similar environmental settings but producing quite different cultures. The third unit deals directly with the subject of human evolution and the general traits that gave man the capacity for culture. The fourth unit deals with the change from the nomadic hunting-and-gathering way of life to the settled form of existence based upon animal and plant husbandry. Study is made of agriculture in this hemisphere in the Tehuacan Valley of Mexico. The fifth unit deals with the origins of urbanism in Ancient Mesopotamia. A film sequence has been developed on the Ancient Sumerian city of Nippur in Iraq. The sixth unit deals with the emergence of a culture which could be called proto-Western in the Bronze Age of Homeric Greece. Units were tested in a limited number of classrooms in the fall and winter of 1964–1965 prior to more widespread dissemination and use in the schools.

The following project has not been thought of as a special project in anthropology for the elementary grades. Nevertheless it has been included in

---

[22] Jerome S. Bruner, *Man: A Course of Study* (44A Brattle Street, Cambridge, Massachusetts: Occasional Paper No. 3, The Social Studies Curriculum Program, Educational Services Incorporated, June 1965).

this section because the program contains many concepts related to developing an understanding of both the physical and the cultural elements of man's development.

The Harvard-Lexington Project was initiated in 1960 as a cooperative research project in the social studies by Harvard University and the Lexington, Massachusetts, School System. Joseph C. Grannis of Harvard University, director of the project, described the development of the project as follows:

> For several years, the writer has been engaged with teachers of two elementary schools in Lexington, Massachusetts, and with his colleagues and students at Harvard in exploring ways of combining the advantages of the chronological, expanding communities, and problem's approaches to social studies. *We began with a sequence of generalizations,* proposed by a member of the Harvard-Lexington research and development staff, Mrs. Beverly Simpson Stone. These generalizations, selected from a number of sources . . . were recommended *not as summary statements of content* but as points of convergence and departure for social studies inquiry. A number of generalizations were suggested for each grade level, together with several units and a general theme for each grade.[23]

The major generalizations K–6 are:

> K The ways of man are more flexible and inventive than the ways of other animals.
>
> 1 Men have many different ways of meeting similar needs.
>
> 2 Human groups and institutions involve various patterns of norms, interactions, and feelings.
>
> 3 Primitive societies have adapted to a variety of natural habitats.
>
> 4 Man finds new ways to control his relationship to his environment.
>
> 5 The industrial revolution has changed the production and distribution of goods and services and has created new opportunities and problems for human society.
>
> 6 Man's acts of inquiry, creativity, and expression evolve from and influence his total way of life.

The sequence of the program moves almost immediately to people and places beyond the child's firsthand experience, but it also establishes bases for relating to this experience. It tries to respect the general principle of involving successively more complex contexts from one year to the next, but there is also an effort to have the learning be more cumulative conceptually from year to year than in the expanding-communities approach. Although it employs chronology it moves more freely through time than a rigorous chronological sequence. And though the curriculum is interdisciplinary, each of the major social science disciplines can be brought into focus at various junctures.[24]

[23] Joseph C. Grannis, "The Framework of the Social Studies Curriculum," *The National Elementary Principal* 42: 24, April 1963.
[24] Ibid., pp. 25–26.

New Developments in Political Science

Many of the new developments in the area of political science on the elementary level have been concerned with identifying the fundamental concepts and ideas to be included in the elementary social studies program.[25] In addition a strong plea has been made by educators and political scientists for more fundamental instruction in government and political processes on the elementary level.

A noteworthy project dealing directly with education in the fundamentals of government has been developed by the Davis County School District, Farmington, Utah. The major purpose of the project is to provide a model program introducing elementary school students to the functioning of government through a student-government program set up as an essential part of the social studies curriculum. Participation in the student-government activities provides the students with the direct experience necessary for the formation and broadening of concepts, while the social studies instruction provides the conceptual framework that is essential for intelligent participation in elections, using the processes of government to affect decision, and participation in discussions of issues. The objectives of the instructional program then are to (1) increase the student's knowledge of the workings of government and (2) to increase his ability and tendency to participate in governmental processes through a student-government social studies program.

The student-government program is organized around the fifth and sixth grades. (Note: A program involving the third and fourth grades has recently been developed.)

Each classroom has established a government modeled after a common form of city government. Different types, e.g., mayor-council, council–city manager, or commission are used as models. All classes in a school do not use the same model and may change models midway in the school year to provide the students experience with the terminology and features of the varying forms of city government in the surrounding communities. The area of responsibility is the classroom. Governmental meetings are held during school time, decisions are made in regard to such classroom matters as housekeeping, bulletin board displays, hospitality, and rule enforcement. The object is to function as nearly as possible like a city government.

Following the organization of each classroom into cities, the fifth and sixth grades have elected representatives to a constitutional convention. At this convention, which is held over a period of many weeks, the students write a school constitution that contains the elements necessary to set up a federal system of government for the school. The constitution becomes the most important document in the school. Ratification of the constitution by each fifth- and sixth-grade class then makes the provisions contained therein binding on the students. Election of a president, vice-president, senators, representatives, and all other officers as mentioned in the constitution is held.

[25] See Appendix A; see also Paul R. Hanna, "The Social Studies Program in the Elementary School in the Twentieth Century," in *The Social Studies: Curriculum Proposals for the Future,* ed. Wesley Sowards (Glenview, Ill.: Scott, Foresman, 1963), pp. 42–78.

The congress meets during the school for three sessions lasting one hour per day for one week.

The responsibility given to the students is in the area of the building outside the classroom and the playground. Intramural activities, as well as outdoor safety and playground regulations, are the concern of the students.

The federal government is modeled after our national government as closely as possible, giving students the correct example of the function of our system of government.

Students carry the responsibility given to them by the constitution but must, of necessity, not enter into areas where school policy is set or where school policy takes preference.

The social studies program is directly related to the student-government program. At both grade levels, the purpose and role of government in society and the governing process are stressed.

Special attention is given to explication and clarifying the values that underlie democratic government. These include commitment to following majority decisions and respect for minority rights. To the extent possible, social studies instruction is based upon the students' participation in the operations of the various aspects of the student government. All students participate as elected or appointed officers and as discussant-voters.[26]

CONSOLIDATING GAINS

One of the major questions has now become How can the results of these many findings be best utilized by local school systems? John S. Gibson states the problem as follows:

> There is much more in elementary grade social studies re-
> search and development—perhaps even too much. Can the
> materials be transferred out of one project and into the main-
> stream of elementary school education? Are the teacher
> guides adequate? Is the content of material being produced
> pitched at too high or too low a level? What about evaluation,
> proliferation of publications several years hence, and creative
> activity in the audio-visual field? Why do not national finding
> agencies or organizations establish a social studies clearing-
> house for the wider evaluation and dissemination of the new
> work in this area? These and many other questions can and
> must be raised by those of us who seek to translate the best of
> the innovative social studies programs to the structure and
> content of the elementary school curriculum—and to do this
> job so that students themselves in the classroom may take away
> the best with them.[27]

It is most likely that there will never be complete agreement as to the one best design for elementary school social studies. This is as it should be. We

[26] *An Exemplary Student-Government Social Studies Program for the Elementary Schools,* Davis County School District, Farmington, Utah. For further information: Ralph H. Davis, Director, American Values Exemplary Center Taylor School, 293 East Pages Lane, Centerville, Utah.
[27] John S. Gibson, "The Big Revolution in Social Studies," *Grade Teacher,* October 1965, p. 135.

have made tremendous progress in our nationwide effort to improve the social studies through diversity in designs. Each design, however, has provided a well-balanced program geared to local needs and preferences, with all of the major social science disciplines brought into focus clearly and effectively at various junctures in the sequence. We now have before us for elementary school social studies more new exciting ideas, concepts, and information on what to teach elementary children than ever before. The test of the future is how well we can utilize and incorporate these advances into our teaching.

A sound word of warning regarding the adoption of new proposals in the social studies has been issued by Preston as follows:

> . . . Periods of change are not only periods of challenge. They are also periods of danger. They are exploited by sloganeers and faddists. If the social studies are to emerge sound and strong from the current ferment, it will be necessary for each new proposition to be scrutinized carefully and experimented with critically—particularly those propositions which are largely organizational in nature. Otherwise, we may find in fifteen years that, instead of having made progress, we have simply experienced another ride on a pendulum.[28]

A SUMMARY OF RECENT TRENDS

Major trends, many of which stem from new developments in the social studies, are summarized in this section to give a concise overview of the nature of the changes that have taken place in recent years.

1. *A trend is to focus instruction on the fundamental concepts or "big ideas" that have been identified by scholars in the various science disciplines.* Many of the fundamental idea relationships of the separate social science disciplines can be taught effectively at the earliest grade levels when organized in a conceptual structure with learning experiences suitable to the maturational level of the pupils.

The Social Studies Framework for the Public Schools of California[29] identifies the "basic ideas" or "concepts" from each of the eight fields of the social sciences. Geographers, economists, and other social scientists have helped formulate statements of important "big ideas" for social study instruction. The most effective instruction in the social studies is that organized around concepts. Children should have opportunities to formulate concepts and generalizations in their own words and to extend and deepen their understandings as they progress through the grades. The old approach of teaching isolated facts and bits of information related to a given topic is no longer defensible. Miel states:

> Conveying bits of information is the dimension that could well receive less "social studies" time. . . . They [teachers] could

[28] Ralph Preston, "The Social Studies: Nature, Purpose and Signs of Change," *The National Elementary Principal*, 42 (5): 13, May 1963.
[29] State Curriculum Commission, *Social Studies Framework for the Public Schools of California* (Sacramento: State Department of Education, 1962).

help children see how facts are interrelated and to draw helpful generalizations.[30]

The process of having the student gather up and memorize isolated facts related to a given topic results in verbal learning with little or no understanding. This may be one of the major reasons so many children have come to dislike social studies.

2. *Closely related to the above trend is a current emphasis upon a multidisciplinary approach to teaching the social studies.*[31] *Formerly, history, civics, and geography were the main areas from which the content of the social studies was drawn. Today, a greater emphasis is given to a balanced program that draws its content from all social science disciplines.* Studies of history and geography in the traditional meaning of the terms are not enough to equip modern-day youth with the necessary understandings, incentives, and skills for solving the problems facing our society, now or in the future. Understandings from other social science disciplines such as sociology, anthropology, and economics have evolved and are demanding a place along with the insights provided from older and more traditional fields.

There is a narrowing of the gap between the curriculum in the elementary school and available scholarly knowledge in all of the social science areas. Scholars are identifying the new and important concepts in their special fields of study and are giving greater assistance in curriculum planning. Thus, the notorious lag between new advances in the various disciplines and their adoption in the curriculum is being reduced. We now have more authentic, up-to-date information available for children than ever before and, therefore, little reason for neglecting a study of the less well-known social science areas.

There is a noticeable decline in emphasis upon the traditional dominance of chronological history in the social studies curriculum.

A new emphasis in geographical studies is appearing, with a stress on man's interaction with his cultural and physical environment. Formal geographical skills will be introduced to children earlier, beginning in kindergarten and primary grades.

Political science content has been expanded in the social studies curriculum. Comparative studies of governments, emphasizing political processes and behaviors rather than descriptions of governmental structure, are recommended.

The economic emphasis has been greatly accelerated, with greater attention given to fundamental idea relationships of economics or with its basic structure on the elementary level.

Materials from anthropology, sociology, and social psychology are being woven into the elementary social studies curriculum.

Comparative studies of family and community are frequently recommended for the early elementary grades as a means of introducing children to such

---

[30] Alice Miel, "Social Studies with a Difference," *The Instructor,* November, 1961, p. 6.
[31] See Paul R. Hanna et al., *Investigating Man's World,* Scott, Foresman's new Social Studies Program. The program is conceptually structured and inquiry oriented. It starts in Kindergarten with a simple investigation of each of the disciplines—sociology, economics, political science, etc. as they affect children in families, school, neighborhood. Similarly, the investigation continues as the children advance in their studies of larger communities of men.

ideas as cultural change and variation in ways of meeting basic needs from one culture to another.

3. *There is a trend toward an earlier introduction of certain ideas, concepts, and skills in the social studies to more adequately challenge the capabilities of children.* It is held by many educators and social scientists that young children are capable of understanding the basic or fundamental ideas of the various social science disciplines at much lower levels of maturity than previously believed possible. Bruner's idea that "any subject can be taught effectively in some intellectually honest form to any child at any stage of development"[32] is widely accepted. There has long been a feeling among educators that something should be done to make the social studies more challenging to children particularly in the earlier grades. According to Wilhelmina Hill:

> There is growing awareness that something must be done about social studies programs for primary grades. It is believed that such programs have been too watered down, much too thin.
>
> Young children today are growing up in an era of television, aviation, and space flight. Their interests and concerns transcend social studies curricula that are mainly local (home, school, neighborhood, community) in character. Practically all children have learned about the far-away from television, and the greatly increased mobility of our population means that many children have lived or travelled in several places.[33]

To meet needs of primary children some units of instruction have been moved downward in the grades. For example, basic units on the home, school, and neighborhood are now taught in the kindergarten. Pupils in the second and third grades make comparative studies of shelters and communities in different cultures. Too, new instructional programs and materials are being developed in connection with new projects in the social studies which will greatly strengthen and improve instruction in the primary grades.

4. *There is increased understanding of how to teach citizenship.* New thought is being given to ways to develop an understanding of our American heritage and a love of country. It is becoming increasingly clear that there is more to the teaching of citizenship than merely having the pupils memorize slogans and participate in patriotic ceremonies in the schools. Loyalty to democratic values can come about through a great variety of content. Although special attention is given to citizenship education in the social studies, children can learn the qualities of a good citizen in the lunchroom, math class, or other activities throughout the school day as effectively as during the social studies period.

The major elements of good citizenship can be taught indirectly, through good programs, rather than always by a frontal attack on citizenship in contrived situations. For example, the scope of civic responsibility includes

[32] Jerome S. Bruner, *The Process of Education* (Cambridge: Harvard University Press, 1961), p. 33.
[33] Wilhelmina Hill, "Major Concerns About the Social Studies," *The National Elementary Principal* 42 (6): 40, May 1963.

helping the child to know what it means to become a good citizen in the home, school, neighborhood, community, state, nation, and world. This kind of knowledge is "built-in" in good social study programs. Also, other elements of good citizenship, such as critical thinking, loyalty to democratic ideals, and responsible behavior are all by-products of social studies well taught. The knowledge and understandings gained by pupils in effective social study programs is the best preparation possible for responsible citizenship, for the ability to make wise decisions is dependent upon clear concepts. Children should, then, be provided opportunity during the school day, as well as outside the school, to practice the ways of democracy.

5. *A greater emphasis is being given to international and cross-cultural understanding.* Modern means of transportation and communication have made the earth smaller. Therefore, it is more important than ever before that we teach children correct concepts about other peoples and how to live together in harmony. George S. Counts has said, "We must remember that the earth today is a little neighborhood."

Children should be taught clearer understandings of other cultures and their contributions to the advancement of mankind. One pitfall is to teach about other countries as they existed yesterday, but not as they exist today. According to Wanda Robertson, teachers, in an attempt to interest children in a study of other countries, often stress the bizarre, the extreme, or the romantic, or present as the norm a picture quite remote from reality.[34] To many children, Holland means windmills, although few are still to be found, and to many children all Eskimos make their homes in igloos. All too often people are presented in a stereotyped fashion; Africans, for example, are described as naked, drum-beating savages living in mud huts in the jungles. Mexicans are often pictured as a backward, lazy people who spend much time sleeping in the sun with little else to do. Such presentations have no place in the social studies, since they only give children distorted views of other countries.

We have learned much in the past few years as to how we can best extend the capacity of children to better understand other peoples. Ethnocentricity has been one of the major blocks to real understanding. A person of one culture responds to a foreign culture in terms of the values and norms of his own culture. One of the major tasks of the elementary school should be that of helping children in the development of cross-cultural sensitivity, whether with regard to other national cultures or in relation to subcultures within a nation. This sensitivity requires an *objectivity* about one's own culture, with the ability to see members of other cultures in terms of *that* culture's values and standards. It requires an extended capacity to understand others, a sensitivity that allows the child to see the "culturally other" in its own right.

Schools generally do not provide children enough opportunity for cross-group association. Children from the same neighborhood social groups are, by and large, thrown together in the same activity groups. According to Preston, teaching world understanding to children should begin with firsthand

[34] Wanda Robertson, *An Evaluation of the Cultural Unit Method for Social Education* (New York: Teachers College, Columbia University, 1950).

experiences at home.[35] Children must learn to relate effectively to other children in the classroom who may differ from them in social, racial, or religious backgrounds before they can extend this understanding on a wider basis. They must also develop a love of their community and their homeland if they are to respect and appreciate the love of others for their countries. These kinds of understandings and attitudes actually become the basis of internationalism.

Traditional social studies programs were orientated almost exclusively to the study of the United States and Western Europe. Presently, there is a strong emphasis on non-Western studies and world affairs. There is a trend in the early grades to include comparative study of families, communities, and regions. This makes it possible to include examples from Asia, Africa, and Latin America.

6. *The modern social studies program has achieved a sensible balance between the content-centered position and the learner-centered approach with its strong emphasis on "process" and children's interests.* According to Hanna:

> In the third quarter of this century we witness balance being restored in the social studies program as the content is once again rooted in social science generalizations that are fed by the less formal experiences of contemporary happenings and by youngsters' responses. Contemporary professional education literature clearly reflects the acceptance of the notion that "today we teach children something." And that "something" is the resultant of a synthesis of content from all three sources built around generalizations drawn from the social sciences.[36]

The renewed emphasis on content to be learned is not a retreat from recognizing the importance of the child and his needs in the educational program. Rather, we can teach the content that society feels is important for children to learn and still do an effective job of helping children meet contemporary social problems and persistent life situations in their daily living. Content and method are recognized as inseparable components in teaching. Jarolimek states:

> It is unfortunate that we have allowed the idea to develop that a social studies program which is rich in content is necessarily hostile to learner-centered teaching. Since ineffective teachers often made poor selections of content, we have tended to associate subject matter with poor teaching—but this does not make the content of social studies any less important, it simply means that a particular teacher is making unwise use of it.[37]

The more sensible position to which we have come in our social studies program has long been advocated by educational leaders. In 1938, John

[35] For an excellent discussion of "how" one might proceed with children to teach world understanding see Ralph Preston, *Teaching World Understanding* (Englewood Cliffs, N.J.: Prentice-Hall, 1955).
[36] Paul R. Hanna in *Social Studies in the Elementary Schools*, Thirty-Second Yearbook, ed. John U. Michaelis (Washington, D.C.: The National Education Association, 1962), p. 64.
[37] John Jarolimek, "Curriculum Content and the Child in the Elementary School," *Social Education* 26: 59, February 1962.

Dewey spoke out against the excesses of an extreme learner-centered position as follows:

> It is ground for legitimate criticism, however, when the ongoing movement of progressive education fails to recognize that the problem of selection and organization of subject matter for study and learning is fundamental. Improvision that takes advantage of special occasions prevents teaching and learning from becoming stereotyped and dead. But the basic material of study cannot be picked up in such a cursory manner. Occasions which are not and cannot be foreseen are bound to arise wherever there is intellectual freedom. They should be utilized. But there is a decided difference between using them in the development of a continuing line of activity and trusting them to provide the chief material of learning.[38]

Essentially the same point of view is summed up by John Childs. He says:

> I consider it important for American educators to recognize that devotion to the ideals of democracy in no way bars us from making a deliberate effort to nurture the young in the essential patterns of democratic life and thought. If our schools are to serve as positive agencies for the maintenance of a free society, they must be concerned today with "society" as well as with the "child," with the "subject matter" as well as with the "method," with "product" as well as with "process," with human "responsibilities" as well as with human "freedoms," with social and moral "ends" as well as with classroom "procedures" and educational "means."[39]

It is not a matter, therefore, of an "either/or" situation in the social studies—a "child-centered" position on one hand as opposed to a "content-centered" position on the other. Rather we can draw from society and from the current life situations encountered by children the materials for a curriculum design that will capitalize on current interests and motivations while assuring the survival and progress of our important values and institutions.

7. *Increased emphasis is being placed on the skills of inquiry, learning by discovery, and creativity.* This type of approach facilitates the improvement of children's ability to think, analyze, and check conclusions. It involves creating inductive learning sequences which start with specific experiences and lead to the discovery of concepts, subgeneralizations, and generalizations by the children. The more traditional approach has been the deductive development that begins with a statement of the general idea and then proceeds to illustrate and develop it.

The inductive type of inquiry enables children to practice the skills of gathering information, classifying and synthesizing the data collected, and perceiving significant relationships. There is evidence that principles which the student learns by "self-discovery" are understood more clearly, retained longer, and utilized more effectively. However, the problem of how best to

[38] John Dewey, *Experience and Education* (New York: Macmillan, 1938), pp. 95–96.
[39] John L. Childs, *Education and Morals* (New York: Appleton-Century-Crofts, 1950), p. ix.

organize teaching materials to provide for an inductive approach to learning remains. Taba states:

> It will require both a different curriculum and a different way of learning from those we have now to achieve productive and autonomous thinking. In the first place, attention needs to be focused on the essential principles and ideas which give structure to thinking. Second, learning experiences need to include more opportunities for inquiry, discovery, and experimentation. Current practices, anchored as they are in transmitting rather than creating knowledge, may be too much concerned with "getting the right answer." One need only look at discussions in which the questions asked are so closed-ended that the main intellectual effort of students goes into guessing what the teacher expects as the right answer or to remembering what the book says on the point, rather than into developing a rational method of arriving at answers and solutions and multiple ways for analyzing and interpreting facts.[40]

Therefore, more effective social studies teaching is becoming dependent upon increasing opportunities for children to discover basic principles for themselves. "Replicating the discovery of knowledge is a prerequisite for acquiring the cultural heritage and is, therefore, a characteristic of the modern social studies."[41]

Learning by discovery facilitates the improvement of children's creative abilities—abilities to think, analyze, and check conclusions. Teaching strategies are being developed to encourage the learner to find out for himself. Inductive approaches, inquiry, and discovery are widely recommended. Emphasis is being placed on helping pupils learn how to apply on an elementary level some of the modes of inquiry and methods of study of scholars in the various social sciences.

8. *There is a trend toward teaching for greater depth of understanding involving a spiraling development of basic ideas from grade to grade.* In the past, in order to cover the whole course of study, often it was just a slimming "Covering a Country in a Day's Recitation"; now the trend is to provide opportunities for study in depth of a selected region and culture. An attempt is made to achieve a more reasonable balance between breadth and depth of coverage by reducing the content to be covered into fewer units of more manageable size and providing for the units to focus mainly on central ideas that have the greatest applicability and transfer. A wide, broad coverage is often inefficient in that content becomes too repetitious and learning too atomized. It is difficult under this kind of coverage to develop important concepts and insure retention of what is learned.

The "spiraling" curriculum[42] is one means of helping children develop

[40] Hilda Taba. *Curriculum Development, Theory and Practice* (New York: Harcourt Brace Jovanovich, 1962), p. 71.

[41] For a complete unit outline of the inductive approach, see N.E.A., *Guiding Children Through the Social Studies* (Washington, D.C.: Department of Elementary-Kindergarten-Nursery Education, 1964).

[42] For a detailed account of the spiral development of generalization, see Hilda Taba and James L. Hills, *Teacher Handbook for Contra Costa Social Studies*, Grades 1–6 (San Francisco: San Francisco State College, 1965).

greater depth of understanding. It provides a vertically orientated framework in which basic ideas that thread throughout the entire curriculum sequence are identified. These understandings cannot be learned in any given unit or even in one year, but rather are developed throughout the total sequence by a series of small steps. Ideas can be dealt with on a concrete or relatively simple level in the early grades. As children move up from grade to grade they extend and deepen their understanding of basic ideas by gathering and organizing information, thus adding new dimensions of meaning to beginning concepts.

Briefly, the spiral development of concepts is a depth method of studying which moves up vertically with each idea from grade to grade, thereby providing opportunity for children to "revisit" each basic idea on higher levels of complexity and abstractness.

9. *There is a greater emphasis upon behavioralizing lesson objectives. Behavioral objectives become a means of evaluation by identifying specific desired outcomes of learning.* When stated in behavioral or operational terms that clearly define the expected behavior, objectives become more tangible and provide a basis for accurate appraisal of student growth and teacher effectiveness.

10. *There is a trend toward emphasis on "learning how to learn" such as reading skills, map-reading concepts and skills, interpreting graphs and tables, locating and appraising sources of information, pooling ideas from several sources of information, outlining, summarizing, reporting, and home study.* Thus the skills involved in the use of textbooks, atlases, gazetteers, indexes, encyclopedias, and library resources can be brought to a high level in the social studies.

11. *Recognizing the inadequacy of the conventional textbook, especially when used as a single source of information for students to consult, there is an increased emphasis on multimedia materials.* This wide range of learning resources includes the use of reading materials, programmed materials, films and kits, maps, globes, artifacts, etc.

12. *The process approach is gaining momentum.* Content becomes the vehicle rather than an end in itself, but this fact does not suggest that it makes no difference what topics or content is selected for study.[43]

13. *There is a trend toward more individualization of instruction in the social studies, more emphasis upon packaged or individual units that children can work through at their own rates of speed, and more emphasis upon interest units where students can have some choice in the selection of topics and units of study.*

14. *There is a new emphasis on helping students gain a realistic understanding of the dynamic factors that have shaped and are shaping the national society.*

15. *Closely related to the above trend, there is a strong emphasis upon a study of present problems rather than a study of the past in an attempt to*

---

[43] See "Explanation on Thought Processes and Applying Knowledge in Functional Situations" (Princeton, N.J.: Edcom Systems, Inc.).

find a new relevancy in the social studies by bringing them back in touch with social reality.

QUESTIONS AND ACTIVITIES

1 / Describe the early developments of the social studies in this country prior to the twentieth century.

2 / When and by what means did the term "social studies" first receive widespread acceptance?

3 / Define "scope" and "sequence." Outline in detail the scope and sequence of the expanding-environment approach.

4 / Identify the basic or fundamental assumptions underlying the life-situations approach. Discuss the validity of the major criticisms of this approach.

5 / Explain why unified social studies programs have continued to gain in popularity on the elementary school level.

6 / Identify some of the criticisms of the separate-subjects approach. Do you agree with these criticisms? In what ways does your opinion differ?

7 / Make a report on "Project Social Studies," listing major purposes and features of the overall project.

8 / Explain why the study of economics, anthropology, political science, and sociology are assuming an important place in elementary school social studies today along with the study of history and geography.

9 / Select one of the basic social science fields. Report to the class the nature of the discipline selected, its major contributions to elementary school social studies, and a promising new development in the field selected.

10 / Make a careful examination of an elementary social studies textbook and the teacher's guide. Determine to what extent the text utilizes concepts from all of the major social science disciplines. List examples of concepts identified under each area.

11 / Select and describe a new social studies project that you feel has made a significant contribution to the future development of the social studies. List the limitations or weaknesses, if any, that you see in the new project.

12 / Evaluate the modern trends which stem from new developments in the social studies. Which of the trends do you consider to be most significant? Why?

SELECTED REFERENCES

American Council of Learned Societies and the National Council for the Social Studies. *The Social Studies and the Social Sciences.* New York: Harcourt Brace Jovanovich, 1962.

ASCD. "Social Ferment and the Social Sciences." *Educational Leadership.* Vol. 22, No. 5, February 1965.

Beals, Ralph L. and Hoijer, Harry. *An Introduction to Anthropology.* Third edition. New York: Macmillan, 1965.

Bruner, J. S. "The Act of Discovery," *Harvard Educational Review.* Vol. 31, Winter 1961.

Calderwood, James D. "Economic Ideas and Concepts." *Teachers Guide to Developmental Economic Education Program,* Part One. New York: Joint Council on Economic Education, 1964.

Chase, Stuart. *The Proper Study of Mankind.* New York: Harper & Row, 1956.

Collingwood, R. G. *The Idea of History.* New York: Oxford University Press, 1956.

Commager, Henry Steele. *The Nature and the Study of History.* Columbus, Ohio: Charles E. Merrill, 1965.

Easton, David. *The Political System.* New York: Knopf, 1953.

Economic Education in the Schools, A Report of the National Task Force on Economic Education. New York: The Committee for Economic Development, 1961.

Frankel, M. L. *Economic Education.* New York: The Center for Applied Research, 1965.

Hanna, Paul R., "Revising the Social Studies: What Is Needed?" *Social Education* 27: 190–196, April 1963.

Jarolimek, John. "Political Science in the Elementary and Junior High School Curriculum." In *Political Science in the Social Studies,* Thirty-sixth Yearbook. Robert E. Cleary and Donald H. Riddle (eds.), Washington, D.C.: National Council for the Social Studies, 1966.

Jarolimek, John. *Social Studies in Elementary Education.* Third edition. New York: Macmillan, 1967. Chap. 1.

Jarolimek, John, and Walsh, Juber M. (eds.). *Readings on and for Social Studies in Elementary Education.* New York: Macmillan, 1965.

Joint Council on Economic Education, *Teachers Guide to Economic Education Program,* Part I, *Economic Ideas and Concepts;* Part II, *Suggestions for Grade Placement and Development of Economic Ideas and Concepts.* New York: Joint Council on Economic Education, 1964.

Kazamias, Andreas M., and Massialas, Byron G. *Tradition and Change in Education.* Englewood Cliffs, N.J.: Prentice-Hall, 1965.

Lee, John R., and McLendon, Jonathon C. (eds.). *Readings on Elementary Social Studies—Prologue to Change.* Boston: Allyn & Bacon, 1965. Part A.

Massialas, Byron G., and Kazamias, Andreas M. (eds.). *Crucial Issues in the Teachings of Social Studies: A Book of Readings.* Englewood Cliffs, N.J.: Prentice-Hall, 1964.

Michaelis, John U. *Social Studies for Children in a Democracy—Recent Trends and Developments.* Englewood Cliffs, N.J.: Prentice-Hall, 1960. Chap. 1.

Michaelis, John U., and Johnston, A. Montgomery. *The Social Sciences: Foundations of the Social Studies.* Boston: Allyn & Bacon, 1965.

Miel, Alice, and Brogan, Peggy. *More Than Social Studies.* Englewood Cliffs, N.J.: Prentice-Hall, 1957.

Morrissett, Irving (ed.). *Concepts and Structure in the New Social Science Curricula.* West Lafayette, Indiana: Social Science Education Consortium, 1966.

Muessig, Raymond H., and Rogers, Vincent R. (eds.). *Social Science Seminar Series.* (Six volumes on anthropology, sociology, political science, and economics.) Columbus, Ohio: Charles E. Merrill, 1965.

National Council for the Social Studies. *New Perspectives in World History,* Thirty-fourth Yearbook. Washington, D.C. NCSS, 1964.

National Council for the Social Studies. *Political Science in the Social Studies,* Thirty-sixth Yearbook. Donald H. Riddle and Robert S. Cleary (eds.). Washington, D.C.: NCSS, 1966.

National Education Association. *Focus on Social Studies.* Report from the 1965 Department on Elementary School Principals Annual Meeting. Washington, D.C.: NEA, 1965.

Rose, Caroline B. *Sociology: The Study of Man in Society.* Columbus, Ohio: Charles E. Merrill, 1965.

Sorauf, Frank J. *Political Science, An Informal Overview.* Columbus, Ohio: Charles E. Merrill, 1965.

Spindler, George D. (ed.). *Education and Culture.* New York: Holt, Rinehart & Winston, 1963.

Stratemeyer, Florence B., Forkner, H. L., and McKim, M. G. *Developing a Curriculum for Modern Living.* Second edition revised. New York: Teachers College, Columbia University, 1957.

Valdes, Donald M., and Dean, Dwight G. *Sociology in Use.* New York: Macmillan, 1965.

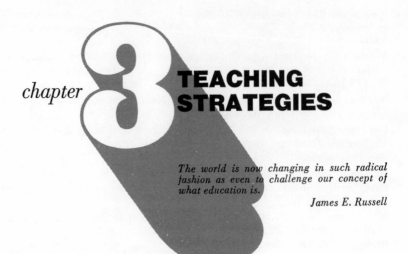

chapter **3 TEACHING STRATEGIES**

The world is now changing in such radical fashion as even to challenge our concept of what education is.

James E. Russell

Social studies have long been among the least popular subjects in the elementary school curriculum. Research has shown that when children have been asked to indicate their preferences among elementary school subjects, they have given social studies a low rating. Chase studied preferences of fifth-grade children. Results of the investigation showed that only 9 percent chose social studies. (The most popular subject was reading, which received 23 percent of the first choices.)[1]

A later study by Mosher bore out earlier findings that social studies was not generally a popular subject with children but was among the "disliked" subjects at both the elementary and junior high school levels.[2]

It is significant, however, that the unfavorable attitudes of children toward the social studies did not arise from a lack of interest in the topics that belong to this area of study. Studies have shown that while children are apparently not interested in the social studies as they are usually taught, they are interested in learning more about things in the world that can be categorized as social study content. For example, Baker collected more than 9000 spontaneous questions of children and found that approximately 50 percent of them belonged in the social studies area.[3]

Another study by Jersild and Tasch showed that when children listed what

[1] W. Linwood Chase, "Subject Preferences of Fifth-Grade Children," *Elementary School Journal,* December 1949, pp. 204–211.
[2] Howard H. Mosher, "Subject Preferences of Girls and Boys," *School Review,* January 1952, pp. 34–38.
[3] Emily V. Baker, *Children's Questions and Their Implications for Planning the Curriculum* (New York: Teachers College, Columbia University, 1945), pp. 27–34.

they would like to learn more about in school the majority of them wanted to know about the kinds of things that might be classified as social study information.[4]

These findings raise an important question: How can teachers salvage social studies from an academic tradition that has tended to reduce them to a body of dry, factual material of little interest to children? It is quite obvious that educators generally and more specifically teachers of social studies have failed somewhere along the way to bring social studies to life, and to make them more challenging to children. When teachers succeed in making social studies attractive and meaningful to children, the children are enthusiastic about the content. Perhaps children's curiosity about and interest in the social studies in the past has been destroyed by indefensible methods of teaching, gross misuse of the textbook, and failure to focus teaching around important understandings and concepts of vital concern to children and society.

NEWER CONCEPTS OF TEACHING

The concept of teaching is changing. We are abandoning the role of the teacher as we have known it in the past. It is becoming quite clear that competent teaching does not include dispensing information verbally and teaching for its mastery, personally directing all classroom activity, or managing student behavior. The evolving concept of teaching competency is being clarified by facts about human behavior and the forces that shape it. These facts come from two sources: (1) innovative ideas over the past decade concerning the elements of the instructional process and (2) studies of human behavior.

New literature related to the instructional process has stressed the importance of teaching children to think analytically and creatively, not just repeat back to the teacher pat answers for pat questions. The bases for new changes have come from imaginative work done during the last decade by such educational leaders as Bloom, Bruner, Guilford, Goodlad, Suchman, Mager, Torrance, Galloway, Getzels, Taba, Woodruff, Bellack, and Flanders, to name but a few. Such work has suggested the following new elements of education:

1 Analysis of verbal patterns within the classroom; a greater emphasis upon divergent thinking

2 Objectives that identify behaviors to be shaped in students (behavioral objectives)

3 The concept of individuation of instruction

4 Nongrading of classes and of subject-matter content

5 Assembling of teachers and teams with differentiated roles

6 Flexible scheduling

7 Having individualized unit packages accessible to students without their waiting for the teacher[5]

[4] Arthur T. Jersild and Ruth J. Tasch, *Children's Interests and What They Suggest for Education* (New York: Teachers College, Columbia University, 1949), pp. 27–34.
[5] See Chapter 4, "Developing Teaching Units in the Social Studies," for an example of individualized units and how to construct them.

8 Emphasis on conceptual learning rather than on storing of verbal information

9 Techniques of simulation to create reality in learning situations

10 Encouragement of inferential or inductive processes of reasoning

11 Developing inquiry skills

12 Cultivation of creative talents.[6]

All of these ideas carry a common message. They present the learner as an aggressive, self-guiding investigator. He has moved from academia where he played a passive classroom-student role to a new setting composed of realities that make up his environment. His teacher no longer "dispenses" knowledge; he plans, sets the stage, diagnoses, prescribes, and troubleshoots. He has stopped trying to "teach." He now produces and adjusts conditions that make it possible for his students to learn. The teacher has traditionally been the most active person. In this new approach, the teacher drops into the background and the learner becomes the active person.

Learning requires conditions that make real behavior and behavior-shaping possible. Traditional teaching methods have consistently violated certain learning principles associated with behavioral change. The acquisition of bodies of verbal knowledge is not likely to influence greatly the learner's decision-making behavior in life.

Influences that elicit student perception, recall, review, conclusions, predictions, and evaluation are indirect and highly educative. Influences that describe, give data, state conclusions, and state moral precepts without allowing students to recognize them from their natural premises are direct and inhibitive of student thinking.

It is most generally agreed that the kinds of questions directed to children by the teacher is of critical importance in developing independent and creative thinking. Gallagher and Aschner have developed a system containing four categories that are particularly useful for thinking about questions.[7] The four categories are: *cognitive-memory, convergent, divergent,* and *evaluative.*

Cognitive-Memory Questions **/** These questions call for facts or other items which can be recalled. A cognitive-memory question is narrow and involves rote memory. Some examples are:

1 What is the largest city in New York State?

2 How did you come to school this morning?

3 Name the ABC countries of South America.

Convergent Questions **/** Questions which ask for "analysis and integration of given or remembered data" are convergent questions. Problem-solving and reasoning are often involved in this category. The answers

[6] Adapted from Asahel D. Woodruff, "A Dynamic Concept of the Learning Environment—'To Learn' Not 'To Teach' " (unpublished mimeographed paper, University of Utah, 1968).
[7] James J. Gallagher and Mary Jane Aschner, "A Preliminary Report on Analyses of Classroom Interaction," *The Merrill-Palmer Quarterly of Behavior and Development,* Vol. 9, no. 3, 1963.

to these questions may be predictable, but convergent questions are always broader than cognitive-memory questions.

> 1 What is there about the position of New York City that accounts for its importance?
>
> 2 Suppose that overnight the school were picked up and moved four blocks away, and you were not told of the move, how could you go about finding it?
>
> 3 What is there about the ABC countries that makes them important in South America?

Divergent Questions **/** Questions in this category call for answers that are creative and imaginative, that move into new directions. Here are some divergent questions:

> 1 How might the lives of the people in New York City be different if the city were located in the torrid zone?
>
> 2 Invent some ways for coming to school which haven't been invented yet.
>
> 3 In what ways might Argentina, Brazil, and Chile be different if they had been colonized by England?

Evaluative Questions **/** These are questions that deal with "matters of judgment, value, and choice." They may be either broad or narrow. "Did you like that story?" is a narrow question; "How did you feel about that story?" is a broad question. Some of the examples of evaluative questions are:

> 1 What would it be like to live in New York City? Would you like to live in New York?
>
> 2 What things would you particularly like to visit in Argentina? Would you prefer to be a cowboy or a gaucho?[8]

The task of helping youth grow in their ability to think rationally, of course, cannot be limited to the learning experiences provided by the social studies of any one subject-matter area. To be completely effective it will require a form of integration or pooling of forces for this development in all subject-matter areas, no matter how diverse the content of these subjects.

APPROPRIATENESS OF MATERIALS

The materials of learning consist of perceptual materials, discussion questions and guides, and any other form of stimulating materials selected because they lead students into desired conceptual understanding. A student can move ahead individually when he can obtain his materials independently from open sources. Materials serve as vehicles for carrying out some intended learning action. Therefore, the materials should be there and ready to use just at the time that learning action is needed.

To contribute directly to a given behavioral or conceptual objective, the material must be right to the point, highly relevant, injecting into the activity just those inputs and meanings needed, and no others that distract attention

---

[8] Adapted from E. Amidon and Elizabeth Hunter, *Improving Teaching* (New York: Holt, Rinehart & Winston, 1966), chap. 3.

or confuse the issue. Learning is fast when the materials are relevant, and it is seriously hampered when they are to some degree irrelevant, misleading, confusing, and misinforming.

TEACHING THE MAJOR SOCIAL STUDIES OBJECTIVES

The three major clusters of social studies objectives—the acquisition of knowledge, the attainment of certain attitudes and values, and the development of habits, skills, and abilities—imply a variety of ways to teach. Each demands a different kind of teaching strategy dictated by the nature of the objectives to be achieved. The following examples are illustrative.

Developing Concepts

The word "concept" is used in various ways by different people. Central to these uses is the idea that a concept is an abstraction or general idea that represents a class or group of things or actions having certain characteristics in common. The mental picture a person has of an object, an event, or a relationship, derived from personal experience with the thing for which the concept stands (the referent), may be termed his concept.

> The human mind is a depository for all of our experience. It has a way of storing experience something like a motion picture record. This stored record makes possible the recollection of past experience almost as if it were happening again. The record is a composite of meaning or understanding, feeling and the value and preference it produces, and the symbols or languages related to them. This combination of meaning, value and symbols is called a concept.[9]

Concepts are built from perceptions obtained through the senses—sight, sound, touch, taste, and smell. A percept is a sensory impression registered on the brain. As continued perception of an object goes on and accumulates impressions, the meaning grows into a picture of increasing significance. This more complete mental picture is called a concept. Concepts give order and meaning to experience. For example, it is difficult to make meaningful to children such concepts as democracy, cooperation, freedom, and justice, as they cannot be perceived in the same way that concrete objects can. Children can use the words "democracy" and "freedom" at an early age without any concept of them. It takes time plus many experiences for them to gain accurate concepts and meanings. Concepts cannot be handed from one person to another; each person must develop his own concepts through experience and learning.

When the basic content to be taught is organized topically instead of conceptually, which, unfortunately, is all too often the case, learning is not pinpointed but can go out from a topic in many different directions. Some of the tendencies that show up when teaching is centered on topics as compared to concepts are identified by Woodruff as follows:

[9] Asahel D. Woodruff, *Basic Concepts of Teaching: With Brief Readings* (San Francisco: Chandler, 1962), p. 80.

Centered on Topics	*Centered on Concepts*
Tends to go in several directions	Tends to concentrate on one vital idea
Produces vague impressions of many things	Produces sharp mental pictures of one thing
Obscures the necessary learning experience	Sharply indicates the required learning experience
Is indefinite as to teaching materials	Identifies the essential teaching materials
Encourages talking about many facts	Selects and organizes facts into a significant idea
Fails to highlight important generalizations	Aims everything at an important generalization
May have a vague relationship to an objective	Makes the concept itself the objective[10]

Concepts are essentially high-level abstractions that encompass specific facts and ideas representative of a lower level of knowledge and abstraction. Therefore, organizing teaching around concepts in no way minimizes the importance of factual knowledge but rather serves to make clear which details are significant and which are not. When a new concept is presented to a student, the learning experience should provide for developing a knowledge of the related facts surrounding it. Specific facts constitute the raw material from which to shape concepts and develop insights with which to make thinking precise. They are the handles whereby a person may grasp a concept. Therefore, a careful selection of the details to study is essential to effective teaching and learning. The emphasis is on selectivity of facts rather than on a broad coverage of small unrelated details.

Facts are rarely important on their own account. For example, how important is it for a child to learn an isolated fact such as how many species of fish are found off the Hawaiian coast? This kind of knowledge is fleeting in nature and, after test purposes, soon forgotten by the student. It is more important to know how to locate this kind of information than to attempt its memorization. The mastery of isolated bits of information and knowledge does not produce new ideas nor lead the mind onward. Even if remembered, isolated and unrelated facts are highly obsolescent. What is being taught as a "fact" today may become the "fiction" of tomorrow. To focus instruction on isolated facts is inefficient—a great waste of precious school time. The mastery of unrelated facts, therefore, should not become the chief focus of instruction or evaluation.

Concepts are a much more durable form of knowledge because they represent principles which do not change as fast as specific information. Knowledge on the conceptual level is much more useful than that of the first level because of its wide applicability. An extremely atomistic content makes it difficult, if not impossible, to see relationships between ideas, and therefore prevents the possibility of developing concepts and applying them. Concepts, on the other hand, are transferable; they provide a kind of knowledge which can be readily applied to new problems and situations. Hence, the

[10] Ibid., p. 241.

importance of planning the unit lesson objective around clear and carefully stated concepts cannot be overemphasized.

Teaching Concepts

Showing the Referent / The first step in concept development is that of providing the student opportunity to take in a number of accurate perceptions of what is being focused on for study. The mind cannot work in a vacuum. All concepts should be presented in such a way that the learner can actually "see," that is, get some meaning about the object, or event, or whatever it is he is expected to learn. The quality of the student's conceptual development depends in great measure upon this and upon his early perceptual experiences that he is able to bring to the learning situation. Unfortunately, some teachers have "short-circuited" or bypassed the first fundamental step of *showing the referent,* assuming that the child's prior experiences alone provided an adequate background for learning concepts.

Whenever possible the teacher should give the student firsthand experience with the referent. Very rapid learning occurs when any object, condition, or force can be perceived directly through the physical senses. This will furnish the student with the basic input of information which he will use in forming concepts. If the referent itself, the thing being talked about, cannot be brought into the classroom, the teacher must vividly represent it with some form of vicarious teaching material or rely upon a verbal description of it. A model, picture, diagram, audiovisual aid, or other similar device may provide a substitute for firsthand experiences. Verbal descriptions are least satisfactory with young children because of their limited experiential backgrounds. In the social studies the curriculum includes many abstract concepts such as democracy, socialism, justice, and freedom. The showing or presentation of abstract concepts poses real problems for teachers as they cannot be perceived in the same way that concrete objects are perceived. It takes time, plus many experiences with these ideas in a variety of situations, before any real meaning can develop.

Discussion / A class discussion is a good method for working over and clarifying concepts which have already been presented. The main purposes of a discussion are to provide for an exchange of ideas among the class members, detect errors in thinking, and clear up any misunderstanding about the concept. The nature of the discussion will vary with the maturity of the students, but it is possible and valuable at every age level. With younger children, the teacher will have to take a more active role in injecting stimulating ideas and suggestions than she might find is necessary for older children. The teacher should provide adequate time in the lesson for the discussion period and not attempt to rush this aspect of concept development.

Memorization / Memorization of properly selected symbols by which concepts are identified and used is essential to good learning. Connected with concepts are names, dates, places, events, or nonverbal symbols that must be learned by the student if he is to communicate meaning effectively to others. When the teacher uses a new term in connection with a concept being learned, the mere hearing of the term constitutes a beginning for the students in the process of verbal learning. After the concept begins to take form, a deliberate effort should be made by the teacher to introduce the vocabulary or symbols related to the concept. If nothing is done to promote thorough learning of symbols, it is most likely that the symbols will not be learned very well. The teaching method for symbolic learning consists of drill and repetition. It is important, however, that the learning of symbolic materials should not precede understanding. Memorization for its own sake, or memorization without some comprehension of the underlying concept, is a most wasteful process. The speed with which memorization can take place is improved by a clear understanding of the concept for which the symbols stand.

Symbolic learning is not confined to single words or combinations of words. It may involve committing to memory a variety of nonverbal symbols such as the following geographical symbols:

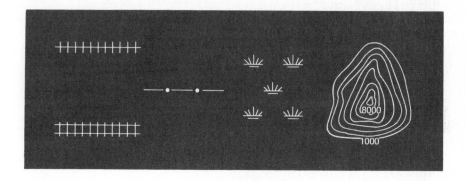

The first is a map symbol used to represent railroads. The second is a symbol commonly used to represent state boundary lines, the third, swampland, and the fourth a mountain peak. Each of them has a meaning that is shared by other people. Also, each of them is related to an important understanding or concept.

More efficient learning takes place if the symbols are presented at the time the concept is learned. The teacher should always use correct terms when referring to the concept and require students to memorize and use them in their speaking and writing. Correct spelling of single terms or words is important and may be assigned to the better students as supplementary words to their spelling lists. The understanding and meaning of the symbols are of vital importance to all students.

Application **/** The fourth step, *application,* has to do with the operational use of knowledge in class projects or in out-of-school activities. Provision should be made in the classroom for children to utilize new ideas in "lifelike" situations as often as possible. Class projects in which important understandings can be put to application should be included in the activities of a unit. Evaluation activities designed by the teacher are a means of testing students' understanding of basic principles and provide opportunity for them to apply what has been learned. Outside assignments can be made that provide children opportunity to use the knowledge they have acquired in functional situations or that provide opportunity for them to observe the principle in operation in real-life situations and to note its effect. It is through the process of application that the real value of a concept is discovered by the student.

The early years are the ones in which the child must gather information in large quantities before he can do much thinking on the higher levels. In order to engage in mental processes involving analysis, synthesis, and problem-solving the learner must be able to assemble individual pieces of information and relate them to one another. An orderly sequence of steps in teaching concepts is essential if children's mental processes are to be raised to these higher levels. Violation of these steps in teaching concepts interferes with efficient learning. Because of the large amount of specific knowledge in the area of the social studies, instructional effort should be directed toward those understandings that can be generalized. This procedure is fundamental to conceptual learning. Table 9 illustrates a plan for teaching concepts.

9   Daily Lesson Plan for Teaching Concepts

I.   Concept: _____

II.   Lesson procedures: _____

Plans for Concept Presentation	Plans for the Discussion Period	Important Symbols	Assignment or Application	Materials
		Symbols: Plan of action to provide for memorization of symbols:		

Evaluation: _____

Developing Attitudes and Values

Providing for the teaching of desirable attitudes and feelings has often been neglected. Mainly, this has been due to the assumption that learning content, or achieving knowledge objectives, will automatically bring about the development of desired attitudes and feelings. Secondly, objectives related to attitudes and values have been more vaguely defined than have cognitive objectives, and the kinds of learning experiences most appropriate to their development have not been clearly understood.

Effective teaching in the area of attitudes and values should be a main concern of the social studies. Never has there been a time in the history of the nation when the need has been greater for the development of informed and desirable attitudes toward basic democratic principles and toward others. Blind emotional reactions and prejudice toward others may result from poor teaching of these objectives or from the exclusion of them from teaching units. It is essential, therefore, that teaching units be all-encompassing— providing for the development of a wide range of objectives including the acquisition of knowledge, the development of desirable attitudes and values, and appropriate skills and habits.

Out of a person's experiences comes certain guides to behavior. These guides, which tend to give direction to life, may be called values. According to Raths, the process of valuing is defined in terms of three major processes:

Choosing
1 freely
2 from alternatives
3 after thoughtful consideration of the consequences of each alternative

Prizing
4 cherishing, being happy with the choice
5 willing to affirm the choice publicly

Acting
6 doing something with the choice
7 repeatedly, in some pattern of life.[11]

Planning for the successful attainment of objectives related to attitudes and social values has been one of the most difficult tasks in writing social study units or lesson plans. Partly, this has been due to the fact that there has been little to guide a teacher in this area as to what kinds of attitudes are most important for development and how they can be learned. Therefore, much planning has omitted the teaching of attitudes and values entirely, or teaching units have offered only meager experiences by which values might be learned. In all too many cases, it has been hoped that proper attitudes and values would emerge as a by-product of obtaining the knowledge objectives. It is little wonder then that we have not been as effective in this area as we might have been.

The development of attitudes and values can come about through a great variety of content. The learning experience, and not the content as such, is of major importance in the achievement of these kinds of objectives as they are relatively independent of any one kind of subject matter. For example, positive attitudes toward democracy can be developed in the lunchroom and on the playground as well as in a social studies classroom. The study of facts in a textbook is insufficient to change attitudes and feelings. The classroom climate and conditions surrounding the classroom need to exemplify democ-

[11] Louis E. Raths, Merrill Marmin, and Sidney B. Simon, *Values and Teaching: Working with Values in the Classroom* (Columbus, Ohio: Charles E. Merrill, 1966), p. 30.

racy. Feelings, values, and sensitivities are matters that need to be discovered rather than taught. Neither democratic values nor feelings of tolerance can be developed solely by teaching about them.

The teaching of democratic values depends partly upon the presentation of intellectual understandings. The methods and major conclusions of the social sciences are the main intellectual means of helping the child comprehend his life and face his problems. However, regardless of the importance of knowledge in helping the child comprehend his heritage, values cannot be dealt with successfully on an intellectual level alone. Central to the changing of values is to find ways to touch or reach the child's deepest feelings and emotions. This may be approached by a variety of means:

1. Using literature and films related to problems students have with feelings and values can greatly extend their capacity to understand human and social situations and identify values. For example, a person who reads the *Diary of Anne Frank* gains a greater empathy for the Jewish people and a clearer understanding of their problems and the inhumane treatment they received during World War II than could be obtained from all of the news accounts of the war.

2. Values may be taught by encouraging youth to identify with the real qualities of national heroes or individuals who have contributed unselfishly to the advancement of civilization. By admiring and striving to be like others, children adopt many of their values. Teachers can capitalize upon this motivating force in youth to foster virtues and appreciations that appear to be essential to our democratic way of life and to the perpetuation of our basic institutions. Models with which children identify can be found in many different fields of endeavor and in many different periods of time, for example, present-day heroes such as the astronauts.

3. Values may be taught through the study of controversial issues—past or present. For example, students involved in an analysis of a past historical problem such as the treatment of the American Indians will acquire a deeper understanding and empathy toward them in their present plight and will gain a greater appreciation for the need for "moral equality" in the treatment of all mankind.

A study of present-day controversies or problems that are shaping the world in which the child will live will help him shape his values so as to be better able to cope with a changing world. For at the heart of controversy lie values—the main basis for controversy. How the child can change his values by rational means is well stated by Joyce:

> He should also become increasingly aware of the values he is absorbing from the culture and develop ways of modifying and extending his values by rational means. When his values conflict with those of other people, he needs to learn to examine carefully the rationale for his beliefs and the rationale for theirs. Then he should have the humility to compromise when that is indicated, the skill to negotiate when that is reasonable, and the courage to stand and be counted when that is appropriate.[12]

[12] Bruce R. Joyce, *Strategies for Elementary Social Science Education* (Chicago: Science Research Associates, 1965), p. 5.

4. Values may be taught through the exploration of the ways of life of other cultures, peoples, and lands of the world. Through this means, a child may gain deeper appreciation of the unique contributions of all races and cultures to the present level of civilization and to his own personal well-being and aesthetic needs.

5. All teaching related to attitudes and values must include opportunities for direct experiences with materials that affect feelings—those which arouse emotions as well as reason. The most appropriate materials and devices include open-group interaction among children of different backgrounds and cultures, role-playing problem stories,[13] cut-off stories where children supply and discuss possible alternative solutions, literature, films, discussion pictures, dramatizations, songs, poetry, letters, diaries, and panel discussions or debates.

6. Providing a classroom environment or climate that fosters democratic values and tolerance toward others.

7. Other approaches to the teaching of values include the use of a wide variety of games which require students to make value choices such as the following:

Rank orders. Rank orders represent an opportunity to practice value decisions in the absence of any consequences. From three alternative choices each person in the group arranges them in order of preference. Each person is to state his rank order and explain why he arranged the items in that manner. At any time a person may choose not to state his ranking or explain his ranking. This is accomplished by declaring, "I pass."

The following are examples of rank orders which might be given:

Would you rather be a:
  Movie star
  Millionaire
  President
Would you rather be a:
  Rose bush
  Cactus
  Lily
Which would you rather do?
  Study for a test
  Do research for a term paper
  Read an assigned book

Value continuum. Two polar positions are identified on an issue and placed at opposite ends of a line on the chalkboard. Examples of polar positions might be Gabby Gertrude and Silent Sandra or Larry Leader and Fred Follower. The range of numbers from one to six is written above the line, then pupils are asked orally to report their positions on the issue by selecting the number on the continuum which represents their choice. Pupils may say "I pass" if they do not wish to respond. Those who have taken a position may take turns telling why they placed themselves as they did.

[13] For a detailed account of how to role-play problem stories see: George and Fannie R. Shaftel, *Role Playing for Social Values* (Englewood Cliffs, N.J.: Prentice-Hall, 1967).

Developing Skills

Objectives related to skill development in the elementary school range from physical-motor skills such as handwriting, typing, throwing a ball, catching a ball, or jumping rope to basic academic skills and skills in democratic citizenship and group living. Social study objectives are concerned mainly with the latter more complex kinds of skills, which require greater intellectual understandings than more simple motor skills. Independent study skill—the ability to use the table of contents and index of a book and the ability to use encyclopedias, dictionaries, and other reference materials in independent work—has received increased emphasis. These kinds of skills are especially important to modern social study programs, which call for the use of a wide variety of reading materials in addition to the basic textbook.

Other skills, perhaps the most critical ones, such as the ability to define problems of investigation, to organize and interpret data, and to improve social and group skills, have too often been neglected or poorly taught.

Because problems in our society caused by hate, criticism, and misunderstanding are prevalent today, the skills of managing interpersonal relations are becoming increasingly important to the survival of our democratic way of life. Greater responsibility for the development of social skills must be assumed by the schools. Regarding the importance of the development of skills in this area of concern Taba states:

> There are children whose homes have not given them much training in the ordinary social disciplines, whose communication skills are at a minimum, and who have only a minimal mastery of such common routines as group listening, controlling the impulses of anger, or following the rules of conduct. For these children, acquiring a "common culture" in the sense of developing a modicum of common social skills becomes a necessity. For the students from minority groups or from homes on lower economic levels, the problem is even more serious. The deficiency in the needed social skills leads to an almost inevitable failure in social situations and to a defensive "chip-on-the-shoulder" attitude, hostility, or withdrawal.
>
> Because the problems of interpersonal relations, especially those of handling interpersonal conflicts, rebuff, misunderstanding, or criticism, are with us everywhere, the skills in managing interpersonal relations have acquired some importance. There is scarcely a child or adolescent who does not face such conflicts with peers, family or adults and who would not benefit from some emphasis on the skills needed to deal constructively with interpersonal conflict, or for the development of constructive human relations.[14]

Another critical area of need in skill-development is that related to group activity. We have much knowledge before us today related to group dynamics —techniques of group deliberation and the kinds of skills required for pro-

[14] Hilda Taba, *Curriculum Development, Theory, and Practice* (New York: Harcourt Brace Jovanovich, 1962), pp. 225–226.

ductive group work. However, group work in the form of committees is often unproductive on the elementary school level and has often floundered because children lack the skills necessary for effective group work. Before children can become productive in committee work, they must perceive what a committee is, its purposes, group roles, and how to function effectively. A variety of specific skills will need development, skills such as assuming leadership roles, initiating ideas, clarifying ideas, understanding group goals, carrying through assignments, and reporting. If these kinds of skills are learned by children, committee work can be greatly improved. Until this can be accomplished, committee work has little to recommend it as a learning device for a group. On the elementary school level much of the time devoted to committee work may have to be spent in helping children learn to work effectively in committees, rather than relying on the hope that they will do so merely by good will and democratic intent.

Teaching Skills

The teaching of a skill should begin with a clear explanation or demonstration of the skill as a means of helping the learner acquire an accurate concept or clear mental picture of the skill involved and of the important principles behind it. A correct understanding of the skill is essential to future high-level performance of it. Subsequent steps involve having the students try the skill while the teacher corrects errors, and then having the students follow regular practice periods to develop the skill. Wherever possible, opportunity should be provided for a student to apply the skill in a natural situation. Table 10 presents a way of organizing a lesson to teach skills.

10 Daily Lesson Plan for Teaching Skills

I. Skill to be developed: _____

II. Plan of action: _____

Describe and Demonstrate Skill	Try Out and Correct Errors	Practice	Application or Assignment
1 Description of action: 2 Demonstration by a skilled performer or audio-visual presentation:	(Initial trial, cues for improvement, identification of common errors)	(Practice according to a schedule of specific drill activities) 1 List of drill activities:	(Provision for use of new skill in total activity or other use of new skill) 1 Nature of assignment or application:

Evaluation: _____

Knowledge of success or failure is important in making progress in learning skills. The more quickly this knowledge comes to a student after an act, the more rapidly he will improve. Information concerning his progress that the learner receives from any source is referred to as *feedback.* The teacher is the best source of this knowledge of progress. In some kinds of activities, such as handwriting and typing, the student may be able to detect improvement by the effect of his act. But when the student cannot detect his progress himself, he needs some kind of feedback to let him know when he is on the right track and is making progress. In more complex skills such as those required for leadership roles in groups, in reporting to the class, and in organizing information, learners must have their performances evaluated if they are to make continued progress.

A careful diagnosis of the level of skill attained by individual pupils in different areas of skill development will make it possible for the teacher to be more effective in properly gearing instruction to meet individual sequences in learning. Too, the process should be a continuous one beyond the elementary level. All succeeding teachers share the responsibility for the maintenance and refinement of basic skills learned on the elementary level and for the introduction of advanced skills.

Developing Habits

Habit formation is another essential objective that concerns teachers at all levels. Unfortunately, little has been consciously done in this area on the elementary level. Among the kinds of habits that apply to social education are: punctuality, accuracy, neatness, cleanliness, courtesy, habits related to classroom routines, correct speech patterns, and study habits. Correct habits can be of great benefit to the learning process. When students are helped to form desirable habits from the beginning of their school experience, the teacher's main task of promoting learning can go forward more smoothly.

The procedures for developing habits are as follows:

1 The learner must perform over and over again a certain action or behavior that it is hoped will become a habit.

2 He must continue to repeat the action time after time until it tends to repeat with less delay or conscious attention.

3 For the habit to continue to occur, it must continue to satisfy the need that sets it off.

Because of the nature of the development of habits, they should be thought of as long-range objectives. Habits cannot be completely developed in any given social study, but rather, they must be worked at in all units of instruction throughout the school year. Valuable work habits and other desirable behaviors do not develop spontaneously; they must be encouraged continuously by all teachers. Old or undesirable habits are easily reinstated. They must be kept from recurring under any circumstances and the desired new habit deliberately used over a period of time long enough for it to become automatic. Unfortunately, many teachers lack the knowledge and persistency necessary to become effective with students in this area of development;

therefore, desirable habit formation in the schools is often poorly taught or neglected.

SIMULATION GAMES

Over the past decade the popularity of simulation games as an approach to learning in the social studies has increased steadily on both elementary and secondary levels of education. Although in the past the number of social science games available commercially for student use have been more numerous on the secondary level, today more attention is being turned to the preparation of games for elementary school pupils. The game technique seems to have considerable value as a teaching tool.

Simulation games are defined by Rogers and Kysilka as follows:

> Last July people all over the world watched man take his first steps on the moon. The success of this amazing achievement can be largely attributed to the elaborate preparation that preceded the actual moon shot. These activities included creating or simulating the environment much like that on the moon. Wearing heavy space suits and packs, astronauts enacted their moon roles in one sixth of the earth's normal gravitational pull. Consequences of actions were observed; alternative procedures were tried; emergencies occurred; mistakes were made and preventive measures developed. . . .

> This same method of practicing what one likely will later encounter in real life has recently been developed for classroom use in the form of simulation games. As you may know, a simulation game is a selected representation of a physical and/or social phenomenon, incorporating a game technique. Players assume roles, interact with other players, and make decisions based on those roles and interactions. Outside forces such as actions by another player or group, may affect a decision and determine its wisdom. Thus, the players can receive feedback throughout the game. Some games need a computer, but most can be played with only such props as paper slips, cards, or play money.[15]

Advantages of Simulation Games **/** There are a large number of advantages that may be listed. Among the more significant ones are:

> 1 From the earliest age children simulate life situations in their play activities. Simulation games and activities, therefore, are of high interest and motivation to them.
> 2 The high interest level and involvement in the excitement of the game lengthens interest span in learning.
> 3 Simulation connects subject matter with real life, making abstract concepts more meaningful.
> 4 Children can come to grips with problems of both the past and present on their own maturity level.

[15] Virginia M. Rogers and Marcella L. Kysilka, "Simulation Games—What and Why," *Instructor*, March 1970, p. 94.

5 Students are given a sense of being able to better understand and affect the world about them.

6 Simulation provides a personal skill-development program in decision-making, strategies, and problem-solving.

7 The students can deal with situations that they may encounter in real life. Through immediate feedback, they can evaluate the consequences of their decisions in a play situation.

8 Through simulation, the teacher can infer what children are learning and how they view the world. It offers an excellent opportunity to measure attitudes and attitudinal changes.

9 Simulation seems to be an appropriate learning approach for pupils at all ability levels and for the culturally disadvantaged as well as for children with richer experiential backgrounds.

Disadvantages / Among the disadvantages are the following:

1 There is the problem of equating effectiveness of learning with enthusiasm. Student emphasis may be on winning rather than on learning.

2 Games must of necessity be an oversimplification of real life.

3 The costs of commercially prepared games may be prohibitive to more widespread use of games.

4 Games may become too time-consuming when not sufficiently understood by the pupils.

Availability of Simulation Games / Some of the present sources of simulation games suitable for elementary school social studies are:

Western Publishing Co., Inc., 850 Third Ave., New York, N.Y. 10022. Kinds of games available:

Consumer / Buying goods on time and through loans.
Generation Gap / A parent player and teen-age player confront each other over conflicting issues.
Economic System / Players become workers, farmers, and manufacturers.
Democracy / As members of a legislature players come to understand how laws are made.
Ghetto / A player is involved with trying to improve the life situation of a person living in the ghetto.

The Learning Center, Social Studies Department, Princeton, N.J. 08540.

Crithaka / Cultural anthropology. Based on social system of the Kikuyus of Kenya.

Abt Associates, 55 Wheeler St., Cambridge, Mass. 02136.

Hunting / Has its setting in the Bushman ecology in the Kalahari Desert.
Economy / Develops an understanding of the circular flow of goods and services in the economic system.
Market / Fosters an understanding of the way prices are determined in a market economy, the laws of supply and demand.
Pollution / Teaches students problems involved in attempts to control pollution.
Neighborhood / Development of an urban area.
Seal Hunting / Demonstrates the chance interaction of the worlds of the seals and the Eskimo.

Sierra Leone / A computer-based game dealing with the role of an American economic adviser attempting to improve various aspects of the economy.

The Slave Trade Game / Deals with slave trade in the eighteenth century.

Edcom Systems, Inc., Princeton, New Jersey 08540. Edcom's curriculum for grades 4–6 is structured around three major ideas—man's location in space, in time, and in human society. This is accomplished by making learning materials that elicit active student participation in a program of inductive discovery attuned to the interests of contemporary children. A number of different games are associated with the program, such as:

Hunting and Tracking Game / Children discover the amazing ability of the Aranda to survive with a limited technology in a harsh, desert environment.

Aranda Marriage Game / Children discover that the Aranda social patterns are far from primitive.

Corn and Cargo Games / To acquaint children with the problems of providing a living in a primitive culture.

Githaka and Market Place / Familiarize children with the problems in founding a community, and the economics of an African market place.

Education Development Center, Inc., 15 Mifflin Place, Cambridge, Mass. 02138.

The Game of Empire / Factors involved in the transformation of British subjects to Americans.

Bushman Exploring and Gathering / Designed to teach the concept of cultural adaptation to a harsh environment.

Caribou Hunting / Simulating difficulties Eskimos experience in hunting caribou.

Board of Cooperative Educational Services (BOCES), Westchester Co., Yorktown Heights, N.Y. 10598.

The Sumerian Game / A computer-based game in which a player assumes a role of ruler of Sumeria and must improve the lot of his people by making decisions.

Western Behavioral Sciences Inst., La Jolla, Calif.

Napoli / Students represent eight geographical regions in the legislature.

TEACHING STRATEGIES FOR CULTURALLY DISADVANTAGED PUPILS

The problem of deprivation exists everywhere in our nation—in all of our big cities, in smaller cities, and in rural counties. Many of the so-called culturally disadvantaged pupils come from impoverished home backgrounds where the social environment is inadequate to prepare them to participate fully in the American society. The real problem that our schools and society generally face is: How do you motivate people who are out of the mainstream to try to lead productive lives; and how do you equip them with the pride, courage, and education to compete for a meaningful place in the world?

One must be careful to avoid the error of always equating the socially disadvantaged children with low-income or working-class families. Socially disadvantaged children are found on all social-class levels. The critical factor is the quality of the home environment, not the amount of family income. It is estimated that the number of socially disadvantaged children make up about 15 percent of the child population generally. In the inner part of big cities, the percentage of culturally deprived children may run as high as double this amount.[16]

According to Havighurst, compared with other children whose families give them average or better advantages for getting started in modern urban life, the socially disadvantaged child lacks several of the following:

> A family conversation which: answers his questions and encourages him to ask questions; extends his vocabulary with words, particularly adjectives and adverbs; gives him a right and a need to stand up for and explain his point of view on the world.
>
> A family environment which: sets an example of reading; provides a variety of toys and play materials with colors, sizes, and objects that challenge his ingenuity with his hands and his mind.
>
> Two parents who: read a good deal; read to him; show him that they believe in the value of education; reward him for good school achievement.[17]

Because a poor home environment retards a child's intellectual development, special preschool educational opportunities are perhaps more essential for underprivileged children than for those from more privileged homes. The effects of intellectual and social deprivation during a child's early years are long lasting and difficult to overcome. Programs such as Operation Head Start and Operation Follow Through, under the Department of Health, Education and Welfare (HEW), are helpful in providing rich experiential backgrounds and needed social skills for children who have suffered cultural deprivation.

In the first place, if the school is to do a better job of teaching the culturally deprived and leading them to productive citizenship, the school must become more adaptable to children as they are when they come to school and more acceptant of their behavior patterns. For example, children of slum areas have different value systems. Often they lack the ordinary social skills necessary for getting along well with others. Because of their narrow experiential backgrounds, they have limited language skills and limited ability in self-expression. These kinds of deficiencies often result in their condemnation by others rather than in the development of positive programs in teaching values and skills designed to meet their specific needs.

More effective strategies for teaching culturally deprived children are continually being developed. Among the principles and procedures that may serve as guidelines to the development of new approaches are the following:

1. Perhaps the characteristic that most often identifies the culturally deprived child is a narrow, impoverished experiential background. This narrow world of the child needs to be widened by a large number of rich firsthand experiences. It is not uncommon to find children in the "inner city" who have

[16] Robert J. Havighurst, "Who Are the Socially Disadvantaged?" reported in *Readings for Social Studies in Elementary Education*, second edition, John Jarolimek and Huber M. Walsh (London: Macmillan, 1969), p. 234.
[17] Ibid., p. 230.

traveled but little outside their own neighborhood. The school program needs to systematically help the child acquire a background of experiences common to most children. Without this background of experience, the child has difficulty in bringing meaning to the printed page. Among other means, a background of common experiences can be built by providing numerous opportunities for disadvantaged children to participate in study trips into the community, and by enriching learning through the use of a wide variety of visual aids. The need for visual aids is most critical for disadvantaged children. Bryan states:

> We cannot assume that all children have had the experience needed to understand what are to us common concepts, and we must develop these concepts through pictures, motion pictures, filmstrips, the use of overhead projectors, etc. I have found it necessary to use twice as many visual aids with these children as with children from middle-class homes.[18]

Another means of reaching the culturally deprived is to provide them with more meaningful books or books that deal with experiences familiar to them. Textbooks dealing with material related solely to the basic human activities of middle- or upper-middle-class families are of little motivation to culturally deprived children. Nevertheless, often their total reading in the social studies is of this kind of material. Little opportunity is provided for them to learn about their immediate environment. There is little wonder that many of them are bored and unsuccessful in their attempts to achieve in the social studies. At this stage in their development, stories about experiences that disadvantaged children share are more meaningful than those about the social-class environment and problems of other people.

2. Culturally deprived children are victims of a social environment that has been deficient in helping them develop the skills needed to deal constructively with interpersonal conflict or for constructive human relations.

Because deficiencies in needed social skills can lead to failure in the classroom and in social situations in society generally, elementary schools have the responsibility, particularly in connection with the skill-development program of the social studies, to provide special training for children from culturally deprived homes in the area of their social deficiencies. This can be done in a variety of ways such as through community cooperative school projects in which the culturally deprived child can identify with other children and work together for productive ends, also through special film and filmstrip programs that provide additional training in human relations, and through literature in which the child can become involved in discussing social-problem story situations.

3. Whether a child is in a high or low reading group is not as critical in the primary grades as is helping the child develop an adequate self concept. Influencing the motivation of the child to make him want to stay in school rather than becoming a dropout may make some differences in his life's chances.

---

[18] Dorothy M. Bryan, "Education for the Culturally Deprived: Building on Pupil Experience," *Social Education* 31: 117–118, 1967.

4. Special education programs for parents and teachers of the culturally disadvantaged will greatly benefit the child in his adjustment problems both in and out of school.

Parents of culturally disadvantaged children could profit from special adult-education classes or programs designed to help them better meet the needs of the preschool child in preparing him for his first formal educational experiences. Special help could be given to a family in the form of free books and other educational materials for children. This would greatly improve the child's chances for success in school.

Through in-service education programs, teachers of culturally deprived children might learn how to deal more effectively and understandingly with problems encountered in the classroom. Special programs are being developed to help teachers better understand deprived children from the "inner city." For example, the *Inner-City Simulation Laboratory* developed by Donald R. Cruikshank with the help of a grant from the NDEA, National Institute for Advanced Study in Teaching Disadvantaged Youth, now published by Science Research Associates, is designed specifically to help student teachers and teachers meet problems encountered in the inner city. The simulated problems presented to teachers are problems that occur daily in inner-city classrooms. They are problems that must be met for teaching to be effective. The participants in the program discover approaches to solving these problems that help them to become more sensitive to the needs of deprived children in the classroom. Teachers can benefit greatly from these lifelike experiences they encounter and, as a result, learn how to work with deprived children in more effective and acceptable ways.

DIFFERENTIATED STAFFING

In the final analysis any plan of teaching can only be as effective as the teacher whose job it is to bring it to life in the classroom. Therefore, the manner in which elementary schools are staffed has a direct relationship to the general effectiveness of teaching strategies, particularly those which foster individualization of instruction, thinking, and creativity. The self-contained classroom in which one teacher is responsible for all of the learning experiences of a given group of children, long a dominant pattern for staffing the elementary school, is giving way today in a number of school systems to a plan of teacher utilization that involves the concept of teaming.[19] Proponents of team teaching believe that the flexible utilization of the teaching staff that teaming provides can better meet the individual needs and varying learning speeds of students than can the one-teacher-per-group arrangement.

Team-Teaching

A teaching team exists whenever two or more professional teachers, working together, assume joint responsibility for all, or a substantial part, of the

[19] See Judson R. Shaplin and Henry F. Olds, eds., *Team Teaching* (New York: Harper & Row, 1964), for a series of discussions on teaming.

instruction of a common group of children.[20] Central to the concept of teaming is the necessity for joint planning and careful coordination for the learning activities for a given group of students. During the first three decades of the present century, there was a tendency toward departmentalization of instruction on the elementary level. This pattern of staffing the elementary school provided for an arrangement in which each teacher taught in only one or two subject-matter areas in which he was most competent. The essential ingredients of teaming were lacking in this arrangement, however, when departmentalization failed to provide for coordination of teaching efforts, integration of subject matter, and for flexibility in the time program.

In a team-teaching arrangement, a "teaching pod" may consist of three teachers with 75 to 90 children. There is a great deal of communication between teachers in such teaming arrangements as they pool their knowledge of children, develop plans for instruction, and jointly evaluate the progress made by the pupils. For specific purposes it is possible to divide students into several groups of varying sizes for desirable lengths of time or to call the entire group together for demonstrations or large-group activity—the size and length of time determined by the teaching task desired.

Methods of Organizing Teams

Teams are classified according to their organizational makeup as "hierarchical" or "synergetic." In the hierarchical arrangement one teacher is designated as the continuing team leader, with responsibilities to coordinate and facilitate the work of the total team. Other team members consist of master teachers who are competent, experienced instructors with specialized talents; beginning teachers who hold standard teaching certificates; and paraprofessionals, teaching aides, or clerical assistants who work under the direction of other members of the team. It is not uncommon for interns from teacher training institutions to serve as members of teams, along with experienced teachers, as a culmination of their preservice preparation for teaching. This hierarchic arrangement allows for a differentiated pay scale in which the leader is paid more, the neophyte is paid less, and the aide is paid at a nonprofessional rate.

The synergetic arrangement is a less formal approach to teaming in which teachers cooperate as professional equals. Often referred to as cooperative teaching, this approach allows the leadership role to shift from one teacher to another as the nature of the task before the team changes. This approach may still provide a place for teacher interns and for the paraprofessionals, but the teachers all have equal status on the team. Pay differentiation is still determined, as in the self-contained classroom, on the basis of experience and training.

Advantages Claimed in Team-Teaching

The concept of teaming for elementary school teaching has been utilized by many school systems throughout the nation over the past decade. Many

[20] Ibid., p. 15.

claims have been made as to the advantages of team teaching over other plans of teacher utilization in the elementary school. Among the major advantages claimed for team-teaching are the following:

1 Greater flexibility in grouping and increased peer and teacher contacts under team-teaching tend to reduce rigidity and encourage more creative and imaginative thought.

2 The quality of instruction that a pupil receives during any one school year is not dependent upon a single teacher.

3 Team-teaching preserves the virtue and avoids the weaknesses of both the self-contained classroom and departmentalized instruction.

4 There is greater utilization of the individual talents of team members. Different teachers' specialties can complement one another.

5 Superior teachers can exercise greater influence in the school and still remain in classroom teaching.

6 Team-teaching facilitates grouping because the basic group is so large that small groups can easily be formed for almost any purpose, and there are enough bright students to make advanced projects feasible.

7 During large-group instructional periods, some teachers may be freed for small-group work, lesson-planning, and parent-teacher conferences.

8 Pupils spend more of their time receiving direct instruction and individualized help than when they are in self-contained classrooms.

9 The diagnostic, planning, and evaluative procedures, when developed by a team of teachers, are generally superior to those developed by a single teacher.

10 Teaming is a very effective means for training teacher interns.

11 The beginning teacher is not left on her own but has supervision and help from experienced teachers.

12 During a team member's illness, the other members of the team can fill the void with less loss of instructional time than when a substitute comes into a regular classroom and often does nothing more than baby sit.

13 More detailed and careful lesson-planning is done.

14 The greater flexibility and increased peer and teacher contacts under team-teaching tend to reduce rigidity and encourage more creative and imaginative thought.

15 There is a tendency for more creative teaching because of the interaction among team members.

Disadvantages Claimed in Team Teaching

1 The frequency and intensity of contact of the team members can lead to complex problems of human relations.

2 In a hierarchical structure, the problem of status pyramiding of teachers under a team leader may work against a healthy climate.

3 Inherent in team teaching is the fact that much time and effort must be spent on the complexities of scheduling and planning.

4 Many of the questions children have during large-group instruction may have to be left until later to be answered.

5 Opportunities for pupil leadership may be lost because of the complexities of the program and the size of the group.

6 Large-group instruction could become more lecture-type and formal.

7 Some confusion may result when groups shift from one area to another.

8 There is the possibility that because of the pressure of time teachers will choose to teach in only one or two subject-matter areas. Thus, the advantages of teaming together in shared instructional responsibilities are lost.

QUESTIONS AND ACTIVITIES

1 / Give three possible reasons why social studies have not been among the most liked subjects of elementary pupils in the past.

2 / Contrast the role of the teacher as a "director of learning" with the more traditional role of the teacher as one who is a "dispenser of information."

3 / List the kinds of classroom conditions or influences that are least educative for the student. Now make a contrasting list of the classroom conditions or influences that are more highly educative.

4 / What kinds of student behavior or thinking abilities are involved in each of the following higher levels of thought: analyzing, reviewing and organizing, interpreting and explaining, concluding, predicting consequences, inventing and creating.

5 / The kind of teaching strategy used in the social studies is directed by the nature of the objective to be achieved. Compare a concept-development strategy with a strategy for developing attitudes and values, habits, or skills and abilities.

6 / How can team-teaching provide for individualization of instruction?

SELECTED REFERENCES

Anderson, Robert H. *Teaching in a World of Change.* New York: Harcourt Brace Jovanovich, 1966.

Bellack, Arno A. *The Language of the Classroom.* New York: Teachers College Press, Teachers College, Columbia University, 1966.

Bruner, Jerome S. *Toward a Theory of Instruction.* New York: Norton, 1968. Chap. III.

Carpenter, Helen McCracken (ed.). *Skill Development in the Social Studies,* Thirty-third Yearbook. Washington, D.C.: National Council for the Social Studies, 1963.

Fenton, Edwin. *The New Social Studies.* New York: Holt, Rinehart & Winston, 1967.

Flanders, Ned A. *Interaction Analysis in the Classroom: A Manual for Observers.* Revised edition. Ann Arbor, Mich. 1966.

Goodlad, John I. "Cooperative Teaching in Educational Reform." *National Elementary Principal* 44 (3): 8–13, January 1965.

Guilford, J. P. "Intelligence 1965 Model." *American Psychologist* 21 (I): 20–26, 1966.

NEA Project on Instruction. *Planning and Organizing for Teaching.* Washington, D.C.: NEA, 1963.

Shaplin, Judson R., and Olds, Henry F. (eds.). *Team Teaching.* New York: Harper & Row, 1964.

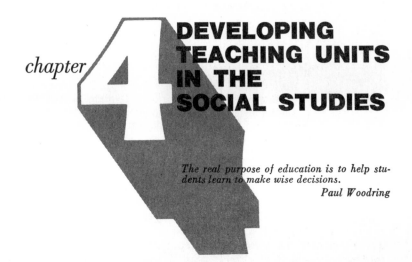

chapter **4** **DEVELOPING
TEACHING UNITS
IN THE
SOCIAL STUDIES**

*The real purpose of education is to help stu-
dents learn to make wise decisions.*

Paul *Woodring*

Effective planning in the social studies
is of major importance, since it provides the needed direction for the teaching-learning process. Good planning has always been basic to good teaching,
but the need today for careful planning is more crucial than ever before. New
ideas are coming from all of the social science disciplines in increasing
numbers. Some initial decisions must be made as to which new ideas are
most durable and valuable and, therefore, worthy of inclusion in an already
overcrowded curriculum.

On the classroom level, this will mean that in order to keep up to date with
new knowledge, teachers will have to continually change and modify existing
lesson plans and units of instruction. Too often, the same plans have been
used year after year. After becoming experienced teachers, many have
viewed written plans as being unnecessary or a waste of time, or as just
something important for student teachers and first-year teachers. Experienced
teachers need to underline the fact that planning is essential to all successful
teaching, and that results cannot be any better than the quality of planning.
Those who fail to plan should stop to consider the effects of careless teaching, brought about by lack of planning, upon the pupils under their charge.
The vital importance of careful planning is stated by Woodruff as follows:

> The complexity of a good lesson is somewhat comparable to
> that of a good building. There are many little situations in the
> flow of a complete lesson. Every one of them involves princi-
> ples operating in a cause-and-effect relationship. Every one
> of them offers an opportunity to perform a work of art, or to
> bungle. The total effect of the lesson is the summation of all

of those moments and effects. The stakes are high in construction work, but they are higher in teaching. An architect can be bankrupted if he makes many mistakes and is forced to pay for them. In teaching it is not the teacher who becomes bankrupt, but the student. His bankruptcy cannot be remedied by money. It is permanently built into him. Each human being is a far more important entity than a building. Our educational system does more to the human individual than almost any other set of forces in his life. The teacher is the chief instrument in that system, and the quality of his lessons is the major determinant of education in America. He should plan every lesson he teaches.[1]

All teachers owe it to their students and to themselves to become thoroughly familiar with planning procedures. Effective planning requires time. However, the time factor need not be overburdening to the teacher if the content she is to cover during the school year in the social studies is organized into teaching units. Well-organized units, once completed, contain daily lesson concepts and activities. With some revision and adapting they can be used by the teacher the following year.

In an attempt to help teachers develop a systematic approach to instruction in the social studies, this chapter examines in considerable detail the nature of unit planning and its advantages for teaching in the social studies.

DEFINITION OF A UNIT

Planning for teaching is usually done by the individual teacher at two levels, the daily plan and the unit. *The unit is composed of a number of closely related objectives or socially significant understandings which have been carefully selected and organized for instructional purposes.* A series of such units may constitute a year's work in the social studies. Although very flexible, the upper grades of the elementary school would cover approximately six major units during the school year while on the primary level a larger number of more simple and informal units of shorter duration might be covered. Daily lesson-planning is a continuous process as the stages of a unit are being developed. The individual lessons that combined make up one large unit of work should be planned so that they lead directly toward the unit goals and objectives.

The basic types of units most frequently used are the *teaching unit* and the *resource unit.* Variations of these patterns have been used and have been classified as "subject-matter units," "experience units," "process units," "problem units," etc. The purpose of each has been to make the unit more functional for the learner by gearing activities to specific kinds of objectives. It is a matter of where the unit emphasis is placed—upon subject-matter content per se or upon a problem-solving approach and action experiences.

RESOURCE UNITS

Resource units are often prepared by group effort—generally involving a committee of teachers from a given grade level who are assigned the re-

[1] Asahel D. Woodruff, *Basic Concepts of Teaching* (San Francisco: Chandler, 1962), p. 174.

sponsibility for its development. Others are prepared by curriculum workers in the central office, state departments of education, or commercial firms. Although resource units have the same general organizational structure as teaching units, they are more general in nature and contain much background information for the teacher on the topic covered. Resource units serve as a storehouse of knowledge for the teacher who is planning a teaching unit. He will find the preparation of units for his actual classroom instruction much less burdensome and time consuming if he first surveys the range of ideas and possibilities presented in available resource units. The resource unit has pulled together under one cover many sources of information, lists of audio-visual materials, community resources, stories, poems, books, and other instructional materials and helps for the teacher that he would be unable to find elsewhere without long hours of search and effort. An effort should be made in school systems to increase the number of social studies resource units available to teachers.

DEVELOPING A TEACHING UNIT

When organized around a conceptual structure with appropriate behavioral objectives, the unit approach to the social studies in the elementary school has become a most promising method for teaching because it provides an opportunity for a more meaningful kind of organization of subject matter involving not only the text as a major source of learning, but a variety of learning experiences. The unit is rich in opportunities for children to satisfy their innate drives to be active, to manipulate and construct, to satisfy curiosity, to dramatize, and to participate in group work. It cuts across subject-matter lines and provides opportunity for children to use fundamental skills from other subject-matter areas in functional situations. It is geared to provide opportunities for children to grow in the skills needed for democratic citizenship. It also offers opportunities for children to work at different tasks and contribute to the success of the unit even though they vary in ability to learn. No other method of organizing teaching-learning situations in the social studies has proved so effective in meeting the needs of children and allowing them to progress at their own rate.

Steps in Developing a Teaching Unit

In order to avoid the haphazard development of a unit, a certain sequence of steps should be followed. The framework or order is as follows:

1 Title (topic, theme, or problem)
2 Initiation or approach (means of motivating unit or stimulating interest in topic)
3 Development of the unit
   a) Major concept
   b) Behavioral objective
   c) Supporting concepts
   d) Learning experiences (developmental activities)
4 Culminating activities (summarizing, drawing conclusions, and clarifying understandings)

5 Evaluation (means of determining if major concepts of unit have been achieved)

6 Related materials (complete listing for unit of books, instructional materials, and other resources).

Each of these main headings will be discussed in turn to provide specific examples of how to develop each aspect of the unit.

Unit Title

The title of the unit may be expressed as a topic such as "Money and Banking," "Shelter for the Family," "Transportation," "Early History of the Americas," "Latin America," "Modern Hawaii," and "The Farm." It is to be noted that the titles of the various units are stated as topics, not as conceptual statements. This is the only place in the unit that a topic may be used. The title of the unit or topic to be studied identifies a general area of knowledge but does not specify the concepts, mental images, or understandings to be developed. Later, in the body of the unit, the specific content to be learned is organized in a definite and clear conceptual structure.

Initiation or Approach

Many different approaches or combinations of approaches are used to arouse interest or curiosity on the part of the children in the unit to be studied. It cannot be safely assumed that all children will be naturally interested in a given unit of instruction. There is potential interest and value in everything in the curriculum, but it is usually up to the teacher, planning with the students, to open up an area of study in such a way that the students can easily find it interesting. A good teacher has then the added responsibility of helping create an interest in the subject matter at hand.

The initiation of the unit is the means of launching the unit or getting it "off the ground" to a good start. The initiating experience should serve five functions:

1 Motivate the study, arousing interest and curiosity

2 Provide students some common experiences that will help bring meaning to their study

3 Help orient the student to the area to be studied

4 Point out areas of interest, questions, and issues that will require further exploration and study

5 Help guarantee the success of the unit by basing learning on things challenging to students.

Michaelis[2] discusses in some detail a number of suitable techniques of initiating a unit of work. Among the most widely used approaches are:

1. *Ongoing study:* In this approach a second unit of study is an outgrowth of the first unit, such as a study of early explorers leading on to a study of the westward expansion or a study of the farm leading on to a study of the

[2] See John U. Michaelis, *Social Studies for Children in a Democracy: Recent Trends and Developments,* third edition (Englewood Cliffs, N.J.: Prentice-Hall, 1960), pp. 224–230, for a discussion of a large number of different approaches.

grocery store. Care must be taken to help children see the relationships or leading-on qualities of one unit to the next, so that a smooth transition between units is made.

2. *Pretest:* A pretest will serve to motivate a unit if properly administered. The purpose is not to find out what the children know about a given topic, but rather to reveal gaps in important areas of knowledge. Finding out what children do not know about a given topic and thereby identifying where they are—their present level of understanding—is an important guide to determining needed areas of emphasis in a unit. A pretest can well be used along with other procedures for initiating a unit in a combination approach. Teachers should develop their own pretests to fit the units they teach.

3. *Audiovisual materials:* There are a wide variety of audiovisual aids and materials that may be used to initiate a unit of work. Among the most commonly used ones are motion pictures, filmstrips, television programs, radio programs, slides, and flat pictures. Most of these are readily accessible to teachers. They are highly motivating to children and can serve as a means to open up problems and to stimulate thinking and discussion about a country or area of study. Teachers should plan carefully for their use and for appropriate follow-up activities. Although audiovisual materials are excellent to initiate a unit, continued and further use of them should be made throughout the unit.

4. *Community resources:* The resources of the community may be utilized to initiate a unit through the means of study trips and resource persons. The community provides a rich source of information for the social studies throughout the entire school year. Generally speaking, study trips and resource visitors are planned for in relation to specific questions and problems already under study. However, a study trip into the community or a visit from a resource person may "highlight" a unit and create a beginning interest not otherwise obtainable. Such visits are particularly effective when used as an ongoing activity to connect two closely related units of work.

5. *Arranged environment:* Another effective way to initiate a unit is through providing a room environment that will arouse the curiosity and interest of children in the new unit to be presented. A social studies bulletin board and table may be used to display pertinent material such as books, pictures, realia, exhibits, maps, and globes. Pictures and realia should be labeled and some of the books displayed with pages opened to places that will attract the interest of children. During the first day that the new unit is begun, children are given the opportunity to look at the well-selected pictures and objects on display and browse through the books on the reading table. The teacher will stay somewhat in the background but should note which kinds of things are of greatest interest to the children. The teacher will follow the period of exploration by the students with a class discussion in which children have opportunity to ask questions, clarify perceptions, and share things of interest to them with others. As a result of this discussion and sharing, interests will become focused on problems of common concern that they would like to find out more about. This will furnish a good lead into the unit of study. Because the arranged-environment approach combines a greater variety of stimuli to

motivate students than other approaches, it has much to recommend it as a means of launching a unit. Nevertheless, it is unwise to infer that one approach is best for all situations. The type of approach selected should be that which will best meet the needs of the group and accomplish teacher purposes.

The following brief example of a unit approach is taken from a unit on modern Hawaii:

> *Initiation of Unit*
>
> *Arranged environment:* Maps, colorful pictures, books, tourist folders, and objects used by the Hawaiian people.
>
> 1 On a bulletin board, display a map of the Hawaiian Islands and pictures depicting the geographic environment and the life of the people today.
>
> 2 On a table in the corner of the room have a selection of books on Hawaii and objects used by the people of Hawaii both in the past and at the present time. Objects might include a model outrigger canoe, a piece of lava, dolls, fabric (tapa cloth and modern Hawaiian prints), a coconut, lei, ukulele, box of sugar, can of pineapple, lahala place-mats, and sea shells.
>
> 3 Read to the class *The Gift of Hawaii, Hawaiian Coffee Picker,* or *Up from the Sea Came an Island.*
>
> 4 Discuss trips that children have taken with their parents to Hawaii.
>
> 5 Teacher-pupil planning—list and discuss, "What we know about Hawaii," "What we would like to find out," and "How shall we go about gathering the needed information?"

Through the introductory experiences of the unit, student interest in the study of Hawaii may be aroused and students may become conscious of major questions and problems that would require further exploration and study. The initiatory phase of the unit also provides for the development of a common background of experiences in a given area of study, a general discussion of a unit area, and preliminary plans for further work.

Development of the Unit

The body of the unit includes the major concepts to be developed, related behavioral objectives, supporting concepts, and carefully selected learning experiences. The function of each in the development of the unit will be discussed separately.[3] Figure 11 illustrates the order of these elements in unit development.

Major Concepts / Major concepts are the large overall understandings that the unit hopes to accomplish. They represent the major generalizations, feelings and attitudes, habits, or skills to be acquired by the student as a result of the unit of work. They also serve as the guidelines for the development of the supporting concepts around which the learning ex-

---

[3] See Appendix C for a sample unit, "Early California Indian Life," illustrating the complete development of the above titles comprising the body of the unit.

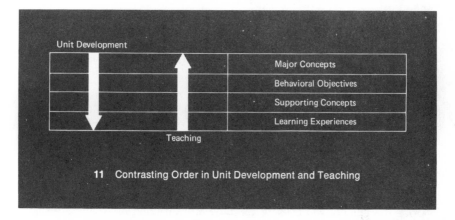

11 Contrasting Order in Unit Development and Teaching

periences for each specific lesson are organized. Upon completion of a given unit of work, each student will be expected to have discovered or inductively acquired each major concept of the unit.

The following major themes, with their related concepts, were developed by the National Council for the Social Studies through the efforts of a task force composed of leading educators and scholars in the various social sciences.[4] They cover the complete scope of social studies instruction and as such provide an excellent source of major concepts. Only the major themes are listed below. Space does not permit the detailed breakdowns under each major heading:

> Theme I Recognition of the dignity and worth of the individual
>
> Theme II The use of intelligence to improve human living
>
> Theme III Recognition and understanding of world interdependence
>
> Theme IV The understanding of the major world cultures and culture areas
>
> Theme V The intelligent uses of the natural environment
>
> Theme VI The vitalization of our democracy through an intelligent use of our public educational facilities
>
> Theme VII The intelligent acceptance, by individuals and groups, of responsibility for achieving democratic social action
>
> Theme VIII Increasing the effectiveness of the family as a basic social institution
>
> Theme IX The effective development of moral and ethical values
>
> Theme X The intelligent and responsible sharing of power in order to attain justice
>
> Theme XI The intelligent utilization of scarce resources to attain the widest general well-being
>
> Theme XII Achieving adequate horizons of loyalty
>
> Theme XIII Cooperation in the interest of peace and welfare

[4] See National Council for the Social Studies, *Social Studies in Transition—Guidelines for Change.* See Appendix B for a detailed breakdown of each major theme.

Theme XIV Achieving a balance between social stability and social change

Theme XV Widening and deepening the ability to live more richly

Behavioral Objectives / A good behavioral objective should be written to accompany each major objective of the unit. If the behavior of the student can be observed while he demonstrates the knowledge he has acquired, or if the product of his knowledge is observable, then the objective is acceptable. Good behavioral objectives are operational statements of intent that enable the students to know what is important and what is expected of them in the learning task.[5] All instruction should be aimed directly at the production of an actual behavior. A well-written behavioral objective taken from a unit of study related to the study of the state of Oregon is as follows: The student will be able to name and describe orally three distinct climates in Oregon and point out their general locational areas on a large map of Oregon.

When it is adequately stated, the behavioral objective in the unit format becomes surprisingly powerful in influencing instruction. Some of the advantages of behavioral objectives or behaviorally stated goals are the following:

1 The teacher can select more suitable learning activities for the class, since he knows precisely what kind of student behavior he is attempting to produce.

2 They provide the basis for a diagnostic preinstructional test as well as the final achievement test. The teacher can more easily select appropriate evaluation procedures, as there is less ambiguity in respect to the meaning of the objective.

3 The specificity of the objectives enables the teacher to determine whether or not he is pursuing the right aims and permits him to continually improve them.

4 They provide a very high transfer value for out-of-school life.

Useful as they are, lists of objectives stated in terms of behavior may become long and unwieldy. They can, however, be made to serve more useful purposes when a single behavioral objective is written for each major concept of the unit. When listed under appropriate major concepts, they become more manageable. This greatly increases their practical usefulness. Thus they become a valuable means of improving content, instruction, and evaluation.

Supporting Concepts / It is through the acquisition of supporting concepts that each of the major concepts or generalizations is arrived at by the student. It is important, therefore, that each supporting concept be directly related to a larger understanding or concept. There is always the danger that supporting concepts will not be adequate in scope to fully develop the major concept from which they are derived. However, there is no set number of supporting concepts required under each major understanding.

[5] See Chapter 9, "Evaluation of Learning in the Social Studies," for a more detailed discussion of behavioral objectives and how to write them.

The number varies according to each major concept and the depth of specific coverage desired. All learning experiences should be directly related to the development of supporting concepts. That is, teaching is organized around the supporting concepts and aimed directly at their development. It is through this means that the student comes ultimately to a greater depth of understanding of the larger generalizations.

The following example, taken from a unit on transportation, illustrates the complete development of one major concept in the body of the unit.

Major Concept   1   People travel for many reasons.

Behavioral Objective

The student will be able to draw a series of pictures showing at least two out of three reasons why people travel, and he will state these reasons orally as he shows his pictures.

Supporting Concepts

1   People travel when they change their residence.
2   People move in order to satisfy basic needs and for social, cultural, or health purposes.
3   People travel for recreational purposes.

Learning Experiences

1   Ask these questions: How does your father get to work? How far must he go? How does your mother get to the store to buy food? How far must she go? Can you think of some people who do not have to move from one place to another?

2   Have the children list some reasons why people go from place to place.

3   Ask these questions: Have you and your family ever moved to a different home? How far away did you move? How did you get to your new home? How did your clothes and furniture get to your new home? Have you ever had neighbors move away or new people move into your neighborhood? How did they travel?

4   Have the children use the globe to explain how they would travel from their home to various places on the earth.

5   Ask these questions: Do people ever travel for fun? How might they travel? Did you ever travel anywhere for fun?

6   Have the children write stories with such titles as "My Most Exciting Trip," "A Trip I Would Like to Take," or "The Day We Moved."

7   Have each student illustrate his favorite way to travel.

Learning Experiences

As previously noted, learning experiences should be closely related to the supporting concepts they are supposed to achieve and should provide for their gradual unfolding. Not all learning experiences are of equal importance in the development of concepts to be learned. Those most basic to the development of a concept should be organized in a logical, sequential order so that one builds on another. Others may be introduced for extension and enrichment purposes. A few may be somewhat unrelated to the others and can be omitted if the pressure of time becomes too great. Care must be taken to see that learning experiences are geared to the maturity level of the class for which they are intended. To be avoided is a cafeteria list of offerings from which teachers may select according to their whims and which are only incidental to the development of main objectives.

The learning experiences comprise a major portion of the unit and require the greatest amount of planning and teaching time. It is in this area of the unit development that teachers can use their previous teaching experience to greatest advantage in planning for a wide variety of meaningful activities geared to meet individual differences of the pupils. It is important to recognize that children can learn best when a number of different ways of learning are open to them. Among other ways, unit activities should provide opportunities for children to learn from books, audiovisual materials, discussions, study trips, analysis, dramatizations, and form-construction activities. If learning is limited to reading from the textbook, which is all too often the case, some pupils may be deprived of their only possible or their best way of learning.

Study Trips / One of the most valuable kinds of learning activities in the social studies is study trips into the neighborhood and larger community. If properly organized and carried out, they can become an excellent means of providing a common background of experience for all pupils and for direct firsthand observation. They are of special importance to children from deprived homes with limited opportunities for the development of rich experiential backgrounds. Often, some of the most valuable trips for primary grade children are within walking distance of the school. However, it is important that every study trip be carefully planned and supervised. The following guidelines are important in planning for study trips:

The Importance of Study Trips

1 They provide opportunities for pupils to observe activities and processes firsthand.

2 They are highly motivating learning experiences.

3 They provide an excellent means of initiating or culminating a unit of work.

4 They provide many opportunities for concomitant learnings such as the development of human relations and social skills.

5 They provide for a follow-up of impressions gained by reading or study with actual experience.

6 They give many opportunities for integrating other learning skills such as letter-writing, reading, outlining and reporting findings, etc.

Selecting Places to Visit

1 It would be well for each school to have a list of community resources available in a central place for the use of all teachers. The list could contain the name of the business, resource person, or place of interest to be visited, the telephone number

and name of person to contact in arranging for the trip. The following kinds of resources might be listed: parks, museums, businesses, government institutions, factories, farms, lumber mills, banks, radio and television stations, newspapers, historical sites, state capitol, schools and universities. This kind of help for teachers would greatly increase the number of visits made each year.

2 Before selecting a place to visit, two major questions need to be asked: Will the information gained be directly related to the ongoing classroom study? and Will the trip be worthwhile considering the time, energy, and cost factors?

Legal Considerations for the Study Trip

1 It is important that the study trip be cleared with the proper school officials and that written permission be obtained from the parents or guardians of the pupils.

2 Regardless of the written statements from the parents, the teacher can be charged with "tort" liability in cases of negligence or lack of proper supervision.

3 Rules of conduct, dress, and safety precautions should be discussed with the class prior to the trip.

4 When transportation is necessary, proper arrangements should be made for the use of the school bus or some other licensed carrier.

5 Only on rare occasions will an individual child be excluded from a study trip. On these occasions care must be taken to see that the child left at school is properly supervised by another teacher.

6 Parents and other responsible adults should be invited to accompany the class on a trip to offer additional help and supervision.

Follow-up Activities

1 Some provisions should be made for the children to take notes or record information while on the trip.

2 Upon returning to the classroom have a teacher-pupil evaluation of the trip, with recommendations of how it might have been improved.

3 Have a class discussion of what was learned by the trip. Where motivation is high have children draw pictures and write reports on the trip.

4 The class should apply what was learned on the study trip to ongoing classroom study.

5 The class should write appropriate thank-you notes to the place of visit and to any parents who accompanied the class on the trip. In the lower grades, the children may dictate a letter to the teacher, who writes it on the chalkboard or chart. This letter is then copied by the children and one is selected by the teacher to be mailed out.

Dramatic Play **/** Dramatic play in the classroom is an educational technique in which children explore an area of human experience by reliving the activities and relationships involved in that experience in their own way, and, under teacher guidance, acquiring needed information and skills so as to increase the satisfactions inherent in play that is meaningful and extensive. Dramatic play encompasses the following procedures:

1 The introductory situation is an arranged environment planned by the teacher.

2 Children explore the arranged environment and are permitted to respond in their own way, to manipulate tools and materials and discuss them.

3 A story may be read by the teacher to further the interest of the children in the selected area.

4 Children are invited to play any part of the story or set their own situation.

5 First play is spontaneous and unguided but carefully observed by the teacher.

6 Play is followed by a sharing period in which satisfactions are expressed and dissatisfactions are clarified, under teacher guidance, into a statement of expressed needs.

7 Planning for meeting the expressed needs includes the processes of problem-solving, making of rules, and assignment of work to be done.

8 A period of enrichment of experiences through such activities as research, excursions, firsthand experiences, and visual aids ensues before, and alongside of, further play.

9 Play proceeds on higher levels (involving more accurate activities and more interrelationships and interpretations) as a result of enriched experience.

10 This is a continuous and expanding experience proceeding on an ascending spiral that may, in the upper elementary grades, eventuate, after weeks of growth, into a structured drama.

Thus dramatic play in the classroom utilizes improvisation, discussion, problem-solving, and generalization, and employs many separate subjects and the entire gamut of educational media (paints, musical instruments, costumes, literature, films, etc.) as needed.

Among the many values derived from dramatic activities are the following:

1 Grow out of and relate to the areas of learning in the social studies, thus enriching total learning

2 Help children get the feel of time and place—"opens a child's eyes to see and heart to listen and understand"

3 Push out the boundaries of the child's "life space"; heighten the child's sensibilities to other human beings

4 Develop positive self-images and provide acceptable ways for children to express feelings

5 Give life, interest, and coloring to learning

6 Develop initiative and creativity

7 Help identify problems for further exploration

8 Help develop social study skills and social study vocabulary

9 Reinforce concepts and understandings

10 Provide an opportunity for the teacher to evaluate social study understandings, skills, and habits in behavioral situations.

Construction and Processing Activities in the Classroom **/** For some time there has been considerable controversy as to the place of construction and processing activities in the social studies. Some have felt that there is no place for these kinds of activities in today's overcrowded classrooms. Others are placing increased emphasis on purely academic and intellectual pursuits in the curriculum, to the virtual exclusion of direct, firsthand experiences of pupils. They argue that we cannot waste good school time on such kinds of activities; there is too much to learn. In spite of the fact that classroom industrial arts are viewed by some with disfavor, they deserve a solid place in a unit-of-work study.

Construction and processing activities may be properly classified as industrial arts processes. They involve the reproduction of activities and processes already worked out by man, activities such as processing raw materials in order to meet his needs for food, clothing, shelter, and protection. In the category of authentic processes fall such activities as making paper, making butter, tanning hides, making candles, and weaving clothing, etc. The importance of having children carry out firsthand some of the life processes of various cultures is stated by Shaftel as follows:

> In a world torn by warring ideologies and the immature struggles of emergent nations, our ability to understand the survival orientation and needs of under-developed nations may be crucial. Can you tell most American children, verbally, what it is like to work all day getting food, clothing, and shelter in order to survive? Or is another dimension to learning needed—a sensing, feeling, "affective" learning such is experienced when you struggle to grind corn by hand on a Mexican metate with a mano and learn by your own sweat what a hard, time-consuming, manual task it is. Perhaps, after such firsthand experience, reading a sentence which states that people who live in a pre-industrial culture have to work very hard simply to provide food each day, will have more meaning.[6]

Today more than ever before, American children living in urban areas and particularly those living in the "inner" city of large metropolitan areas need to be helped to understand the relationship between natural resources, industrial processes, workers, and the finished products that are delivered to their doors or to the local stores.

Construction activities in a unit-of-work study become the vital channels through which children can learn through experimentation and inductive thinking to arrive at major concepts or generalizations. According to Shaftel:

> . . . Industrial arts activities provide the concrete experiences that enable the child to view and explain the world to himself in his own way, when part of the unit-of-work approach to learning.
>
> The construction products, in this rationale, then become props (small houses, streets, delivery trucks; or a setting for a peon's

[6] Fannie R. Shaftel, *Industrial Arts in the Social Studies Program,* reported in *Social Studies in Elementary Schools,* Thirty-second Yearbook, ed. John U. Michaelis (Washington, D.C.: National Council for the Social Studies, 1962), p. 214.

hut) to help the child get inside an area of human experience, in a childlike way, in order to explore relationships between institutions and people. *They become children's models for thinking!* For as children run trucks, they need streets; as they build streets, they discover the need for traffic rules. They may conclude, for example, that when there is traffic on streets, rules make it safer for people.

. . . Each activity is selected for its significant contribution to important ideas. Construction, in this framework, is subordinated and modified. It is done simply, on a child's level, to facilitate his thinking, to create an atmosphere in which to take on the roles of people. It contributes, as does a stage set, to identifying with a time, a place and a people, but does not dominate the program.[7]

There are many teachers who recognize the educational value of construction experiences but who are hesitant to use them because of lack of space for materials, lack of tools, or lack of skill in industrial processes. Regardless of the many reasons for not using construction activities in the social studies program, they serve important ends. A creative or resourceful teacher will find ways to utilize these more meaningful kinds of activities in her social studies program.

Culmination of the Unit

Culminating activities are used to summarize, clarify, assess, evaluate, and apply what has been learned during a unit of instruction. Perhaps their most valuable function is to clinch basic understandings, attitudes, and skills developed in the unit. This is accomplished best through procedures involving practical applications of what has been learned. Culminating activities also may focus on what has been left unfinished and direct discussion toward the next unit, thus serving as a kind of ongoing activity between one unit and the next.

Occasionally, a major activity such as a dramatic presentation, a program, or an informal party is used as a means of helping pupils round off a study. Often, another class or parents are invited to this part of the culmination. Care must be taken to see that these kinds of activities do not become the goal of the unit. Otherwise, they tend to become superficial and staged and not a good learning situation. The amount of school time spent in their preparation is often difficult to defend in relation to the educational value realized through them.

Listed below are examples of culminating activities commonly used. They may, of course, be modified, expanded, or combined for most effective use.

1 Having a teacher-conducted discussion in which key points related to basic concepts and understandings are reviewed

2 Having students present summary reports based on main ideas and problems developed in the unit

3 Displaying children's stories, charts, pictures, maps, scrapbooks, and other materials that highlight important learnings

[7] Ibid., pp. 217–218.

4 Presenting a group activity in which all members can take part (The activity should be related to the main ideas studied throughout the unit. This may be in the form of a program, creative play, or dramatization.)

5 Planning a study trip to the community to observe an activity related to the study or to put into practice conclusions reached by the class, such as safety measures in getting to and from school, etc.

Evaluation

Evaluation is the means of obtaining data on student progress in achieving major objectives of the unit of work. It is an essential process throughout all of the unit from the initiation through the culmination. It can be accomplished most effectively when unit goals are related to specific behavioral outcomes. Stated in behavioral or operational terms that clearly define the expected behavior, objectives become more tangible and provide a basis for accurate appraisal of student growth. It is only at this level that the growth of the class toward unit objectives can be appraised with some accuracy.

Continuous diagnosis throughout the different phases of the unit will call for the use of a wide variety of evaluative devices. Early in the unit a sociometric test may be used to determine the quality of interpersonal relations and to form work groups. Evidence of improvement in group work can be noted by informal rating devices used by the teacher. Charts on work standards and checklists for children to use in self-evaluation may be prepared as the unit progresses. Evaluation of daily progress may be accomplished through teacher-pupil planning sessions in which committees and work groups report progress and plan for future steps.

Among the many different kinds of evaluative devices or procedures used, the following are most common:

1 Behavioral objectives

2 Sociometric tests

3 Informal teacher observation

4 Anecdotal records

5 Pupil self-check lists and rating scales

6 Folders containing samples of individual work

7 Work-standard charts

8 Tape recordings used to compare concepts and attitudes expressed in final discussions with those expressed earlier in the unit

9 Objective tests

10 Essay tests.

Related Materials

At the end of the teaching unit it is most helpful to include a complete listing of books and other related instructional materials and resources. They should provide a list of suitable related materials for students who may want to study further on their own. Also, they should include the sources of materials called for in the learning experiences and those kinds of materials that are of a special nature or that require some advanced preparation for use. It is helpful if materials are categorized under the following kinds of major headings: Bibliography (teachers' and children's books), Reports, Films, Filmstrips, and other materials and sources of information.

When the teacher has developed a social study unit or a number of units covering the basic content of her grade level, she is well prepared, with some minor adjustments, to teach on a day-to-day basis. Generally speaking, a good lesson should be limited to one clear concept, attitude, or skill taken from the unit, which can be managed with a class period or within a relatively short time. There is a tendency on the part of some teachers to cover too many concepts or understandings within one class period. Concepts, if learned effectively, must be developed through carefully planned steps. They require time to develop and should not be rushed.

In summary, the following steps are essential in planning a good unit of work in the social studies:

1 Determine the area of study. *Examples:* Early California Indians, Hawaii, Transportation, The Farm, Money and Banking.

2 Find out all you can about the topic through reading, research, etc.

3 Decide what major concepts you want to teach related to the unit topic. *Example:* The climate and materials available in a region influenced the types of houses built by early California Indians.

4 Determine appropriate supporting concepts for each major concept developed. *Examples:* Plank houses built of redwood were used by the northern Indians; grass houses were built by the southern Indians.

5 Develop a behavioral objective for each major concept. *Example:* Upon completion of the unit, the student will: (a) draw pictures depicting at least three types of Indian homes and (b) describe orally or in writing the kinds of materials used in building each of these homes.

6 Select appropriate techniques for evaluating the extent to which students are able to achieve the desired behaviors for each major concept.

7 Determine the most effective ways to teach each concept. *Examples:* field trip, demonstration, discussion, reading, etc.

8 Plan the initiation. An aroused interest in an area makes learning easier and more effective.

9 Consider an appropriate culmination. *Examples:* exhibit, exam, sharing program.

10 Determine appropriate related activities. *Examples:* Make a list of new vocabulary that will be used frequently in the unit. List books and reading materials, etc., that can be suggested to students who may want to do further research and study on the topic.

INDIVIDUALIZING SOCIAL STUDY UNITS

The same conceptual structure used in a group unit, with accompanying behavioral objectives, may be used as the basis for the organization of a "packaged" individualized unit. From that point, the unit as previously outlined in this chapter may be individualized by three basic steps.

1 Develop a pretest or preassessment instrument to determine where the child is at the present time. That is, which major concepts he has already acquired or understands and the areas of his deficiencies. This pretest may be in the form of an oral test or discussion on the lower grade levels.

2 Provide for a choice of learning activities. This will require a different format for the organization of learning experiences than is found in the traditional unit of work geared for the whole class. Learning experiences are categorized under a number of different headings such as reports, creative activities, etc., and are keyed back to specific major concepts and behavioral objectives. (An example of choice-of-learning activities will follow later in this chapter.)

3 Provide a means of evaluation to determine the extent to which all major concepts of the unit have been achieved by the students. Provide for reteaching and additional work in areas of deficiencies.

Any attempt to individualize social studies must take into account three basic steps or principles of individualized instruction:

I. Free Selection of Topics for Study in a Choice-of-Units Approach **/** It is essential that each child have an opportunity to select from a number of topics or units his own areas of interest for study. This provides a high motivation for learning and helps meet the individual needs of each learner. Teachers can be more effective in their teaching of the social studies when areas of study are directly related to the interests and background of preparation of individual pupils. Under the context of free selection or choice-of-units approach, the content of the social studies serves mainly as a means to an end. The broad goals of the social studies related to social study skills and the development of positive habits and attitudes become the more significant goals to be attained. The following social study skills, habits, and attitudes should be continually stressed and worked on throughout any individualized study, regardless of the nature of the content covered:

Social Study Skills
1 Following specific directions
2 Planning, working at, and completing tasks
3 Working independently
4 Reading skills essential to effective research
   a) Reading for specific information
   b) Reading to remember and understand
   c) Skimming for general ideas
5 Library skills utilized in research
   a) Use of card file in the school library
   b) Use of the Dewey decimal system
6 Use of reference books and material
   a) Using a bibliography
   b) Using indexes, tables of contents, and glossaries

    7 Use of a dictionary in research

    8 Use of an atlas and an almanac

    9 Use of maps and globes
       a) Construction of maps, use of commercially made maps
       b) Use of geographical terms
       c) Use of geographical keys
       d) Use of globe skills

   10 Effective writing skills
       a) Taking meaningful class notes
       b) Outlining material effectively
       c) Writing meaningful reports
       d) Keeping individual pupil records
       e) Developing creativity in written work

   11 Pupil problem-solving in a variety of settings

   12 Working cooperatively with others, recognizing the worth of other pupils' ideas, accepting criticism, recognizing and accepting the responsibilities for solving the problem at hand.

Significant Habits and Attitudes

1 Being willing to assist in the planning and execution of activities

2 Taking initiative in looking up pertinent information and sharing it with the class

3 Being attentive and courteous in listening to teachers, classmates, resource persons

4 Sticking to the subject and raising only pertinent comments or questions

5 Being free of interrupting or monopolizing tendencies in discussions

6 Being open-minded when presented with new sources of information

7 Having the desire to check the reliability of sources

8 Being willing to give an attentive and courteous hearing to those who may disagree.

II. Self-pacing / Materials should be individually paced so that each child can progress at his own rate of learning. Each individual pupil reacts to a stimulus and initiates action at his own rate and depth.

III. Choice of Learning Activities / Provide for a variety of learning activities under a number of different categories from which a child may select. Not all children can learn equally well from a single approach to learning such as the textbook approach. To be successful with all children, teachers must see that many avenues of approach to a given concept are open to children. The following suggested categories of learning activities will provide a choice necessary for individualized study. A point system may be assigned for each category of activities as a means of motivation or grading. This is to be left to the discretion of the individual teacher. Perhaps a point system would be more valid as a means of motivation for pupils on the upper-grade levels. Communication through written activities may pose a problem for children on the lower-grade levels, particularly for those in the kindergarten and first grade. In these grade levels perhaps oral and pictorial instruction can be given to the pupils.

In an individualized unit approach, learning activities that are specifically geared to the development of major concepts and behavioral objectives of the unit are categorized under the following nine headings:

1 *Knowledge sessions:* Basic knowledge sessions conducted by the teacher cover all large understandings or major concepts of the unit. All students may be required to attend each session, or it may be left open for students to attend according to individual needs and deficiencies as determined by the pretest.

2 *Independent research reports—oral and written:* It is left to the pupil's judgment as to whether he wishes to do an oral or a written report. Although all pupils should be encouraged at times to give an oral report, some find it a most difficult task.

3 *Creative activities:* There are a wide variety of creative activities in which children may engage in each unit of work, such as writing stories or poems, drawing pictures, etc.

4 *Individual projects:* Individual projects include such activities as making maps, dioramas, models, etc.

5 *Look-and-listen sessions:* These sessions involve viewing films, filmstrips, etc., and listening to records and tapes.

6 *Readings:* A list of pertinent reading references related to each unit should be provided from which the student may choose.

7 *Questions for answer or discussion:* A list of key questions related to each major concept may be provided for pupils as a guide for their reading and study. They may also be used in small or large group discussions.

8 *Vocabulary:* Vocabulary development should be an integral part of each unit of work. On a point system, two points are awarded for each new word that the student learns.

9 *Culmination activities:* There are a wide variety of summarizing activities such as making scrapbooks, movie rolls, etc., that students may engage in near the completion of a unit of work.

As an alternative approach to the above format, learning activities may be typed on individual 5-by-8-inch cards and filed according to the above categories for individual pupil use.

The following student study guide depicts the complete organization of an individualized unit of work, including major concepts, behavioral objectives, and choice of learning activities.

1. Every Monday the student will fill out a contract like the one shown. He will contract what he plans on getting done in a one-week period. This gives the teacher an opportunity to plan ahead and prepare relevant materials. This also gives students a goal to work toward.

2. At the end of each social studies period, if the student has completed some work, it is turned in along with his study-guide folder. This gives the teacher an opportunity to check work and record points in the student's study guide.

Student Contract   Name _____

Choice of Activities	SOCIAL STUDIES Daily Schedule

1 Creativity
 	
    pictures ☐
 	
    chart ☐
 	
    stories ☐
 	
    poems ☐
	Monday *Date* _____
	
	(Knowledge session: 35 minutes)
	(Contracting session: 15 minutes)

2 Reports ☐ 3 Individual project ☐ 4 Readings ☐ 5 Films ☐ 6 Vocabulary ☐ (student checks the work he has completed at the end of the week)	*Tuesday* *Date* _____ (Independent study: 45 minutes) Creativity: pictures Picture showing how the California Indian looked
	Wednesday *Date* _____ (Independent study: 45 minutes) Filmstrip: *Early California Indians*
	Thursday *Date* _____ (Independent study: 45 minutes) Readings: "Food of the California Indians" folder
	Friday *Date* _____ (Independent study: 45 minutes) Creative writing: "Indian Legend"

Major Concept or Main Idea	Supporting Ideas	Behavioral Objective	Vocabulary
1 Geography and climate of Calif. affect where Indians live.	1 Many varied climates are found within borders of Calif. 2 Calif. possesses many natural resources. 3 Topography influences the location of settlements. 4 There is no written record of when, how, or why the Indians came to Calif.	I will understand the climate and topography of Calif. and why it affected where the Indians lived. I will be able to locate and fill in my own outline map showing the topography features and the natural resources of California.	1 coastal 2 desert 3 valley 4 river 5 lake 6 bay 7 island 8 climate 9 topography 10 Asia 11 tribe
2 People of a different culture often look different from people of our own culture.	1 Calif. Indians are of a short stature, stocky, and strong. 2 California Indians are flat-nosed and broad-faced. 3 Calif. Indians have black hair that is very straight and eyes that are very dark. 4 Calif. Indians' skin coloring varied from light brown to dark.	I will be able to show in a drawing what the Calif. Indians look like. I will be able to describe in a written paragraph the characteristics that differentiate the Indian from people of my own culture.	1 stature 2 structure 3 stocky
3 California Indians' environment determined their manner of dress.	1 The clothing of the Indians was very scanty. 2 Plants and animals provided the materials used to make clothing. 3 Calif. Indians wore feathers, headdresses and robes only for ceremonial occasions. 4 Shell beads were their favorite article of ornament.	I will be able to describe in a written report the characteristics of the Indian's dress and explain why he dressed as he did. I will be able to show in picture how the men, women, and children dressed and report orally the reasons. I will be able to explain from which plants and animals the different types of Indian clothing were made.	1 ornament 2 apron 3 loincloth 4 scanty 5 tules 6 implement
4 Food and how it was prepared. (Nature helps to satisfy man's basic needs.)	1 Plants were the Indians' main food. 2 Meats and fish were important foods. 3 Indians built storehouses for food. 4 Indian foods required little preserving.	I will be able to chart out the types of food the Indians ate and illustrate the source from which they came. I will be able to demonstrate, by acting it out, the different methods of preparing food.	1 preserve 2 storehouse 3 acorn 4 Chia 5 utensil 6 granary

Major Concept or Main Idea	Supporting Ideas	Behavioral Objective	Vocabulary
	5 Baskets were used for cooking utensils. 6 Indians cooked out of doors.		
5 The climate and materials available in a region influenced the types of Indian homes built by the California Indians.	1 The wickiup was common to most sections. 2 A village of wickiups was called a "rancheria" 3 Plank houses built of redwood were used by the northern Indians. 4 Grass houses were built by the southern Indians.	I will be able to make a model of the different types of Indian homes. I will be able to illustrate in drawing the different utensils and materials used in building each of these homes.	1 implement 2 fertile 3 settlement 4 wickiup 5 plank 6 assembly house 7 sweat house 8 rancheria
6 California Indians used tools, weapons, and utensils for their survival.	1 Implements were primarily made of stone, bone, and shell. 2 Implements and utensils were primarily used to make houses, boats, rafts, baskets, bowls, ornaments and in cooking.	I will be able to illustrate on a chart the implements and utensils and weapons used by the Indians and will be able to explain and illustrate what each was used for.	1 weapon 2 hatchet 3 flaked knives 4 wedge 5 mussel-shell adz 6 bone awls 7 scraping stones 8 fire stick 9 fire stone 10 metate-mano 11 mortar-pestle 12 atlate 13 forked hunting stick 14 forked fishing stick
7 Indian men, women, and children participate in many activities.	1 The Indians govern themselves. 2 The Indians amuse themselves with many games. 3 Storytelling was a favorite entertainment. 4 The Indian men, women, and children work hard for their survival. Ex. cooking hunting. . . .	I will be able to play an Indian game. I will be able to sing an Indian song, and make either a basket, piece of pottery, or a piece of jewelry. I will be able to write an Indian legend.	1 amusement 2 entertainment 3 chant 4 government 5 legend 6 ceremonial 7 pottery

Choice of Learning Activities Name _____

Knowledge Session (10 points) All knowledge sessions must be attended.	Date	Points Earned
1 Climate and geographical features affect where the California Indians settle.		
2 People of a different culture often look different from people of our own culture.		
3 California Indians' environment affected the way they dressed.		
4 Food and how it was prepared.		
5 The climate and materials available in a region influenced the types of homes built by the California Indians.		
6 California Indians use tools, weapons, and utensils for their survival.		
7 Indian men, women, and children participated in many activities.		
Research Reports (written - 25 points; oral - 15 points) Must choose at least one written report and one oral.	Date	Points Earned
1 Write a report describing the California Indian men, women, and children's manner of dress. Explain what they used and why they dressed as they did.		
2 Write a report on the Indian houses. Explain what materials were used and what tools and implements were used. Explain in which region of California each could be found. Explain how the climate affected the type of house they built.		
3 Write a report on how the Indians governed themselves.		
4 Give an oral report explaining how the topography and climate of California affected where the Indians lived.		
5 Give an oral report explaining the different plants and animals that were used for food. Be able to tell how they were prepared.		
6 Compare the modern and early California methods for preserving food (written or oral report).		
Creative Activities (5–25 points) Must do at least one map, chart, story, and activity.	Date	Points Earned
Maps		
1 Fill in an outline map of California. Include topographical features and natural resources. Use symbols and labels.		
2 Fill in an outline map of California showing where each of the different tribes was located. Show the different crops located in each region.		
3 Fake your own map showing the possible routes the Indians may have taken to get to California.		
Pictures		
1 Draw a picture showing how you think the California Indian looked.		

Choice of Learning Activities (*Continued*)

"Creative Activities"	Date	Points Earned
2 Draw a picture showing how the men, women, and children dressed.		
3 Draw a picture showing the three different types of houses the Indians built.		
4 Draw a picture of the weapons men used for fishing and hunting.		
Creative Writing		
1 Write a story explaining why you would or would not like to dress like the California Indians.		
2 Write a story about yourself and explain how you would spend one day in an Indian village.		
3 Write an Indian legend.		
4 Write a play about the California Indians and present it to the class.		
Charts		
1 Make a chart showing the animals and plants used for making clothing and beside each draw a picture of the article of clothing.		
2 Make a chart showing the different kinds of Indian foods and indicate in which region each would be found.		
3 Make a chart showing the different implements, weapons, and utensils used by the Indians and show what each was used for.		
4 On a chart list the activities of the men, women, and children.		
Activities		
1 Learn an Indian game.		
2 Learn an Indian song.		
3 Learn an Indian dance.		
4 Make a folder on California Indian life.		
5 Write a poem about California Indian life.		
Individual Projects (10–25 points) **You must choose at least two projects.**		
1 Make a puppet of an Indian man, woman, or child. Dress it appropriately.		
2 Arrange a display of foods that are seeds, roots, stems, and leaves.		
3 Make a model of either a grass house, a plank house, or a wickiup.		
4 Make a mural showing Indian life in each of the different regions of California.		
5 Make a piece of Indian pottery.		
6 Weave an Indian basket.		
7 Make a piece of Indian jewelry.		
8 Make a diorama of an Indian village.		
Look-and-Listen Section (10 points) **View any three filmstrips you would like.**		
1 Filmstrip: *Early California Indians*		
2 Film: *Indians of California, Part II, Food*		
3 Film: *Indian Dances*		
4 Other		

Choice of Learning Activities (*Continued*)

Readings (10 points) Read any five of your own choosing. Answer question in folder.	Date	Points Earned
1 Climate and topography of California		
2 How California Indians look		
3 Clothing of the California Indians		
4 Food of the California Indians		
5 Storehouses and preservation of food		
6 Methods for preparing food		
7 The rabbit drive		
8 Weapons used for hunting		
9 Materials used for building homes		
10 The plank house		
11 The grass house		
12 The wickiup		
13 Implements, weapons, and utensils, and the use of each		
14 How Indians lighted fires		
15 Government of the Indians		
16 Activities of the California Indians		
Books to be used for research		
1 Richards, *California Yesterday*		
2 Flower, *A Child's History of California*		
3 Buell, *California Stepping Stones*		
4 Marcy, *The Indians' Garden*		
5 Hoffman, *California's Beginnings*		
6 Sneddon, *Docas, Indian of Santa Clara*		
Culmination of Unit (10 points)	Date	Points Earned
1 Plan a California Indian feast day.		
2 Complete folder or scrapbook on Indian life.		
3 Complete the outline map on the classroom wall.		
4 Make a mural showing all the different phases of the California Indian's life.		
5 Take Posttest.		

QUESTIONS AND ACTIVITIES

1 / Give three major reasons why careful planning is basic to good teaching.

2 / Explain the major differences between a teaching unit and a resource unit.

3 / Give a number of basic reasons why the content of a unit should be organized around a conceptual structure.

4 / How does a unit of work provide for individual differences?

5 / Examine some social study units which may be found in the curriculum library and evaluate them in terms of the steps for developing good teaching units found in this chapter. Are any provisions made for unit evaluation? Why is evaluation important?

6 / Arrange to visit a classroom where a unit of work is in progress. Note any strengths and weaknesses of the unit approach to learning. Discuss with your teacher.

7 / Develop a group unit of work according to the suggested format in this chapter. Using the basic conceptual structure of the group unit, individualize it according to the steps outlined.

SELECTED REFERENCES

Carpenter, Helen M. (ed.). *Skill Development in the Social Studies.* Thirty-third Yearbook. Washington, D.C.: National Council for the Social Studies, 1963.

Fraser, Dorothy McClure, and McCutchen, Samuel P. (eds.). *Social Studies in Transition: Guidelines for Change,* Curriculum Series Number Twelve. Washington, D.C.: National Council for the Social Studies, 1965.

Goodlad, John I., and Anderson, R. H. *The Nongraded Elementary School.* Revised edition. New York: Harcourt Brace Jovanovich, 1963.

Hanna, Lavone A., Potter, Gladys L., and Hagaman, Neva. *Unit Teaching in the Elementary School.* New York: Holt, Rinehart & Winston, 1963.

Hill, Wilhelmina. *Unit Planning and Teaching in Elementary Social Studies.* Washington, D.C.: U.S. Office of Education, 1963.

Hill, Wilhelmina (ed.). *Selected Resource Units in Elementary Social Studies: Kindergarten–Grade 6.* Curriculum Series Number Eleven. Washington, D.C.: National Council for the Social Studies, 1961.

Jarolimek, John. *Social Studies in Elementary Education.* Third edition. New York: Macmillan, 1967. Chap. 3.

Jarolimek, John (ed.). "Social Studies Education: The Elementary School, Focus on Concepts, Values, Skills, Individualizing Instruction." Reprinted from *Social Education.* National Council for the Social Studies, November 1966.

Lee, John R., and McLendon, Jonathon C. (eds.). *Readings on Elementary Social Studies—Prologue to Change.* Boston: Allyn & Bacon, 1965. Pp. 316–343.

Michaelis, John U. *Social Studies for Children in a Democracy.* Third edition. Englewood Cliffs, N.J.: Prentice-Hall, 1963.

TEACHING CHILDREN THE USE OF GLOBES AND FLAT MAPS

chapter 5

> *One day we gave the child a colour'd sphere*
> *Of the wide earth,*
> *that she might mark and know,*
> *By tint and outline,*
> *All its sea and land.*
> *She patted all the world;*
> *old empires peep'd*
> *Between her baby fingers;*
> *her soft hand*
> *Was welcomed at all*
> *frontiers.*
>
> *Charles Tennyson-Turner*

The word "geography" is derived from *geo* (earth) and *graphy* (writing). Thus, geography is concerned with a study and description of the earth. However, the scope of geographic inquiry cannot be limited to only a consideration of physical phenomena. "Earth writings" can be of no significance except as they relate to the human condition. According to Hartshorne, "The relations between the world of man and the non-human world are of the greatest concern in geography."[1] Therefore, the study of geography focuses upon the forces at work in both the physical and cultural environments of mankind. The nature of geography is defined by Servey as follows:

> Geography as an area of study encompasses both science and social science. As a science, geography is usually referred to as physical geography. It includes the definitive study of the following factors as they operate in the various regions of the world: (1) location on the globe in relation to the location of other geographical regions and political divisions; (2) topography—the lay of the land and its manifestation of richness in terms of soil, minerals, wildlife, and vegetation; (3) climate—its causes, and its manifestations in terms of temperature, precipitation, winds, and seasons; (4) the interrelationships among location, topography, and climate; and (5) the general influence of these factors on the life of man.

[1] Richard Hartshorne, *Perspective on the Nature of Geography* (Skokie, Ill.: Rand McNally, 1959), p. 48.

As a social science, geography is usually referred to as cultural geography, or as a more specific aspect such as economic or industrial geography. Basically, it is a study of patterns of application of physical geography principles in terms of the utility of geographical factors, in the life of man in specific regions. The student of cultural geography usually is guided toward a review of physical geography, utility patterns, the relationship between geographical factors and utility, and the significance of these in terms of world economy, political structure, and the structure of world culture.[2]

The foundations of modern geography were laid by nineteenth-century German scholars Humboldt, Ritter, and Ratzel. Humboldt was primarily a physical geographer who was concerned mainly with the character and interrelationships of physical phenomena. Ritter and Ratzel promoted the development of human geography by showing the dependence of man on his physical environment, thus laying the foundation of cultural and regional geography.

According to Douglass, modern geographic study involves three major factors:

First, it is concerned with *description*. That is, the things which occur in the environment may be described with accuracy, whether they are within the immediate view or whether they are far over the horizon. To aid in this process, concepts have been invented and terms developed. For example, at one level of generality, words like "delta," "mountain," "plateau," and "valley" assist in the process of description. . . .

Second, geographic study is concerned with the *location* of things, with the *direction* of these things, and with the positions and relations of these, each to the other. . . .

Third, geographic study is concerned with attaching significance or meaning to the things which may be described, located, and related to each other. The geographer always asks the question, "Why is this relationship important and in what ways it is of significance to man?"[3]

Geography has been called the "Mother of Sciences," since other disciplines such as geology, climatology, and anthropology have arisen from geographic study. Yet geography has become more vigorous all the time and has continued to gain in importance as one of the subjects comprising the social studies curriculum of the elementary school. Because of its nature, geography has been correctly termed the bridge between the natural and the social sciences. Like history, geographic phenomena cannot be explained meaningfully without the aid of the various social science disciplines and the natural sciences. Unless geography can utilize knowledge from these fields it remains incomplete. Thus, geography is distinguished not so much by the

---

[2] Richard E. Servey, *Social Studies Instruction in the Elementary School* (San Francisco: Chandler, 1967), pp. 44–45.
[3] Malcolm P. Douglass, *Social Studies from Theory to Practice in Elementary Education* (Philadelphia: Lippincott, 1967), p. 230.

nature of its subject matter as by the ways in which that knowledge is utilized.

Social studies have appropriately been the major area of the school curriculum concerned with teaching children the skills of reading and interpreting globes and flat maps. Every social study that children are engaged in involves concepts related to understanding spatial relationships. That is, every problem children approach deals with the study of people or things occupying a place on the earth's surface. The physical geography of an area—its location, topography, climate, and distance from other places—takes on great significance as one examines the interrelationships of these factors and their influence on the life of man. Thus the globe and flat maps are among the most useful instructional tools in the social studies.

The need for skill in the use of these tools goes beyond the social studies program. Newspapers, magazines, and television news broadcasts often rely upon maps as an effective means of communicating world happenings more clearly. Thus, the need for acquiring a basic understanding of maps and their common uses has taken on additional importance for people generally today. Too, an increasingly mobile population that travels widely over the earth's surface is dependent to a great extent upon the accurate and intelligent use of maps in getting from place to place.

The present need for improved map-reading skills and related abilities points up the importance of a development program in this area, beginning at the earliest grade levels. There is some evidence that in the past many of our schools have failed to provide a systematic program for developing effective map-reading skills on the elementary level.[4] However, with many new materials available for teachers, this need not be the pattern for the future.

If a map program is to be effective, it must be developmental in nature, beginning with kindergarten children and continuing throughout the elementary grades, the junior and senior high school, and even on to the college level. The complete mastery of a given map skill is not expected at any particular grade level. Many basic understandings related to maps can be introduced to children early in their school experience, but each succeeding year should bring an extension and deepening of these understandings or concepts.

The cartographer, or map-maker, uses a wide variety of symbols to represent the natural and man-made things in the environment that are shown on maps. To effectively use or construct maps, children must therefore be introduced to the special "language of mapping." Learning to use and read map symbols calls for more than rote memorization of the arbitrary associations that have been given them. If learning is to be meaningful and effective children should have firsthand experience with reality and should be able from this experience to visualize the things for which the symbols stand. In other words, the teaching-learning sequence should be such that children do not encounter the abstract symbol prior to the development of concepts about the reality for which the symbol stands. The ultimate concern of map-reading is to develop in children the ability to infer relationships that exist among the physical and cultural elements symbolically represented on the map.

[4] See Malcolm P. Douglass, "Some Relationships Between Laterality and Knowledge of Directions," *Elementary School Journal* 66 (2): 68–74.

BASIC UNDERSTANDINGS TO BE DEVELOPED IN MAP-READING

During the elementary school years teachers should be concerned with helping children develop the following understandings and skills in map-reading:

1 Developing the ability to use and understand the globe as the most accurate representation of the earth's surface

2 Developing accurate concepts about directions in space and on globes and flat maps

3 Developing concepts related to distance and scale

4 Developing the ability to interpret map symbols of various kinds and to visualize the realities for which they stand

5 Developing the ability to recognize and express relative location

6 Developing the ability to use and understand the basic kinds of map projections.

Using and Understanding the Globe

Since the globe is spherical, similar to the earth, the map that is drawn on its surface is a more accurate representation of the earth's surface than can be shown on a flat map. Concepts shown on a model globe are important to the earliest stages of geographical education. For example, the globe correctly reveals the comparative size of continents and oceans. It is the best tool available for showing worldwide relationships, inasmuch as it depicts most accurately the shapes and sizes of land areas, distances, and direction. Concepts that can be taught from a model globe are basic to the geographical understandings of elementary school children. Therefore, it is important that a globe be available to every elementary classroom. If the globe is readily accessible to children in the classroom, it will be used in many informal situations and will become the means of helping them visualize true global relationships. Of course, in addition to the incidental references made to the globe by children, the teacher will use the globe in teaching in more formal social studies activities. Nevertheless, as children make reference to the globe, they may note the size and shape of major land and water bodies and their relative locations. Of interest to the individual child may be the approximate location of his home and the location of nations and cities that are prominent in the news of the world. As he becomes familiar with the basic roundness of the earth, he will become acquainted with the true shapes, distances, and directions of many different areas of the world. He may plot the shortest distance between two given points on the earth's surface as a means of illustrating the closeness of many parts of the world that seem to be farther apart when viewed from a flat map. Thus, through the use of the globe in both formal and informal learning situations, the child may gradually acquire a basic and accurate understanding of worldwide relationships.

Although the globe is an important tool for helping children acquire true global concepts, it cannot be made large enough to show much detail of the earth's surface. Flat maps are superior to the globe in depicting small surface areas because of the greater detail that can be shown on them. But even a flat map is understood most effectively when used in conjunction with the globe. Although the globe has *some* limitations for classroom use, it is the most valuable tool available in developing a global view of the world. Its superiority as an instructional aid in teaching basic geographical concepts cannot be overestimated.

The child should be introduced to the globe early in his school experience in informal activities. This will provide a background for the more formal instruction in the upper elementary grades. The following classroom experiences will help children develop global concepts:

> 1 A globe should be available in the lower grades for much informal use. Children can discover many accurate relationships about the planet on which they live from continued references to the globe. Have children note that the globe is a good model of the earth, that the distance around the globe is the same in all directions, and that the surface is uniformly curved.
>
> 2 Have the children find land areas and water bodies. They can gradually learn the names of the continents and oceans, the names and location of the poles, the equator, and major cities.
>
> 3 Talk about flying around the earth and the paths of satellites. Discuss how the oceans and land would look.
>
> 4 Count the large land masses. Center attention upon North America. Note ways it differs from other continents in shape. Point out the United States and the approximate location of where we live.
>
> 5 Have the children discover that water covers more of the earth's surface than does the land. Point out that most of the land of the world is located on the northern half of the world north of the equator.
>
> 6 Have children refer to the globe often in connection with class reports and discussions. Have them locate places they have studied, places in the news, places they have visited, and other places of special interest.

Developing Accurate Concepts About Direction

Maps drawn on either a sphere or a flat surface are reduced-scale symbols of the earth's surface that serve to bring space under control for close scrutiny. Because the surface areas depicted on a map represent a series of connected points within space, directional abilities are essential to the clear interpretation of the area shown. The ability to orient oneself to a map and to acquire a correct sense of direction is a prime skill of map-reading.

Unfortunately, man has not developed the keen senses associated with directional relationships that are evident in many of the lesser forms of life. For example, giant turtles off the east coast of Africa travel wide areas of the ocean yet return unerringly year after year to the same breeding areas and to the same beaches to lay their eggs. Similarly, the Pacific Coast salmon travels many miles in the sea before returning to spawn in the river where he himself was given life. Other of the earth's creatures such as horses, pigeons, swallows, bees, and ants all exhibit keen directional sense. Animals apparently have special senses and mechanisms that aid them in finding their way from place to place. As yet, man has not been able to fully understand or explain such amazing phenomena.

Because of the nature of the senses with which man is equipped, developing a good sense of direction requires special training and experiences with directional relationships beginning in earliest childhood. Since directional skills are not inborn but learned, children need experiences that will help them learn to express accurate ideas about direction and the relationship of one thing to another in space.

The need for the ability to express directions accurately is illustrated by the story of the farmer who was driving a tractor along a country road when he was stopped by a motorist who was apparently lost and who asked for directions to the nearest town. The farmer began, "Well, you just go down the road a piece and turn left on the first road you come to, then you go—no, you can't get there that way." Finally after a number of unsuccessful attempts to explain clearly how the motorist could get to town, the farmer replied, "I am sorry, mister, you just can't get there from here."

Developing directional concepts on the elementary school level can be most effectively accomplished when the learning experiences are specific and geared to the developmental level of children. Following is a list of developmental activities appropriate for developing directional concepts at the elementary level:

1 Talk about the cardinal directions. Have the class face north. Teach them that if one knows the direction of north, he can place the other directions. When facing north, one's back will be toward the south, east to the right, and west to the left. Specific attention should be given to the fact that the sun rises in the east and sets in the west.

2 Place a map of the local area on a table or on the floor and have the children orient it to the north with the aid of a compass. In this connection, experiment with the compass and other devices that tell direction.

3 Mark arrows on the classroom floor showing the cardinal directions, or place labels showing directions on classroom walls.

4 Directions should be discussed after children have taken short trips into the neighborhood. Give children opportunities for making simple statements in answer to questions about direction. For example: "The freeway is *west* of our school." "I walk *south* and then *west* to get to my home from school." "The large shopping area is *east* of our school." "The fire station is *south* of our school."

5 Introduce the concepts that north is toward the North Pole and south is toward the South Pole. Help children avoid the misconceptions that "north is always at the top of the map," and that north is "up" and south is "down."

6 Teach children how to find directions by shadows (the principle used in making sundials) and by locating the North Star at night.

7 Have children construct maps of familiar areas such as their neighborhood, playground, or school area. Have the children

note directional relationships such as the route they take to and from school, directions to nearby towns, etc.

8 Help children learn the cardinal directions and the "in-between" directions on a compass and to use them accurately in referring to directions.

9 Introduce children to the concept of parallels and meridians or the map grid. Give children experience in locating direction on various kinds of map projections. Explain how the area shown and the directions represented on it differ from one map to the next.

10 Using the grid system of the globe, ask directional questions such as, "What direction is California from the country of Brazil?" etc.

Developing Concepts Related to Distance and Scale

Whenever the earth's surface or any portion of it is portrayed on a globe or flat map, a concept of scale must be employed if accurate earth-map relations are maintained. In mapping, the scale used is determined to a great extent by the size of the paper on which the map is drawn and by the amount of the earth's surface that is depicted. This fact may make it difficult for elementary school pupils, especially during the primary grade years, to understand scale and to visualize the distances represented on maps of varying sizes, particularly when they depict the same geographical area. This same problem may exist also with maps of uniform size that depict different size areas of the earth's surface. Therefore, the process of developing concepts related to scale and distance is a prolonged and gradual one beginning with the child's earliest school experiences and extending throughout the elementary school grades. In addition to a knowledge of direction, concepts related to scale and distance are essential to effective map construction and interpretation. As such, they are an important aspect of the elementary school map program.

Scale may be defined as the relationship of distance measured on the map to the distance it represents on the earth's surface. Three closely related methods of expressing scale on maps are the following: the inch-to-mile statement, the graphic scale, and the numerical scale or representative fraction (see Figure 12).

Perhaps the easiest scale to understand and to use on the elementary school level is the graphic scale. Distance in miles between two points on a map can easily be determined by a simple measurement between points and applying this distance to the scale in miles. The "inch-to-mile" statement is more difficult for children to understand because the ratio of inches to miles continually changes as different size areas of the earth's surface are drawn to fit a standard page size. The representative fraction (RF) scale, too, is a complex scale for many elementary school pupils inasmuch as it involves the use of fractional units that are too advanced for many pupils at this age level. The following activities are appropriate for developing concepts on the elementary level related to distance and scale:

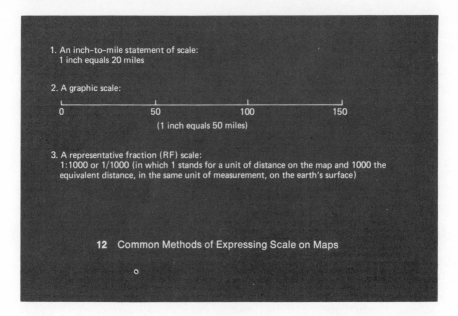

1. An inch-to-mile statement of scale:
1 inch equals 20 miles

2. A graphic scale:

0	50	100	150

(1 inch equals 50 miles)

3. A representative fraction (RF) scale:
1:1000 or 1/1000 (in which 1 stands for a unit of distance on the map and 1000 the equivalent distance, in the same unit of measurement, on the earth's surface)

12 Common Methods of Expressing Scale on Maps

1 Because many miles can be covered in a few hours by airplane, the concept of distance is not clear to many younger children. Have children note how long it takes to travel from one place to another by different modes of transportation or by walking. For example, give them practical experience in noting the time it takes to cover various distances such as coming from home to school by walking, riding a bicycle, or by car or bus. Have them note the different measures of distances such as blocks or miles. Have them discuss the westward movement of many of the early pioneer groups of our country. Compare means of travel, distances covered, and time taken with modern means of travel over the same distances.

2 Collect examples of the ways distances have been measured. Identify different kinds of tools and devices that are needed to measure distance. Discuss how they are used to measure distances accurately.

3 Have children give approximate distances between places on the school grounds and in the neighborhood community. Their estimates of distances on the school grounds can be easily checked with a tape measure or by a wooden wheel with spokes cut to the same length. Distance can be measured with the wheel by measuring its outside circumference or distances between the spokes. By attaching a handle to the wheel, it can be rolled between distances on the playground. By counting the number of revolutions of the wheel between various points, exact distances can be determined.

4 Show the class an aerial photo of the neighborhood and have them pick out the location of their homes, school, and other prominent landmarks. This will help them to see more clearly that a map represents on paper a certain amount of space on the ground.

5 Have the children make a three-dimensional map of the school grounds or the school neighborhood. Discuss scale and distance and how they may be shown accurately.

6 Build model cars or model airplanes to show concept of scale as viewed in relation to larger cars or airplanes.

7 Using a Polaroid camera, take pictures of students up close and then at a greater distance to show concept of scale. Note the area included in each picture.

8 Compare maps made to different scale that depict the same geographical area. Note the differences in the amount of detail that can be shown on each.

9 Make a scale drawing of the classroom showing the windows, doors, and furniture.

10 Using the same scale as the equator on the globe in your classroom, find the great circle distances from your home to Moscow, to Paris, and to Tokyo.

11 Have the child place the edge of a piece of paper between two locations on a map, mark them, and lay the edge of the paper alongside a graphic scale of miles in order to determine the distance between the two points.

12 Make a comparison of various kinds of map projections, noting differences in distortions of distance and scale. Then compare with the model globe to account for the variations in distortion.

Interpreting Map Symbols and Visualizing the Realities Symbolized

The cartographer, or map-maker, uses a wide variety of symbols to represent places and things shown on maps. Therefore, learning to use and read map symbols involves knowing this special language of mapping and understanding the meanings of the symbols used. In many ways this is a difficult task for children, since a great variety of symbols is used at different levels of abstractness. This complexity is apparent when we consider that the map itself is a symbol that must be interpreted through the use of other symbols. The task of interpreting maps is further complicated owing to the fact that not all symbols used on maps are standardized.

Map symbols vary in abstractness ranging from those that bear some resemblance to the object represented to those that designate more abstract associations such as boundary lines and elevations. Figure 13 gives some examples. Although color shadings that show elevations on maps have been standardized, they show only the range of elevations and therefore may be somewhat misleading to children inasmuch as they do not reveal the topographical features of an area. However, in recent years good maps have been developed that combine relief-like qualities with the standard color scheme. This conveys much more realism than does a system utilizing the color shadings alone.

Because of the limited experiential background of elementary school pupils, symbols that are closely related to the object being represented will make early map-reading experiences more meaningful to them and will lay a solid foundation for the study of more abstract map symbols in the later elementary school years.

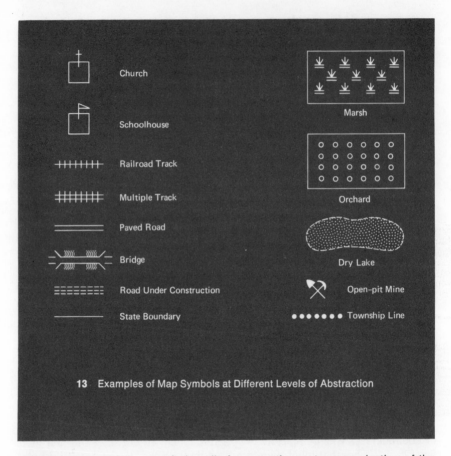

13   Examples of Map Symbols at Different Levels of Abstraction

Learning to read map symbols calls for more than rote memorization of the arbitrary associations which have been given them. If learning is to be meaningful and effective, children must have firsthand experience with reality. For the meaning which a child attaches to a symbol is directly dependent upon his experiential background and upon the concepts he holds in his mind of the world about him. The early years of the child's school experience, therefore, should focus mainly upon the development of concepts related to his immediate geographical environment. In the use and construction of maps at this age level, he will use pictorial and semipictorial symbols almost entirely to represent the commonly observed features of the landscape. As the child progresses in competence in map-construction and in map-reading, he will learn to use and understand the conventional map symbols used by cartographers. The following learning experiences will help children grow in their ability to understand and use map symbols:

> 1 Take children on a walk around the school. Discuss the different things we can see when we go for a walk (trees, houses, highways, railroads, etc.). Have the children make a map of the school area using three-dimensional symbols.

Then prepare a map of the same area replacing the three-dimensional symbols with abstract symbols.

2 Prepare a series of charts showing map symbols. Have children bring photos or magazine pictures to accompany each symbol being represented.

3 Have students draw a map of the school playground and make up their own symbols. Display the maps and discuss the difficulty of reading maps without legends to guide in understanding the symbols. Then have the students put legends on their maps.

4 Make two outline maps of the same country or geographical area, for example, the country of Australia. Leave one as just a plain outline map without any symbols on it. On the second outline map mark in a number of symbols showing location of mountains, rivers, lakes, and deserts. Add a legend showing the meaning of symbols used. Display both maps on the board in front of the class. Have a class discussion about the maps, pointing out how symbols make a map more useful and meaningful.

5 Using a road map, have each student compile a list of:
 a) Symbols that look somewhat like the things they represent
 b) Symbols that stand for man-made features
 c) Symbols that do not resemble the things they represent
 d) Water features
 e) Vegetation features
 f) Elevation features
Compare these symbols with those of a map of the United States and discuss the differences.

6 Provide each child with a plain outline map of a selected country. Have them make a legend for the map and place symbols on it for each of the following kinds of areas or features:
 a) A delta, oasis, or swamp
 b) Desert regions
 c) Mountains
 d) Capital city; other important cities
 e) Important rivers
 f) Fertile cultivated areas
 g) Highways and railroads, etc.

7 Name, locate, and list the greatest ocean depth and the highest elevation above sea level shown on a world map.

8 Refer to the world map to determine whether there is any relationship between land elevation and other natural features such as rivers and harbors and the location of large cities.

Recognizing and Expressing Relative Location

Traditionally geography was taught as a separate subject, with a major emphasis of study upon the physical environment and place location. It is now recognized that place location or the ability to locate major physical features of the earth on a map is not among the more meaningful kinds of geographical activities. Relative location is a much more important geographic consideration that involves more than place location in that it is concerned primarily with the functional significance of a place. That is, learning to understand relative location is a process that includes not only the ability to read exact locations as shown on maps but the ability to interpret the interrelationships among location, topography, and climate, and the general influence of these factors on the life of man. For example, because of its unique geographical location, the country of Korea has been a land-bridge to Asia from the Pacific area. As a result, it has been the scene of conflict for hundreds of years as warring nations have invaded the country. Too, the food-producing areas in the south and the mineral resources of the north have caused other nations to be interested in the country. Today, Korea is a power in world politics because of its strategic position.

The significance of physical factors of a land or an area, however, does not always remain constant. Improved means of transportation and communication may reduce the problem of isolation caused by natural barriers such as mountains, deserts, and oceans. But there are other barriers and restrictions, devised by man himself, which greatly affect relative location and which in many instances are more difficult to modify or change than the conditions determined by nature.

In the elementary school, children can begin gradually to acquire an understanding of both dimensions of relative location: exact location and the functional significance of a place. It is expected that children will gain experiences which will lead them to an understanding of the grid system. This system consists of a series of east-west lines referred to as parallels of latitude and north-south lines referred to as meridians of longitude. The nature of this imaginary grid system over the earth is important to understand when consulting a globe or flat map, as it provides the means of expressing location with great precision.

Latitude may be defined as a means of measuring distances by degrees north or south of the equator. The phrases "low latitudes," "middle latitudes," and "high latitudes" are locational terms that children can acquire in connection with a study of latitude. The low latitudes are located between $23\frac{1}{2}°$ north and $23\frac{1}{2}°$ south of the equator. The east-west line at $23\frac{1}{2}°$ north is the Tropic of Cancer, and the east-west line at $23\frac{1}{2}°$ south is the Tropic of Capricorn. Middle latitudes are between $23\frac{1}{2}°$ and $66\frac{1}{2}°$ north and between the same degrees south. The areas extend north from the Tropic of Cancer to the Arctic Circle and south from the Tropic of Capricorn to the Antarctic Circle. The high latitudes are between $66\frac{1}{2}°$ north and the North Pole, and the same degrees south and the South Pole. The above terms should be substituted for torrid, temperate, and frigid zones, which are climatic rather than locational terms and are misleading to some extent in that they do not always accurately describe the climatic conditions of the zones which they are used to designate.

Concepts related to longitude may be more difficult to teach to young children than those related to latitude inasmuch as the meridians converge at the poles. However, children can develop accurate understandings related to longitude as it is taught in connection with time zones and specific locations. The meridians of longitude are used to measure distances in degrees east and west of the prime or Greenwich meridian. Children can discover that meridians on a standard size globe are spaced 15° apart showing one hour of time (360° ÷ 24 = 15°). With the prime meridian and the international date line as main points of reference for longitude, children can learn the time zones of the United States and relative time in other places of the world.

The concept of degrees as a means of measuring distance may be taught in relation to both latitude and longitude in connection with the location of specific places. The use of an imaginary grid over the earth makes exact location possible. Children can be taught how to use degrees in locating cities or other places being studied. For example, New Orleans is located at approximately 30° north latitude and 90° west longitude. However, the location of one place in relation to other places or surface features should not be overlooked. In addition to distance, factors related to accessibility of a place, such as natural barriers and transportation facilities, need to be considered.

Of course, not all children can be expected to attain the same level of understanding in relation to latitude and longitude and location. However, their abilities in this regard can be greatly improved as they deal with these concepts in the intermediate and upper grade levels if the basic geographic understandings are introduced early in the child's school experience and developed cumulatively from grade to grade.

The following kinds of learning experiences may be used to develop concepts related to locational abilities:

> 1 Have children look at pictures of different areas of the world, noting such features as mountains, oceans, plains, rivers, etc. Have them note some of the leading cities of the world and the natural features surrounding them. Discuss how long it would take to get there by modern means of travel. Consider how difficult it would be to cross natural barriers without our modern means of transportation. Follow up with a discussion of how the location of a place affects its growth and development.
>
> 2 Demonstrate the need for a grid system as a means for locating places on the earth. Mark an X on a playground ball with a piece of chalk. Ask the children to describe the location of the mark. If the children say that the X is on the upper half of the ball, the ball can be turned making the statement incorrect. The need for a grid system with reference points as a means of locating places on the earth's surface with some precision becomes apparent.
>
> 3 Using the grid system of the globe, north-south and east-west lines, demonstrate how precise locations are determined. Upper-grade children can locate important cities of the world in terms of degrees. For example, have them name the large cities located at approximately:
> a) 30° north latitude; 90° west longitude
> b) 38° south latitude; 145° east longitude
> c) 15° south latitude; 48° west longitude
> d) 7° north latitude; 80° east longitude
> e) 39° north latitude; 9° west longitude
>
> 4 Study how airplanes and ships follow their course of travel from one location to another.
>
> 5 Consider questions related to the relative location of dams, highways, and cities. What factors are important to their locations?

6 Discuss the meaning of home addresses of pupils in the classroom and of people living in other countries.

7 Study the means by which elevation is determined on maps (color shading and contour lines). Discuss the relationships between elevation and climate, temperature, human living conditions, and the use of land.

8 Make a model mountain from styrofoam and color according to desire. Slice the mountain into 2-inch layers. (Styrofoam can be cut easily with a power saw. This should be done by an adult who can use the saw safely.) Take the mountain apart and trace each layer separately on a piece of paper to make a contour map. Compare the model mountain made of styrofoam with the contour map. Discuss what a contour map shows us about the slopes and heights of a mountain.

9 Have children practice reading single-purpose maps. (This is most appropriate for upper-grade children.) Note the location of natural resources, population, vegetation, transportation routes, climate, etc.

10 Teach children the locational terms and special geographical vocabulary related to understanding maps and globes.

Using and Understanding Map Projections

An understanding of the spherical nature of the earth and a clear understanding of the global relationships acquired from a study of the model globe are essential to the development of concepts related to map projection. The map drawn on the surface of a globe is the most accurate representation of the earth's surface and as such provides the basis of other kinds of maps projected on a flat surface. A map projection is a method of representing the surface of the earth upon a plane through a system of parallels and meridians. The major problem in attempting to project a curved surface, such as that of a model globe, to a flat one is distortion. Every flat map projected from the globe is distorted to some extent. Obviously, the larger the area shown on the flat map, the greater the distortion is going to be. This problem can be illustrated by attempting to flatten out an orange peel or by cutting up one half of a rubber ball to make it as flat as possible. The difficulty of transferring a sphere to a flat surface becomes evident. If this principle is not understood, some kinds of map projections can be confusing to children. For example, the Mercator projection distorts the size of the Soviet Union over 300 percent, and Greenland appears larger than the continent of Africa. Different projections distort the earth's surface in other ways.

Flat maps of small areas of the earth's surface can be constructed with little or no distortion. For this reason they are valuable maps for use in the classroom. Larger projections that provide a view of earth as a whole are useful for many occasions, but it is most helpful if they are used in conjunction with the globe, particularly when attempting to develop global concepts. Children can discover that the model globe is not always the best tool for classroom use for the following reasons: (1) We can never see more than a part of it at one time, (2) the globe is too large to show significant details of small nations or small areas of the earth, and (3) it is not a convenient map to carry about when traveling.

Children should be taught how to use a variety of maps—not just one kind. Atlases are a good source of maps of many different kinds. Learning how to use the atlas effectively is an important social study skill. Unfortunately, many pupils have never learned how to use them to the greatest advantage. If used properly, the atlas can become a source of much valuable data in connection with the study of geography. Children's contact with maps can be further broadened through the use of maps that appear in newspapers, textbooks, and other sources.

Of course, it cannot be expected that children of elementary school age will acquire a sophisticated understanding of map projection. Altogether there are over 200 kinds of projections, and the concepts related to many of them are very complex. Considering children's maturational level, at best they can only be expected to gain a limited understanding of a few common types of projection—their limitations, areas of usefulness, and how they relate to the globe. Elemenatry school pupils, particularly those on the upper-grade levels, may become well acquainted with some of the principles related to the construction and use of three basic types of projection: cylindrical, conic, and azimuthal.

Cylindrical Projection / Most projections are derived from mathematical formulas designed to afford the properties desired. Since maps are made for many different purposes, a large number of projections have been devised. Each has a special usefulness and each one chosen for use distorts least for the purpose for which it was intended.

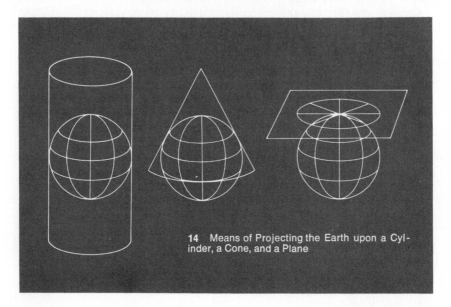

14 Means of Projecting the Earth upon a Cylinder, a Cone, and a Plane

Cylindrical projections are constructed by casting the earth's surface upon a tall cylinder of paper that completely encircles the globe. The point of contact is at the equator (see Figure 14). When the cylinder is cut and unrolled, it forms a plane surface. Meridians and parallels are opened up so that the grid system appears as straight lines. All longitude lines are parallel, equal in length, and equally spaced. Latitude lines are parallel and equal in length. They do not decrease from the equator poleward, as on the globe. Therefore, distances and areas grow rapidly larger with increase of latitude until the distortion becomes enormous in the high latitudes. While there is considerable distortion of the polar areas, the equatorial regions are relatively true to shape. It is impossible with a cylindrical projection to show the entire surface of the earth, the poles being at infinity.

Mercator's projection is one of the most common and widely known of the cylindrical projections. The projection was designed by Gerard Mercator in the year 1567, primarily for the use of navigators. Today it is still known for the important contribution it has made to navigation. On it, navigators can draw a straight line (called a rhumb line) between two points, set a compass to the angle at which the rhumb line crosses a meridian, and sail directly to a given destination without change of compass. Although a useful projection for navigators, it has many inconsistencies that make it of limited value for classroom use with children. For example, aside from distortions of land and water bodies, direction is also badly distorted. Great-circle routes are shown as curved lines, whereas on a globe they are straight lines. On the Mercator projection the Soviet Union appears to be a great distance east of the United States. When viewed from a globe, its true geographical relationship becomes apparent. Actually, the U.S.S.R. is across the North Pole and is the nearest land mass to the United States.

Although the Mercator projection is not used in the schools today as often as it formerly was, it is sometimes used in books to show the areal distribution of phenomena over the earth's surface. For this reason children should be introduced to this kind of projection so they understand its strengths and weaknesses. It is important that they see how flat maps of the world are related to the globe and thus learn how to interpret them more accurately.

Conic Projection / A conic projection is developed by projecting a portion of the earth's surface upon a cone tangent to the earth (see Figure 15). The map is drawn on the part of the cone that touches, or almost touches, the cone. Parallels are arcs of concentric circles; meridians are equally spaced straight lines that tend to converge. At the parallel of tangency, scale, shape, and area are depicted accurately. Use of two standard parallels provides an area in which elements are reasonably accurate.

Conic projections are relatively easy to construct and are particularly useful for depicting land areas in the middle latitudes with large dimensions in an east-west direction. Meridian scale errors, however, increase rapidly with increasing distance from the central meridian. Thus, this projection becomes of little value for representing areas of wide longitudinal extent. Modified conic projections such as Alber's equal-area projections, with two standard

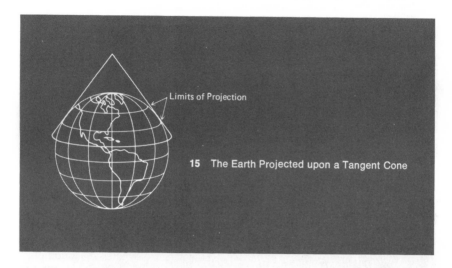

Limits of Projection

15 The Earth Projected upon a Tangent Cone

parallels, are particularly useful for mapping distributions where areal size-relationships are important at continental or lesser areas. This projection is often used in mapping the United States, inasmuch as there is very little distortion for area, size, and shape.

An interrupted equal-area world map projection constructed around a number of central meridians, one for each major world land mass, presents the entire earth's surface with a minimum distortion of the sizes of areas (see Figure 16). Most notable in this regard is Goode's interrupted homolosine projection. Where interruptions will not complicate presentation, no other map has been devised that shows to better advantage the distribution of world phenomena.

Azimuthal Projection **/** An azimuthal projection is developed from a plane tangent to the earth at one point. The projection can be made with the plane tangent to any given point on the globe. One of the most useful projections of this kind is a polar projection. Radiating from the North or South Pole as straight lines are the meridians. Parallels are shown as concentric circles. Shapes are increasingly distorted from the center outward. The opposite pole is the largest circle, making it an impossible concept to depict. A projection of the North Pole accurately shows the proximity of high-latitude Eurasian and North American continents (see Figure 17). Great-circle routes that extend across the polar regions, such as the route between San Francisco and Moscow, are correctly shown with a straight line. Distances along the parallels appear too long in comparison with north-south routes, as scale is correct only along meridians.

On a Gnomonic azimuthal projection the shortest distance between two points on the earth's surface is shown by a straight line. This is an outstanding advantage and is most useful for plotting great-circle routes.

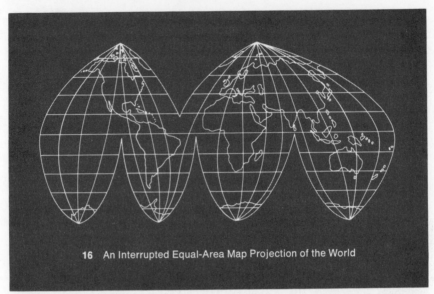

16 An Interrupted Equal-Area Map Projection of the World

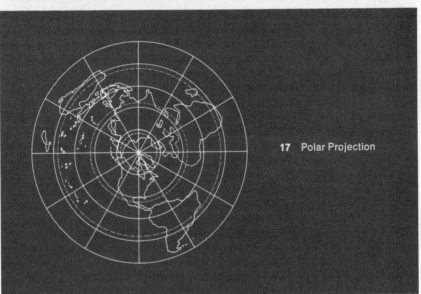

17 Polar Projection

Teaching Concepts Related to Map Projection / The following are suggestive of the wide variety of activities that may be used in helping children gain a basic understanding of map projection:

1 Cut an orange in half and squeeze out the juice. Place the empty hull, face down, on a flat surface and press down until it is absolutely flat. Observe that some edges will be torn and stretched out of shape. The difficulty of transferring a sphere

to a flat surface without considerable distortion becomes evident.

2 Compare a Mercator projection with the globe and discuss the differences.

3 Point out the specific purposes of cylindrical, conic, and azimuthal projections. Show how each is well suited for the purposes for which it is intended. Discuss uses of each kind of projection.

4 Show a polar projection and discuss the areal relationships this map shows. Point out the distortions of land shapes as you look at the outer edges.

SELECTING MAPS FOR CLASSROOM USE

The geographer uses the map as a major tool to communicate geographical knowledge and understandings to others. Among the major goals of map-reading are helping children acquire the needed skills and abilities to interpret the various signs and symbols used on the map, to accurately perceive geographical relationships, to draw inferences, and to generalize findings. The development of these skills and abilities to a high level is a slow process extending throughout the elementary school experience and beyond. Of course, among any given group of children there is to be expected a wide range of differences in understanding and rate of learning. But each child can profit most toward obtaining the above goals if systematic use is made in the elementary classroom of maps and globes that are appropriate to the developmental level of children. This requires a careful selection of maps for classroom use. For example, if too much information is crowded into the surface of a small map, it may confuse children and be of little value. Most map companies producing maps for elementary schools are cognizant of this fact and therefore offer simplified series for both the primary and intermediate grade levels.

The elementary school should make use of a wide variety of maps, including globes, large wall maps, maps in atlases, and maps in social studies textbooks that are especially prepared to accompany textual material. Ideally, the following kinds of commercially prepared maps should be easily available for use in all elementary classrooms:

> 1 A physical-political globe
>
> 2 A slated globe (can be written on with chalk; perhaps one or two of these globes to be shared by the whole school would be sufficient)
>
> 3 A physical-political world map
>
> 4 A physical-political map of the home state
>
> 5 A plastic relief map of the United States (one per school may be adequate)
>
> 6 A geographical terms map (this map would be most appropriate for use in the intermediate- and upper-grade levels).

The following list includes some of the better-known producers of geographic teaching aids for schools:

1 AERO Services Corporation, 210 East Courtland Street, Philadelphia, Pennsylvania 19120.

2 Geo. F. Cram Company, Inc., 730 E. Washington Street, Indianapolis, Indiana 46206.

3 Denoyer-Geppert Company, 5235 Ravenswood Ave., Chicago, Illinois 60640.

4 Farquhar Transparent Globes, 3727 Spruce St., Philadelphia, Pennsylvania 19104.

5 C. S. Hammond and Company, Inc., 515 Valley Street, Maplewood, New Jersey 07040.

6 National Geographic Society, 17th and M Sts., N.W., Washington, D.C. 20036.

7 A. J. Nystrom and Company, 3333 Elston Ave., Chicago Heights, Illinois 60618.

8 Rand McNally & Company, P.O. Box 7600, Chicago, Illinois 60680.

9 Replogle Globes, Inc., 1901 N. Narragansett Ave., Chicago, Illinois 60639.

10 Weber Costello Company, 1900 N. Narragansett Ave., Chicago Heights, Illinois 60639.

For a free list of maps approved for public sale, the teacher should write to Army Map Service, Corps of Engineers, U.S. Army, Washington, D.C.

MAKING MAPS

In addition to using commercially prepared maps in the classroom, children should have many opportunities to make their own maps. Mapping activities should begin early in the child's school experience and continue systematically throughout his elementary school years. There are many educational purposes that can be attained by having children construct maps, if done in meaningful learning situations, that cannot be attained in any other way. Unfortunately, map-making activities traditionally have been quite meaningless and have left much to be desired as far as contributing to the major goals of map-reading. For example, past emphasis was often upon the size and shape of major countries, which demanded that children be able to make a "freehand" outline or drawing of the country under study. The map was then used largely for place-location exercises, with children being required to locate principal cities, rivers, and mountains. Such map experiences were of dubious value because they dealt almost entirely with a limited concept of place location and with land shapes. To be of value, map-making activities should be related directly to specific problems in the unit of study, not carried on as busywork or as something isolated from a study of basic human activities.

Growth in map-reading can begin with children in the kindergarten and primary grades. They begin by mapping those things that are within their immediate environment, which can be directly and continuously experienced while they are engaged in map-making. For example, children may make a simple drawing or sketch of the floor layout of their classroom or a room at home. Through this means, they discover that a map is a representation of a given space or area drawn to reduced scale on which things can be shown in proportion to each other. Model blocks or furniture may be used in making a simple sand-table layout of the classroom or school. Following a study trip into the neighborhood, children in the primary grades may make a neighborhood map on a large piece of paper placed on the floor, showing the important buildings and the children's homes adjacent to the school. Gradually, these kinds of activities can be extended, as children further develop skills in mapping, to include the community and areas beyond. As larger areas such as the state, nation, and the important countries of the world are studied, a wide variety of maps and map-making techniques may be used, depending on the purposes of the study and the maturity of the children.

Making Map Outlines

Many occasions arise in the teaching of the social studies when the use of both large and small map outlines is most appropriate for the development of given geographical concepts. For example an outline map of the United States might be used by children in plotting the early trails of pioneer groups, to discover why these trails followed the routes they did and to note the natural barriers encountered along the way. When the need for an outline map arises, it should be provided as quickly and efficiently as possible. Little would be gained from having children struggle with a freehand outline. The teacher may provide a small dittoed outline map for the children's use. If a larger outline map is needed for class use, the opaque projector may be used. Enlargements can be projected from textbooks, magazines, or from other similar reference material. The overhead projector may also be used as a useful means of clear enlargements, but it requires that the necessary overlays or transparencies be prepared in advance.

Large outline maps can be traced directly on a chalkboard by utilizing cardboard or light plywood patterns of the desired land area. A chalkboard map stencil may be made by punching small holes at regular intervals around the borders of a large map outline drawn on tagboard or chart paper. A dotted outline map can be made on the board by patting over the holes with an eraser containing chalk dust. A chalk line may be traced over the dotted outline if a heavier outline is desired.

The proportional-squares technique is a useful method of enlarging or reducing by squares (see Figure 18). This technique employs the principle of "similar figures." The size of the squares can be varied as desired as long as the outline shown in each small square matches that shown in the corresponding larger square.

Making Relief Maps

Maps that show topographic features are useful tools in helping children learn accurate concepts about the surface features of the earth. Molded relief features help children visualize the earth's surface more clearly and provide

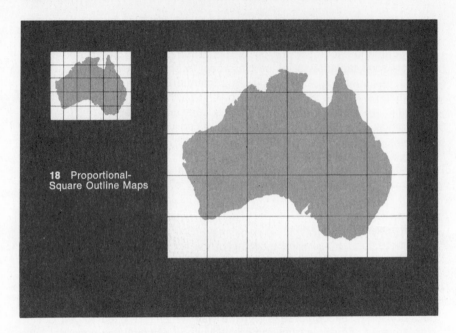

18 Proportional-
Square Outline Maps

the means whereby they may learn through another dimension—the sense of touch.

As children construct relief maps of the county, state, nation, or other areas, they gain valuable experience in understanding scale. One of the major problems in making relief maps is related to helping children understand that the relationships of height to distance on relief maps are often exaggerated to show the desired topographic features of the land more clearly. Of course the larger the area shown on the map, the greater the vertical distortion must be. For example, on a relief map of the United States that is made to a horizontal scale of 6 feet, or 72 inches, the highest mountains drawn to correct vertical scale would appear only as tiny pin points on the map. Therefore, if topographic features are to be emphasized, there must be some distortion of the vertical scale. Exaggeration on commonly used commercial plastic relief maps of the United States is 20:1. On model globes the ratio is as high as 100:1. This principle can be shown clearly by drawing a horizontal line on the chalkboard to represent the distance across the area being mapped. Vertical lines can then be drawn to scale to show the relative height of mountains. By applying this to their own relief maps, children can decide how much vertical exaggeration they may wish to show. Thus, they can discover that elevations on relief maps must be made relatively higher than they should be if they are to be clearly shown.

Relief maps should be constructed on a plywood base or some similar sturdy material cut to the desired dimensions. Lighter bases made of cardboard or heavy paper will not adequately support a relief map and have a tendency to buckle in the center and curl up at the edges as the modeling material dries.

Make an outline map on the board by means of a projector. It is helpful if a second outline of the same map is made on a large sheet of paper or piece of tagboard. This can then be used as a working guide or reference while the modeling material is being placed over the outline drawn on the board. Sketch in rivers, lakes, mountains, and contour lines on both outline maps where needed, showing ranges in altitude. Use standard colors to note changes in elevation between contour lines. Color rivers, lakes, and other water bodies blue. Check wall maps or an atlas to insure accuracy in the height and placement of mountain ranges and other natural phenomena. Small finishing nails may be driven into the base board every few inches at varying heights along contour lines and at points where mountain peaks are to be represented. They should extend about a quarter of an inch less than the desired height of mountains, hills, and upslopes so as to be completely covered by the modeling material.

Upon completion of the modeling and after the map has thoroughly dried, the surface can be colored to highlight features and to show contrasts. The use of the international color scheme for maps should be encouraged. Many different kinds of paints may be used to color the map. For permanent coloring, tempera-type water paint is most commonly used. After it has dried, shellacking will give it a protective covering.

Modeling Materials for Relief Maps

There are many different recipes used for modeling relief maps—some much more expensive to use than others. Inasmuch as many of the major purposes for the construction of relief maps are accomplished upon their completion, they are generally not preserved for long periods of time. Therefore, many may prefer some of the more simple to use and least expensive recipes. Among the most practical and useful ones are those noted below.

Papier-mâché **/** A widely used modeling material

1 Cut newspaper sheets (or paper toweling) into 3/4-inch strips. Soak overnight in water.

2 Drain off excess water and tear paper strips into small pieces. If a finer texture is desired, material may be pulverized by rubbing it over a washboard.

3 Add wheat paste until material becomes of good modeling consistency. It is then ready to apply to outline map. When dried several days it becomes almost rock-hard.

A cooked paste may be used, if desired, in the place of the wheat paste. It can be made by mixing one cup of flour with two cups of cold water. Stir until free from lumps. Add one teaspoon of powdered alum and one tablespoon of table salt. Stir into one quart of boiling water. Cook until the milky look changes to a clearer mixture.

Paper Strips and Paste **/** This method is as follows:

1 Cut paper toweling and newspaper into 1-inch strips.

2 Build up the terrain on the outline map with crumpled paper held in place by masking tape.

3 Dip 1-inch newspaper strips into wheat paste.

4 Remove the excess paste from the strips with thumb and index finger. Place the strips over the crumpled paper forms on the map until it is covered with one layer of newspaper strips.

5 Add a second layer of covering by the same process, using the paper-toweling strips. This will give a smooth, clean finish to the map.

6 After the two layers have been placed on the map, allow to dry. It may then be painted with tempera paint.

Sawdust and Paste / Use sawdust and paste as follows:

1 Mix wheat paste to the consistency of heavy cream.

2 Stir fine, sifted sawdust into the paste; mix well.

3 When the mixture is the consistency of biscuit dough (kneaded well) it is ready for modeling. Experience will help you know how much sawdust to use. Apply to the map and let dry for four or five days.

Any cracks that occur may be filled with some freshly mixed sawdust and paste. A wood glue is excellent to fasten parts that may come off in drying. When dry, this material can be sanded, filed, or cut with a saw.

Asbestos pulp or paper dust is excellent for modeling materials and can be substituted for the sawdust in this recipe. Asbestos pulp may be obtained from a home-insulation company. Paper dust may be obtained from printing companies or similar establishments that use large paper-cutters in their business.

Salt Clay / Prepare this mixture as follows:

1 Assemble 1 cup salt, ½ cup cornstarch, ⅔ cup water.

2 Combine in a saucepan and cook over a low flame, stirring constantly until the mixture thickens into a doughy mass.

3 Remove from the heat immediately and cool until it can be handled.

4 Place on aluminum foil, wax paper, or formica table top and knead well.

It is ready for use, or it can be stored several days if carefully wrapped in foil, saran wrap, waxed paper, or placed in a wide-mouthed jar with a lid. If it has been stored, it should be kneaded well before using.

Magic Modeling Dough / Prepare this mixture as follows:

1 Heat 2 cups of salt, 1 cup water.

2 If colored modeling dough is desired stir in powdered paint (2 tablespoons makes a very bright color).

3 Add, all at once, 1 cup of flour. Stir and knead well.

Modeling dough will keep for a few days if put in a jar with a lid or in a plastic bag.

Liquid Starch and Detergent **/** This recipe is quick drying and, therefore, most useful where a finished product is desired within one day's time.

1 Mix 1 part liquid starch with 4 parts powdered soap.

2 Beat the mixture until it is fluffy.

3 Apply it to the map outline immediately. The mixture dries hard but crumbles easily if dropped or bumped.

Conglomerate **/** Prepare as follows:

In a gallon can mix 1 cup of wheat paste with 4 cups of water to make a thin mixture. Mix in 1 cup plaster of paris, 2 cups fine sawdust, and 1 gallon of fluffed, torn toilet tissue strips (1- by-1 inch). Mix thoroughly. Makes a lightweight, adhesive, and durable modeling material.

A SUMMARY OF MAP AND GLOBE UNDERSTANDINGS: GRADES K–6

Understanding Earth Relationships

The globe is the most accurate map of the earth's surface.

A flat map shows part of the earth's surface flattened out.

Portraying the earth's surface on a flat map involves distortion of land and water areas.

The earth is a huge sphere which can be divided into hemispheres.

There are four hemispheres—eastern and western; northern and southern.

The earth is made up of large bodies of land and water called continents and oceans and is surrounded by air.

The earth rotates on its axis from west to east once every twenty-four hours.

The sun appears to move across the sky during the day.

The moon, planets, and stars appear to move across the sky during the night.

The length of day and night changes with the seasons.

Understanding Directions

Down is toward the center of the earth; up is away from the center of the earth.

Directions on a map are determined by the poles. North is toward the North Pole; south is toward the South Pole.

North is not always at the top of the map. North may be shown on a map at places other than the top of the map.

The North Star can be used to determine the direction of north.

East-west and north-south lines on a globe or map form a grid system which helps us determine directions.

All places on a north-south line (meridian) are exactly north or south of one another.

All places on an east-west line (parallel) are directly east or west of one another and are the same distance north or south of the equator.

The northern latitudes are north of the equator; the southern latitudes are south of the equator.

The Eastern and Western hemispheres are divided by the prime meridian and the 180th meridian.

West longitude is measured to the west of the prime meridian from 0° to 180°, which is halfway around the earth.

The low latitudes lie on both sides of the equator and are bounded on the north by the Tropic of Cancer and on the south by the Tropic of Capricorn.

The high latitudes are located near the poles north and south of the Arctic and Antarctic circles.

The middle latitudes lie between the high and low latitudes.

There is a slight variation in direction between true north and magnetic north as shown by a magnetic compass.

A great circle is any circle that divides the earth into hemispheres.

Great-circle routes (air routes) are the shortest distance between any two points on the earth's surface.

Understanding Location

The latitude and longitude of any place show its exact location on a globe or map.

Each hour the earth rotates through 15° of longitude (360° every 24 hours).

The world is divided into 24 time zones, each 15° of longitude.

The international date line located along the meridian 180° from Greenwich is the place where each calendar day first begins.

There are four standard time zones in the continental United States.

Landmarks can be seen upon the earth and drawn upon a map.

Landmarks or other conspicuous natural features can be used to help locate places on a map or globe.

Natural barriers, ocean currents, and natural resources influenced exploration, the movement of people, and settlements.

Understanding Symbols

A globe is a symbol that stands for the earth.

Maps use legends that give the meaning of the symbols used on it.

Distance on maps and globes are relative to differences in distance on the earth.

A scale drawing shows things smaller than they really are so they can be put on a paper.

The scale of miles used on a globe or map makes it possible to determine the distance of one place from another.

Distances between various locations on a map can be compared.

Mileage scales are expressed in different ways on different maps.

Distance from the equator may be measured in miles or degrees.

Large-scale maps show more detail than small-scale maps.

Some toys are small-scale models of real things.

Small things on a map represent large things on earth.

Places distant from one another on the earth appear to be close together on a map or globe.

Pictorial symbols on a map stand for real things on earth.

Map legends are the keys for interpreting various maps.

An international color scheme is commonly used on maps and globes to show elevation or altitude.

The keys in a map legend may vary from map to map.

Maps are made for different purposes, to give different kinds of information about the earth.

More than one map can be consulted for information about a given area.

A relief map enables one to tell the altitude of the land, its general slope, and the general direction in which a river flows.

There is a direct relationship between the climate of a place and other factors such as elevation, ocean currents, or location.

Through the use of maps one can increase his understanding of current and past history.

QUESTIONS AND ACTIVITIES

1 / Choose a basic map or globe concept on the grade level of your choice. Plan a lesson, including appropriate learning experiences, which will meaningfully present the understanding or concept selected.

2 / Compare the advantages and disadvantages of a flat map and the globe as instruments in developing geographic concepts.

3 / Discuss some of the difficulties involved in presenting the concept of map projection to elementary school pupils. How can a study of map projections be made most profitable for children in the upper-grade levels of the elementary school?

4 / What desirable educational outcomes can be obtained by having children make relief maps as compared to making other kinds of maps?

5 / Experiment with the different recipes for modeling relief maps. What are some of the advantages and disadvantages of the various recipes tested?

6 / Construct a chart depicting pictorially some of the major map symbols.

7 / From your outside readings, set up criteria for evaluating maps in terms of their suitability for use with elementary school children.

SELECTED REFERENCES

Bacon, Phillip. "A Straight Line Isn't Always the Shortest Distance." *Grade Teacher* 83 (2): 104, October 1965.

Bagrow, Leo. *History of Cartography*. Revised and enlarged by R. A. Skelton. Cambridge, Mass.: Harvard University Press, 1964.

Greenhood, David. *Mapping*. Chicago: University of Chicago Press, 1964.

Hanna, Paul R., Sarbaroff, Rose E., Davies, Gordon F., and Farrar, Charles R. *Geography in the Teaching of Social Studies—Concepts and Skills*. Boston: Houghton Mifflin, 1966.

Harris, Ruby M. *Handbook of Map and Globe Usage*. Skokie, Ill.: Rand McNally, 1959.

Kennamer, Lorrin. "Developing a Sense of Place and Space." *Skill Development in Social Studies*. Thirty-third Yearbook. Washington, D.C.: National Council for the Social Studies, 1963.

McAulay, J. D. "Second Grade Children's Growth in Comprehension of Geographic Understandings." *Journal of Geography* 55 (1): 33–37, January 1966.

Michaelis, John U. *Social Studies for Children in a Democracy*. Third edition. Englewood Cliffs, N.J.: Prentice-Hall, 1963. Chaps. 13 and 14.

National Council for the Social Studies. *New Viewpoints in Geography*. Twenty-ninth Yearbook. Washington, D.C.: National Council for the Social Studies, 1959.

Raisz, Erwin J. *Principles of Cartography*. New York: McGraw-Hill, 1962.

Sarbaroff, Rose. "Map Making in the Primary Grades." *Social Education* 24 (1): 19–20, January 1960.

Sarbaroff, Rose. "Improving the Use of Maps in the Elementary School." *Journal of Geography* 60 (4): 184–190, April 1961.

Thralls, Zoe A. *The Teaching of Geography*. New York: Appleton-Century-Crofts, 1958.

Whipple, Gertrude. "Geography in the Elementary Social Studies Program." *New Viewpoints in Geography,* Twenty-ninth Yearbook. Washington, D.C.: National Council for the Social Studies, 1959.

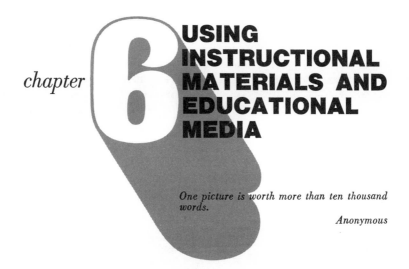

6

chapter

USING INSTRUCTIONAL MATERIALS AND EDUCATIONAL MEDIA

One picture is worth more than ten thousand words.

Anonymous

For a relatively long time, schools have had in their instructional program printed materials such as textbooks, paperbacks, dictionaries, encyclopedias, and the resources of the library. In addition, there have been available some nonprint media such as motion pictures, filmstrips, slides, recordings, flat pictures, and graphic materials. Today, other educationally valuable media are available for use, including such exciting innovations as computers and remote information-retrieval systems, 8mm single-concept films, programmed instructional materials, games, and multimedia social study kits.

But as yet many teachers have gone little beyond the textbook and an occasional film in the utilization of what is available to them. The failure of teachers to make use of newer media may be due in part to factors related to cost, selection, and distribution-utilization problems. But mainly, it can be attributed to the lack of preservice and in-service training of teachers in the use of these new tools. As teachers become more "media-minded," secure and adequately trained in the use of new materials, utilization will increase proportionally. In some instances, utilization has been hampered by the unavailability of materials at the time they are most needed. The present trend toward establishing an instructional-materials center (IMC) or learning-resource center within each elementary school will greatly reduce the gap between pupil need and availability. It will also provide more opportunities for the individualization of instruction. Pupils will have ready access to learning materials needed for individualized study and research.

MAJOR PURPOSES OF INSTRUCTIONAL MATERIALS

As stated by Joyce, instructional materials have two purposes. One is to give children access to data. The other is to help them draw meaning from the data.[1] Although the two operations are closely related, a dichotomy of purpose highlights the importance of the teacher's responsibility to the child beyond that of merely bringing within easy access a wide array of learning resources. The instructional media must be carefully selected and wisely used. The teacher's role is one of a guide to learning rather than a dispenser of facts.

There are a number of reasons why the utilization of a wide range of learning resources can meet class and individual learning needs in a superior manner.

1. Because of individual differences, not all children can be reached successfully by the same approach to the social studies. The traditional textbook approach, for example, has failed to reach and motivate many pupils, particularly culturally disadvantaged children, slow learners, and those with reading difficulties. To some others, the approach has been narrow and somewhat stifling to learning. Books and other printed materials may be effective tools to understanding for some pupils, but the vast majority of pupils will profit most when multiple or combination approaches are used, involving the use of study trips, films, printed materials, tape recordings, filmstrips, self-directed programmed materials, etc. There is no one best strategy for teaching the social studies. Each learner requires individual diagnosis and special use of materials. The need is to find and use the right materials tailored to individual needs. Students who have the advantage of well-selected and wisely used audiovisual media learn more effectively than do those who have access only to verbal and abstract materials.

The social studies curriculum today is shifting from memory of names, dates, and events to inquiry as an approach to learning. A wide variety of audiovisual materials will aid in this direction in that it will provide the means for the student to become an inquirer, a discoverer, an analyzer, and a seeker of knowledge. A wealth of material will also make it possible for children to explore topics in greater depth.

2. Remote information-retrieval systems and other new developments in computer-assisted instruction have made it possible for the student to assume more responsibility for his own learning. These kinds of learning devices can provide instruction on an individualized, self-directed basis, allowing opportunity for the student to obtain much needed information without the direct help of the teacher. Many routine and drill types of materials can be handled by machines, thus freeing the teacher for more creative kinds of teaching and guidance.

3. Multimedia approaches to learning are highly motivating to children. We have a generation of children today who are immersed, saturated, and "turned on" by the many new audiovisual developments. They permeate the child's total life inside and outside of school. The average student today perhaps spends more hours per week in front of television sets, movie

[1] Bruce R. Joyce, *Strategies for Elementary Social Science Education* (Chicago: Science Research Associates, 1965), p. 192.

screens, and record players than he does in the school classroom. New developments in the use of media are fascinating to the child in school. Well-chosen educational media present concepts in such a manner as to create interest and high motivation. This tends to bring to life social studies instruction, to make it more enjoyable and vital.

Of all the areas of the school curriculum, none is more suitable for the meaningful use of a wide variety of instructional materials and audiovisual aids than the social studies. Reviewed in the following pages are the resources, audiovisual aids, and newer developments in educational media that hold promise for the development of a more vital social studies program. A number of them have long been used in social studies programs, although perhaps not as meaningfully as they might have been.

TYPES OF MATERIALS

Flat Pictures

Perhaps one of the most common but useful visual aids in teaching the social studies is flat pictures. Effective use of pictures in teaching requires that they be utilized as integral parts of the lesson. A brief or casual reference to a picture implies to the pupil that it is of little importance. They should be recognized as sources of information along with books and other media. A few carefully chosen pictures of high quality are of greater instructional value than many pictures of low quality. Pictures are appropriate for use at almost any time. One of their most valuable uses is in the initiation of a social study unit in which they can be used to stimulate interest, problems, and questions for study.

Through the planned use of well-selected pictures it is possible to achieve many purposes:

> 1 Pictures may serve as a substitute for direct or firsthand experience.
>
> 2 Misunderstandings and wrong impressions can be corrected.
>
> 3 Critical thinking can be improved as children examine and discuss pictures.
>
> 4 Reports by children can be improved and be made more meaningful through the use of pictures.
>
> 5 They enrich reading, particularly when children are immature or have limited experiential backgrounds.
>
> 6 They increase retention of learning.
>
> 7 They can develop skill in viewing, observing, and interpreting.
>
> 8 Pictures can teach comparisons such as size and can show processes that might be virtually impossible to explain verbally to young children.
>
> 9 They provide for individual study at the learner's own rate and interest level.

There are many sources from which pictures may be obtained, such as magazines, newspapers, travel agencies, and business concerns. In addition, there are a number of commercial publishers that produce pictures specifically for elementary social study units. Pictures and collections should be organized around major topics or units and kept on file in labeled folders where they will not become bent or mutilated. Small pictures such as some obtained from magazines may be enlarged for close examination of specific details by the use of an opaque projector.

Realia

The term "realia" refers to real objects such as tools, utensils, art objects, clothing, etc., that are made and used by people in a given culture or society. The social studies program can be enriched greatly through the proper use of realia. For example, in planning a unit of work on Mexico, the teacher might obtain many different kinds of realia common to the Mexican culture, such as sombreros, sarapes, pesos, utensils, ornaments, and musical instruments for use in building accurate impressions and concepts of the people in Mexico. Children obtain a much greater depth of understanding and a far more accurate picture of a culture or society if they can see, research, and discuss real things or objects that are used in the daily life of the people. Realia are particularly valuable at the beginning of a study or unit of work to create student interest in the topic under construction and to inspire inquiry. Later, after a study of a culture in more depth, they may be used most effectively in connection with special reports and with special programs and dramatizations.

A wide variety of realia are generally available for classroom use from school instructional-material centers and from parents in the local community. When not obtainable from these sources, they may be viewed at public museums, universities, and commercial firms.

Dioramas

A diorama is a three-dimensional scene, made by children, which depicts a basic human activity or way of life typical to a given culture or people. A medium-sized pasteboard box with one end cut out serves as a good three-dimensional area for constructing a realistic miniature scene depicting some aspect of living in a culture. The background scenes are painted on paper, which is pasted to the sides and back of the box on the inside surfaces. The landscape, human figures, trees, etc., are made by paper-sculpturing and are connected to the floor so as to stand, thus giving a three-dimensional effect to the scene. The scenes may be used to depict ways of living in different places and eras. The construction of realistic and authentic scenes is dependent upon much prior careful study and research of a culture. The greatest values in preparing dioramas are found in this kind of highly motivated, meaningful research activity.

Movie Box

For elementary school pupils, a movie box can be a valuable learning device. It can be constructed simply from a pasteboard box with an opening at one end, approximately 14 inches high and 18 inches wide. Place a wood dowel,

1 inch in diameter and 15 inches long, down through the box near both sides of the 18-inch opening. These two dowels, with small handles on top to serve as a turner, are holders for the movie roll that is to be shown. A movie roll can be made on a long strip of butcher paper cut 14 inches wide to fit the opening of the movie box. The long strip of paper is divided into a series of 18-inch spaces or frames. Children can draw pictures in each frame telling a story or depicting life activities of a people under study. When completed, the movie roll is attached to the dowels in the movie box so that it turns as a scroll. As each frame is shown, the pupils who have prepared the roll give a narrative explaining each picture. This kind of activity correlates art and language skills, as well as teaching social study content. It is highly motivating for pupils in the middle or upper grades of the elementary school.

Textbooks

With the present knowledge explosion, the school finds itself with more and more subject-information to teach. No longer can the textbook, the chief instructional medium of the past, be relied upon alone to communicate all this new knowledge efficiently. This does not mean that the textbook should be eliminated, but rather that other communication techniques or newer educational media should be utilized as additional aids to learning. There is general agreement that, if properly used, the textbook is a valuable tool in teaching the social studies. But in proper perspective, it is just one tool among many. Along with the text, a wide variety of audiovisual materials and other teaching aids should be used in teaching the subject matter.

In the past, in the more traditional social study programs, the textbook dominated instructional procedures. When one·recognizes that many beginning teachers are not directly prepared to teach the subject-matter content of the social studies, there is little surprise in the fact that the textbook has long dominated classroom procedures. The textbook was looked to as a basic guide that determined the selection of content to be covered, the pattern in which it was to be covered, and the teacher's selection of learning activities. The misuse of the text consisted in having the children read the text sequentially, beginning with page one, and answer questions at the end of each chapter. It was essential that each unit of the textbook be "covered" within a strictly set time limit so that the complete text could be finished within the school year. This approach tended to treat children as though they were all exactly alike, each needing the same dosage of the same required material. Little or no provision was made for individual differences. This kind of practice may be termed the "old" social studies. Fortunately, today this approach to teaching the social studies is rapidly disappearing. A concise statement that well describes the narrowly conceived textbook approach is given by Muessig as follows:

> Textbook-centered teaching has a medieval heritage. The teacher who could secure a book or commit the contents of a manuscript to memory was "in business." The text was a source of authority, often unquestioned and unchallenged. The more faithfully the learner could return its contents to his teacher, the more approbation he earned. This approach, therefore, has

been with us a long time. . . . The facts contained in the single sources have some kind of magical intrinsic value—worthy in and of themselves. The assign-study-recite-test procedure is generally followed. The teacher generally originates, directs, and passes judgment upon all learning activity. Only those evaluation techniques which attempt to assess the degree to which names, dates, places, and events have been "learned" are employed. Motivation is provided by the teacher by way of grades and other extrinsic rewards. The teacher's main aim in life seems to be "covering the text." More and more facts accumulate as research continues over the years and as man's stay on earth is extended; textbooks get larger; and it gets harder and harder for the teacher to reach first, page 523, then page 678, and later, page 751 by the end of the year.[2]

Reliance on the textbook to the exclusion of other kinds of learning resources is an unfortunate practice that has existed far too long. It has been said that a student working with textbooks alone is like a traveler abroad who keeps his nose in the guidebook and never looks at the life around him. But if properly used in connection with other learning resources, the textbook can become a valuable aid to learning. Modern texts are greatly improved over what we have had in the past. They are valuable source books which contain a wealth of basic information, although highly condensed, on a variety of topics included in the social studies curriculum. They contain a wide variety of maps, tables, charts, pictures, and other reference materials. However, they are written with the intention that teachers will enrich them with supplementary materials and firsthand pupil experiences. The critical need in a good social studies program, therefore, is for a multiplicity of nontextual material representing many levels of reading difficulty and comprehension. The use of a single textbook in the hands of every child, as the sole source of learning, is one of the unfortunate practices that has stifled meaningful teaching in the social studies over the years. The textbook was not intended to become the complete social studies curriculum. The more varied the forms of learning that can be provided—reading, study, trips, audiovisual materials, dramatization, etc., the more meaningful, individualized, and thorough teaching in the social studies may become.

The Place of the Textbook in the Social Studies Program **/** It is quite likely that the textbook will remain a basic tool for teaching the social studies for some time to come. Basic textbooks are a main source of information for teachers and pupils. Every teacher should be acquainted with multiple texts and their manuals for the excellent suggestions they contain on how to teach the social studies. Newer adoptions are much improved over older textbooks. There have been notable improvements in the nature of content focused on more significant concepts related to the various social science disciplines, better presentation of material and control of levels of reading difficulty, suggested learning activities that are more meaningful and less

[2] Raymond H. Muessig, "Bridging the Gap Between Textbook Teaching and Unit Teaching," reported in *Readings on Elementary Social Studies—Prologue to Change,* eds. John R. Lee and Jonathon C. McLendon (Boston: Allyn & Bacon, 1965), pp. 329–330.

stifling to pupils, improved map study, and increased use of visual materials and attractive illustrations—many of which are in color. The following principles serve as a guide to more effective use of basic textbooks.

1. The textbook is one of many tools to assist the teacher in presenting social study information to his pupils. It cannot assume the role of teacher and relegate him to the role of an assistant. The teacher must help direct the pupil in the use of the text. Without guidance from the teacher, much of the value of the text may be lost.

2. Because of the wide scope of material covered in social study textbooks, they cannot treat any subject in great depth. For example, the coverage of different cultures or countries is often brief and highly condensed in nature. Therefore, there is need to enrich and supplement the textbook with a variety of other materials that permit study in greater depth. The textbook remains, however, the most valuable single source of social studies information. But children should go to it, as any other reference book, when specific information on a topic is needed. The textbook can in no case become the total social studies curriculum, nor should it determine the sequence of topics to be studied or the amount of coverage required.

3. A single textbook in the hands of each student is an unfortunate practice that has persisted far too long. This practice often leads to the misuse of the text. The reading-difficulty levels of social study texts are geared to the average student or above. This makes it difficult for slower students to profit from the text without special help. What is needed is a large collection of supplementary texts and story books with parallel content on easier reading levels. The answer to reading problems in the social studies lies in the careful selection of supplementary reading materials to accompany each unit of study. A good collection of supplementary books, along with a few basic textbooks from a number of different major publishing companies, will meet the needs of a social studies program far better than reliance upon one basic textbook for all pupils.

4. Social study textbooks should contain a balance of content drawn from each of the several social science disciplines. The emphasis of the textbook should be on helping the pupil learn how to apply on an elementary level some of the modes of inquiry and methods of study of scholars in the various social sciences. The typical factual-type questions at the end of each chapter in most textbooks are of little value in helping students accomplish this aim.

5. The textbook is a useful tool in the social studies in introducing children to some of the key ideas of a unit of study. From this point, children can be involved in study at greater depth, requiring the use of encyclopedias, supplementary reading materials, maps, globes, charts, and other reference materials.

Supplementary Texts

There are a large number of supplementary books available for use with social study units. A good selection of supplementary books, rich in social meanings, to accompany each unit of work is invaluable. They make it possible to provide parallel reading materials for a wide range of reading abilities and also provide opportunity for students to study a topic in greater depth than would be possible through the use of the basic text alone. Although basic textbooks give an overall view of the required topics, many of the interesting details and explanations must be omitted because of space. It is through the use of well-selected children's books or "trade" books that the social studies are brought alive by providing children opportunity to read interesting and detailed accounts of the daily lives of boys and girls in other times and places. A good selection of books to accompany a unit of work in the social studies should be readily available on the shelves or the reading table for pupil use. If enough good books are made available, there is no reason why each child cannot find a book that interests him.

A number of excellent bibliographical guides are available to aid in the selection of supplementary books. *Children's Books to Enrich the Social Studies,* Bulletin No. 32, compiled by Helen Huus and published by the National Council for the Social Studies (Washington: National Education Association, 1961), contains annotated lists of 618 books for the elementary grades. The bulletin is divided into five sections as follows:

> I Our World—dealing with geographical backgrounds, products, and conservation
>
> II Times Past—including prehistoric and ancient history, medieval times, early explorations, colonial America, and nineteenth-century America
>
> III People Today—containing listings on the twentieth-century United States, other parts of North America, the Arctic and Antarctic, Latin America, Europe, Africa, the Middle East, Asia, and Australia
>
> IV The World's Work—treating business and industry, communication and transportation
>
> V Living Together—including both at home and in our land, as well as in the world, and celebrating holidays.

All major publishing companies of social study texts also publish a good selection of supplementary texts. Of particular note is a series of supplementary books on various countries of the world published by Fideler Company of Grand Rapids, Michigan. Each book is beautifully illustrated and concentrates on a single nation in great detail. Also, the American Heritage Publishing Company issues a series of excellent books on American history. They are particularly well adapted to the present social study programs of the fourth and fifth grades. Six new titles are scheduled for publication each year.

Motion-Picture Films

Both school administrators and teachers have recognized the power of the motion-picture film as a communication tool for educational purposes. Through the use of films, one can bring the entire world of meaning into the classroom at the time it is needed. Today, there are unlimited numbers of educational films available for use. They are obtainable from school instructional-material centers, loan libraries of universities, service and manufacturing industries, state and federal governments, governmental embassies, private business firms, and from film-production organizations such as McGraw-Hill Films Division, Coronet, Encyclopaedia Britannica, United World, Academy, and the International Film Bureau.

Motion pictures enable teachers to become much more effective in their roles as instructional leaders. Through the film medium, social studies teachers can bring events of the past and present into the classroom. They can help students learn about peoples in the farthest reaches of the earth.

There is increased pupil interest in subject matter when motion-picture films have been woven into the curriculum. Careful selection and integration of teaching films in the social studies program can also result in positive changes in students' motivation, involvement in learning, retention, and free-reading activities. Films make it possible for students to observe natural phenomena in slow or fast motion and in magnified or diminished representation. These advantages, along with the fact that it is "natural to learn by seeing and hearing," make the use of films an exciting path to learning in the social studies.

Educational motion pictures appeared first as the silent 35mm motion-picture film and next in the form of the silent 16mm film. The addition of sound to the motion-picture film during 1929 and 1930 began the era of the 16mm educational sound motion-picture films used in the classroom. The production and use of the 16mm sound film has advanced steadily in both quality and quantity since that time.

Today, a new development in instructional films has appeared in the 8mm format. The 8mm film is gaining in acceptance and is attracting the attention of educators everywhere. The emergence of 8mm sound films has been a factor in this growth, but an even greater factor, found also in silent 8mm films, is the combination of inexpensive, continuous-loop cartridge-loading projectors with the idea of increased instructional efficiency through the presentation of a single concept at a time. The 8mm film is projected onto a small screen or onto a rear-view screen to produce a highly visual and well-defined image. A common approach is to use 8mm films to present information to individuals or to small groups of students. This type of utilization can be achieved with either a cartridge-loading projector or the conventional reel-to-reel projector. Special facilities are not essential, just a convenient viewing situation associated with the students' working area.

The trend toward individualized instruction was perhaps largely responsible for this new movement. The development of a new "Super 8" film and the advent of the technicolor continuous-loop cartridge-loading projector was heralded by many with immediate acceptance. The frame size of the picture in "Super 8" film has changed as compared to the older format, now called "Regular 8." Like modern refrigerators, the picture is larger on the inside without being larger on the outside. These developments provide an excellent way to present a short sequence of instruction that can be viewed as many times as the learner requires in order to master the concept. Many of the silent film sequences are from three to five minutes in length. Sound 8mm films are now becoming increasingly available in greater lengths, from ten to twenty minutes. Just a few years ago, there were only a few hundred single-concept films available from commercial sources. Now, there are over 5000 loops available in subject matter ranging from art to zoology, with steady increase in production anticipated.

As previously noted, single-concept films are particularly appropriate in the area of individualized instruction. An exciting application, appropriate for teaching values in the social studies, is the open-end film. Here a small group of students watch a film presenting a situation or incident without a conclusion. They then suggest or work out solutions individually or through group discussion.

Still-Projection Materials

The term "still projection" refers to several methods by which visual materials, both transparent and opaque, can be projected onto a screen or flat surface for viewing. Still-projection techniques and materials permit the creative teacher great flexibility in providing meaningful learning experiences for children. Some of the most useful kinds of still-projection materials for social studies instruction are filmstrips, slides, transparencies, and non-transparent materials such as flat pictures, book illustrations, drawings, diagrams, tables, and charts.

Filmstrips / A filmstrip is a related sequence of pictures, in color or in black and white, contained on a strip of 35mm film. They provide the classroom teacher with a convenient and effective means of communicating instructional content visually. Some of the major advantages of filmstrips are:

> 1 Filmstrips are available in a wide range of subjects at relatively low costs. In addition to low cost and their ease of storage, filmstrips are easy to use. Good pictures can be projected on the screen without complete room darkening.
>
> 2 Filmstrips lend themselves well to small-group or individual use. They can be used effectively by children in a small study area without disturbance to others.
>
> 3 The filmstrip is a flexible teaching tool that can be used at any desired pace. The teacher can move through a filmstrip rather quickly or, if desired, hold each frame as long as necessary for detailed analysis.
>
> 4 Filmstrips lend themselves well to use with other media. For example, when they are accompanied by prerecorded tapes and headsets, individualized instruction can be facilitated. More and more publishers of textbooks are producing filmstrips closely correlated with text materials.

Filmstrips should always be available at a convenient location where children can have ready access to them for individual or small-group study as needs arise.

Because of the large number of titles available, one can select filmstrips related to any topic of study in the social studies from geography to current affairs. As in the selection of other types of teaching materials, filmstrips need to be carefully selected according to their appropriateness for children, particularly those on the primary grade level.

Slides / Ever since the development of the 35mm camera and color film, the 2 x 2 slide has become available on almost any topic. Because of their relative ease of procurement, low cost, and excellent color qualities, 2 x 2 slides have gained in popularity as a teaching tool.

There are many sources available for obtaining slides for use in the social studies. In addition to commercial sources, teachers and parents have often traveled widely and have readily available a good selection of slides covering many foreign countries and places of interest in the United States.

One approach to obtaining slides for specific topics or units of study in the social studies is to develop on a school basis a collection of slides of the local area. Industries, farming, transportation, and historic sites make excellent subjects. When slides in each area of study are organized sequentially, children can write captions for each slide. The narrations for each slide can be placed on tape to accompany the slide presentation. Even the preparation of the slide presentation alone can be a valuable learning experience for children in social studies and the language arts.

Stereoprojection / Stereographic slides have a lifelike quality that regular photographs do not possess. When they are viewed through a stereoviewer, a highly realistic and vivid three-dimensional effect is obtained. This fact alone makes them highly motivating to children of all age levels.

A modern form of the stereographic slide is the more popular stereodisk. Seven pairs of 16mm transparencies taken with a stereographic camera and mounted on a flat disk make up a stereodisk. The disks are viewed in compact and inexpensive viewers that children can operate.

For some time stereodisks have been available for children on such subjects as scenic wonders, famous people, nature, and children's stories. Today, disks have become increasingly available on a wide variety of subjects, including a coverage of people and places in all areas of the world. Because many stereodisks are available on topics related to social studies units covered in the elementary school, they have become of special value to the program by providing increased opportunities for individual viewing, study, and research.

Overhead Projectors / Overhead projection with large transparencies is probably the most significant development in still-projection techniques of the last decade.[3] Because of its great versatility and convenience, the overhead projector is among the most useful tools available for presenting social studies information. Overhead transparencies are available from commercial producers in a wide variety of subject-matter areas. But perhaps the most valuable transparencies are those made by the teacher himself for his own specific teaching needs. The teacher can make his own transparencies from written or typed materials, drawings, diagrams, maps, and opaque materials in books and magazines.

[3] Walter A. Wittich and Charles F. Schuller, *Audiovisual Materials—Their Nature and Use,* fourth edition (New York: Harper & Row, 1967), p. 357.

Some of the major advantages of using the overhead projector are these:

1 Transparencies projected on a screen can be seen clearly by all members of the class.

2 The fact that the overhead projector is operated from the front of the room makes it possible for the teacher to face his class and to maintain direct eye contact with them at all times during the presentation of a lesson.

3 The teacher can present his materials progressively by means of overlays.

4 The teacher, from his position beside the projector, can easily indicate any point on the transparency he wishes to emphasize. By using a felt pen or grease pencil he can write on the transparency any additional information he wishes.

5 The teacher can project charts, diagrams, outline maps for geography, etc., without spending long periods of time copying them on a chalkboard. He also has all of the flexibilities indicated in no. 4 above, which adds to the effectiveness of the presentations.

6 The teacher can develop a large number of transparencies that are easily filed and always ready for use at the time they are needed.

Opaque Projection / The opaque projector is a valuable instructional tool in the social studies. A teacher with access to an opaque projector has available an almost unlimited amount of illustrative material at little or no cost. Opaque materials such as printed pages of a book, pictures in a magazine, photographs, postcards, pupils' work, drawings, diagrams, tables, maps, specimens, and other solid objects can be reflected on a wall or screen for group viewing.

The opaque-projection technique permits the projection of nontransparent materials just as they are with a minimum of mounting or other kinds of preparation for use. Another unique advantage of opaque projection is the convenience with which outline maps and other kinds of illustrative materials can be enlarged and transferred to chart paper or to the chalkboard in any desired size for class use. For example, when a large outline map of our country is needed for class use in the study of geographical relationships, it should be provided as quickly and efficiently as possible. In this case, there would be little to be gained by having children struggle with a freehand outline. Finally, a principal value of opaque projection is the large amount of readily available and cost-free materials that can be utilized through this media.

Tape Recorders

The tape recorder can be used in a variety of ways to improve instruction in the social studies. Through the use of prerecorded tapes much valuable information can be presented to individual pupils, small listening groups, or to the total class.

Prerecorded tapes are a highly adaptable medium for individualizing instruction. Tapes are available commercially on a wide range of subjects.[4] But perhaps the most valuable tapes are those prepared by the teacher to meet the needs and interests of individual pupils. A recent development that has greatly aided this kind of program is the cassette, a small tape within a cartridge, which can very easily be used without any skilled training. When the cartridge is placed into a cassette tape recorder or playback unit, it provides the student with an opportunity to learn at his own pace and at his selected time and place. He can receive all the repeated playings desired for his own individual learning needs. It is rather foolproof in that the material on the tape cannot be erased by the student. Because of its ease of use in both recording and playback operations, the cassette tape recorder is rapidly becoming one of the most useful tools available for individualizing social studies instruction.

For small-group listening, most standard tape recorders equipped with standard phone jacks for external speakers or headsets can accommodate an eight-station listening system with a volume control for each headset. This offers a simple, convenient method of isolating group activities—one group can listen to a tape without interfering with or disturbing the other members of a class. Pupils having difficulty reading basic text material could follow a teacher-made tape of selected social study content.

A recent modification of the continuous tape reel is the "Language Master," which presents words, sentences, and symbols on 3-by-5-inch index cards. A short strip of recording tape is attached to the lower portion of each card, providing a "sound track" that describes the printed material on the card. When placed into a slot on top of the recorder, the card automatically moves slowly from right to left across a magnetic head, thus effectively combining visual and aural learning. Although first applications have been in the area of the language arts and reading, "sound cards" could be adapted to many uses in the social studies. For example, they might be used effectively in helping students learn symbolical material related to social study concepts, such as geographical terms, map symbols, names, and dates. This approach would be highly motivating to pupils, thus greatly improving learning, and would provide increased opportunity for individual study and drill.

Educational Television (ETV)

Over the past decade there has been a notable increase in the number of closed-circuit television systems installed by local school districts. This great expansion in educational television across the nation was given impetus by federal bills that provided sizeable appropriations to assist school districts, colleges, and universities in improving ETV programs. From the inception of television, educators have recognized its potential as a means of improving learning in the classroom. However, there have been some serious problems related to how it might be used most effectively.

The television set is an inadequate substitute for the classroom teacher. Its greatest instructional value lies in the fact that it can assist classroom instruc-

---

[4] See "National Tape Recording Catalog" published by the Department of Audiovisual Instruction, National Education Association.

tion in a way not possible through the use of other media. Through the use of the medium of television, children can be eyewitnesses to significant events that occur in our nation and throughout the world. History as it occurs —the first moon walk, presidential elections, new advances in science—may be a classroom television experience. Thus, television is a means of bringing many kinds of enriching experiences to the social studies program.

Outside of school, children spend many of their waking hours before a television set. They are, therefore, well acquainted with this medium and are greatly attracted by it. To capitalize on this same high motivation in a classroom learning situation, care must be taken to integrate television with other learning activities. Children must be prepared with an adequate background of information and follow-up activities for every program they observe.

Television is available to schools through two main avenues, closed and open circuit. Closed-circuit television uses a network of coaxial cables and covers only limited areas. Open-circuit television broadcasts its signals into the atmosphere to be picked up by antennas. Both systems can be used effectively in conjunction with each other by a school district. Closed-circuit equipment will make it possible for school systems to use, at the time they are needed in the classroom, selected commercial programs that have been videotaped.

A great promise for the future in educational television relates to the comparatively new 2500-megacycle instructional-fixed television system. Microwave broadcasting at 2500 megacycles makes it possible for a school system to send over five or six different programs simultaneously at no increase over the cost of a single channel. This will overcome two serious obstacles to the rapid growth of educational television in the schools, the shortage of funds and the potential shortage of frequencies. The design of this new system is fairly simple, requiring mainly the installation of a frequency converter to raise the television signal up to the 2500-megacycle band and the installation of receiving antennas at the various points of reception. Microwave broadcasting at 2500 megacycles serves well to bring educational television to limited areas within a 20-mile radius. This new system was first experimented with and tested at Plainedge, New York, in 1962. After the first successful tests, the Federal Communications Commission established the instructional-fixed television service for educators generally throughout the country beginning in September 1963. Since this time many school districts and universities in the United States have established extensive microwave networks that serve large numbers of students.

Educational Television—An Aid to Individualized Instruction / Many schools have provided individual study areas or carrels in each classroom and in special areas such as the library or media center where students can be engaged on their own independent study and research. The installation of a video monitor in each study carrel, along with a loudspeaker or headset, makes it possible for the student to listen to and observe video tape recordings on a wide variety of subjects, according to his individual needs. Adding the visual dimension greatly improves learning efficiency of the student. Video tape recordings can be prepared by the teacher for specific learning needs or can be obtained from commercial sources.

The video tape recorder is a most exciting innovation in educational television use. When used with videocon cameras, it permits teacher and pupil self-evaluation. The video tape recorder may be used to record performance, and to provide immediate playback for viewing. In the social studies program this will allow children to see and hear video recordings of role-playing episodes, class discussions, class reports, panels, and debates for purposes of analysis and self-evaluation.

Information Retrieval

Through the use of a new innovation known as "Remote Information Retrieval System" (RIRS) and sometimes "Dial Access" (DAIRS) the student at a study carrel may use a touch-pad system similar to telephone touch-tone systems to select one of many programs of audiovisual instructional material for individual study. Both hardware (the equipment necessary to store, select, and transmit information) and software (the program materials from which the student receives information) should be designed specifically to help meet individualized instructional needs. The amount of material per course that a RIRS can provide may vary from entire course segments to supplementary lecture materials or isolated excerpts. In addition to course content RIRS can provide services such as news broadcasts, recorded speeches, stereo music, long-range weather forecasts, and shortwave news broadcasts from foreign countries. Workbooks and other educational aids may be used to supplement the audiovisual coursework.

COMPUTER-ASSISTED INSTRUCTION (CAI)

As early as 1960, educators began to look at the computer as an aid in education. Today, CAI has emerged as a specific, demonstrable, and potentially powerful instructional tool. A major drawback to widespread use of computers in education has been the cost factor. In the past it has been available in the schools only on a subsidized basis. However, it is hoped that in the future new developments in CAI will make it possible for schools to obtain computer services at greatly reduced costs. Some computer-based advantages to teachers and pupils are:

1 Removing much of the burden of paperwork and reports

2 Making information concerning the progress and needs of each student immediately available

3 More rapid scoring and analysis of tests and furnishing immediate data for use of counselor and teacher

4 Enlarging the sources of information, supplementing the school and classroom libraries

5 Providing individualized instruction, permitting each student to go as far and as fast as his unique capabilities will allow—perhaps the single most powerful argument for CAI

6 Allows flexibility of instruction through a multimedia approach, i.e., a combination of printed materials, pictorial, and auditory presentations

7 Will provide for a variety of responses on the part of the student, including auditory, written, multiple choice, etc.

8 Statewide informational networks may extend to nationwide networks and then may extend to tie in with worldwide informational services.

At the present time there are three possible levels of interaction between the student and the computer.

1. Individualized drill and practice to supplement the regular curriculum taught by the teacher. The introduction of concepts and new ideas is handled in conventional fashion by the teacher. The role of the computer is to provide regular review and practice on basic concepts and skills. These exercises can be presented on an individualized basis, with the brighter students receiving exercises that are harder than the average, and the slower students receiving easier problems. A large computer with 200 terminals can handle as many as 6000 students on a daily basis in this instructional mode.

2. A deeper level of interaction between student and computer is the tutorial system, which presents a concept and develops skill in its use. The intention is to approximate the interaction that a patient tutor would have with an individual student. Every effort is made to avoid an initial experience of failure on the part of the slower children. Yet the program has enough flexibility to avoid boring the brighter children with endlessly repetitive exercises. As soon as the student manifests a clear understanding of a concept on the basis of his handling of a number of exercises, he is moved on to a new concept and new exercises.

3. The deepest level of interaction is the dialogue system, aimed at permitting the student to conduct a genuine dialogue with the computer. This system is presently in the experimental stage.

Computers will not replace teachers, nor reduce the number of teachers needed. But teachers will look on computers as a new and powerful tool for helping them teach their students more effectively. For the teachers, computer-assisted instruction can mean more time for creative teaching and relief from the time-consuming routine of drill and review. The computer offers perhaps the most practical hope for a program of individualized instruction in the school classroom.

PROGRAMMED INSTRUCTION

Programmed instruction provides the means whereby specific subject-matter content may be provided for the pupil in a step-by-step sequential learning order. Each single step or "frame" asks a question directly related to the idea or information presented and calls for the student to make a response to it before proceeding to the next segment of information presented. The student receives immediate "feedback" or knowledge of his performance by being supplied with the correct answer to the question, which he can compare with his own response. A correct response provides reinforcement of the idea learned. In the case of an incorrect response the student can repeat the learning sequence. The program is constructed so that each segment or "frame" leads logically to the information contained in the next. Each learning step between "frames" is small so that the child may proceed on his own with a high degree of success. One of the greatest advantages of programmed material is that it provides opportunity for the child to proceed at his own pace, freed from the restrictions placed upon him by the pace established in group learning.

Programmed material may be presented in a variety of forms including workbooks and textbooks, or the material may be presented by the use of teaching machines. However, in either case, learning from programs is a quite different kind of learning experience for the pupil than the usual class discussion or consensus opinions. Because of their verbal quality, programmed materials require a certain degree of reading proficiency on the part of the child using them. In fact, the progress that a student makes with most kinds of programmed materials is greatly influenced by his reading ability. To be successful with programmed materials, each child must be able to work on his own with little help from teacher or other students.

The concept of programmed instruction includes the basic assumption that subject matter can be organized into clearly defined segments. Although certain kinds of social study materials, such as place geography, and names, dates, and places in history, lend themselves well to segmentation; other kinds of learnings that call more for value judgments and analysis are not as easily adapted to programming.

While as yet there are few programmed materials available in elementary social studies, availabilities are rapidly mushrooming in all areas of the curriculum.[5] As new programmed materials in the elementary social studies become available, it will become increasingly possible for programmed instruction to take over a larger fraction of the time-consuming tasks of the teacher, tasks involving information-giving per se. If much of the information-giving role of the teacher can be assigned to teaching machines, this will free the teacher to engage in more creative activities that challenge the talents of students and will also provide opportunity for the teacher to offer more individual attention to special problems.

GRAPHIC REPRESENTATIONS

A number of different types of graphic materials are used in the elementary school, for example, graphs, diagrams, charts, posters, and cartoons. Graphic materials are designed to present information clearly, concisely, and in simplified form through a combination of drawings, words, and pictures. The main educational values of these kinds of materials lie in their capacity to attract immediate attention and convey certain types of information in condensed, summarized form. For example, a threading diagram may be of con-

[5] See *A Guide to Programmed Instructional Materials* (U.S. Office of Education, 1963).

siderable help to a person in learning how to operate a movie projector. A poster may serve as a needed reminder to a pupil not to run in the hallways. In each case, the main emphasis is a sharp focus on key information, highly informative and motivating to the student. Today greater use has been made of graphic materials in elementary social study textbooks, weekly newspapers, and reference materials of all kinds. Because of the increased use made of graphic materials on the elementary school level, teachers have the added responsibility of helping pupils develop the concepts and skills needed for more accurate understanding and effective interpretation of these materials.

Graphs

A major purpose of graphs is to present comparative quantitative data quickly and simply. For elementary school pupils, particularly those on the beginning grade levels, graphic concepts must be kept simple and easy to read. Skill in interpreting graphs is extended gradually as the child progresses through the elementary school. The basic skills involved in effective interpretation of graphs include the ability to understand the significance of the title, to understand the basic units of measure used in the construction of the graph, to interpret the relationships shown, to draw inferences and important generalizations based on the data, and to relate information derived from graphs to that gained from reading and other sources of information. The process of having children compare, contrast, and evaluate contributes greatly to the development of skill in critical thinking.

A number of different kinds of graphs have significance for the elementary school social studies program, including bar graphs, pie or circle graphs, and line graphs. In the early grades, a simple bar graph related to the experiences of the children is most meaningful to them and is a good place to start in developing their ability to understand graphic relationships. For example, a simple bar graph depicting the number of parents of children in the classroom who are producers of goods and the number who are producers of services can be readily understood by primary-grade children. When pictorial symbols are used in a bar graph, such as small stick figures to represent each parent, the relationships become more evident even to the youngest children.

Bar graphs may be constructed with bars running either horizontally or vertically. Although one of the more simple kinds of graphs to use with children, they have some serious limitations that should be understood. One may encounter some difficulty in reading them accurately with children when exact numbers of quantities represented are not given and when the symbols used or data presented are not related to the personal experiences of children. However, it is hoped that these factors will become less critical as the child progresses in his ability to understand graphic material.

Circle or area graphs are constructed on a percentage basis showing the fractional parts of a whole. Their interpretation depends in some measure upon an understanding of percentages. Therefore, children in the upper grades of elementary school are able to grasp the relationships shown much more readily than younger children. If circle graphs are used with children on the primary grade level, they should be limited to data which have reality to children from their firsthand experiences, and they should deal with large fractional proportions which are within the range of understanding of children at this age level. As in the case of other graphs, it should be remembered that the circle graph is only a relatively accurate form of presenting data. It should be emphasized that graphs are intended to show relationships rather than exact, specific figures.

A major problem associated with the interpretation of circle graphs has to do with understanding perspective. The angle from which a circle graph is shown can seem to change the proportions. This can be misleading to children and can result in some incorrect impressions if they are not informed about such possibilities. Also the circle graph can be difficult for children to interpret when it is divided into too many small fractional parts or divisions.

Perhaps the most accurate form of graph is the line graph. This kind of graph is used to show changes of quantity in relation to time. For example, a line graph might be used to depict changes in population over a period of time or increases in production of goods or services over given periods of time. In this sense it is often used as a means of revealing and predicting trends. This kind of graph is most appropriate for construction and use by children in the upper grades of the elementary school. The grid on which it is constructed is often too difficult for younger children to understand or interpret.

Skill in the interpretation of line graphs depends upon understanding accurately the scale used in their construction. For example, the slope of the line will vary considerably depending on the kind of grid used. The degree of increase can be made to appear greater by narrowing the size of the horizontal scale and increasing the steps in the vertical scale. Using the same data, the degree of increase can be made to appear smaller by reversing the process, by increasing the size of the horizontal scale and narrowing the size of the vertical scale. Understanding this problem has a direct bearing on children's ability to develop skill in interpretation of line graphs.

Because of the symbolical nature of graphs and the kind of data they present, the child should be exposed to them throughout his elementary school years. He should have direct experience in constructing graphs of all types during his school experiences. It is only through the construction of graphs that the child gains real skill in their interpretation.

Charts

Like graphs, charts are an especially valuable tool for use in social studies. They serve as an excellent means of classifying important information that is to be referred to a number of times. They also help summarize and simplify complex ideas that children encounter in their reading, especially in social study textbooks. Jarolimek has classified charts used in the elementary school social studies under two basic headings: Formal Charts and Informal Charts.[6]

Formal charts are commonly found in textbooks, newspapers, and other reading materials. Formal charts include the following kinds:

[6] John Jarolimek, *Social Studies in Elementary Education,* third edition (New York: Macmillan, 1967), pp. 260–265.

Narrative charts portray historical developments or depict steps in a procedure, such as how a bill becomes a law.

Tabulation charts present data in a table form in order to facilitate making comparisons.

Relationship charts show cause-and-effect relationships such as factors related to the pollution of the environment.

Pedigree charts show developments that have a single origin, such as the lineage of a family.

Classification charts point up various kinds of relationships such as those in basic food charts.

Organization charts show the internal structure of organizations such as corporations or governmental bodies.

Flow charts show steps in a process such as the manufacture of steel.

Informal charts are developed by the teacher and students throughout a unit of study as a means of developing standards or summaries of materials related to the ongoing study. Such charts may be grouped into the following kinds.[7] *Experience charts* based upon study trips and other firsthand experiences; *group-standards charts* to set forth rules and standards of work; *creative-expression charts* to record songs, poems, and stories; *vocabulary charts* for listing new words and terms associated with the concepts taught; and *direction charts* providing guidance in using reference tools and construction materials.

Elementary school pupils, beginning with the primary grades, should be encouraged and taught how to make and utilize charts of different kinds in collecting and reporting data. Skill in interpreting charts is a means to this end. For upper-grade pupils, construction of charts provides an added value of helping to extend manuscript-writing skills which were discontinued by many during their primary-grade years.

Cartoons

Cartoons are among the most symbolic and abstract types of pictorial materials. They are drawings and sketches in which the subjects are presented in caricature, with a considerable amount of exaggeration and often humor present. It is important for the child to begin to develop some understanding of the symbolism associated with them, as he is confronted by an endless succession of them in public places, on billboards, and in magazines, newspapers, and books. Skill in understanding and interpreting cartoons is essential for children in a democracy. The cartoonist can use his creation to communicate a meaningful message, or he may use it as a means to foster prejudice, to indoctrinate, or to arouse emotion rather than critical thinking. Children need to recognize this and the fact that cartoons present only one point of view. They need to be helped to evaluate cartoons critically and to become acquainted with the symbolism used. Otherwise, they may be unduly subjected to propaganda of all kinds.

[7] For a complete listing of informal classroom charts see John U. Michaelis, *Social Studies for Children in a Democracy*, third edition (Englewood Cliffs, N.J.: Prentice-Hall, 1963), p. 385.

A knowledge of the symbolism used in cartoons is essential to their interpretation. The kind of symbolism used may be confusing to those with literal minds, both young and old. However, little difficulty should be encountered in teaching most children to recognize and understand the common symbols used to represent the United States, such as Uncle Sam, a tall bearded man with striped pants and a tall hat, or the American eagle. Symbols representing other countries, such as John Bull, the English lion, and the Russian bear can be taught through repetitive experiences with cartoons throughout the elementary school years.

Cartoons can become a means of stimulating research on the part of the student as he attempts to find data to check the viewpoint set forth or to explore both sides of the issue involved. Again, as in working with graphs and charts, student-made cartoons are the best route for helping children develop skill in their interpretation. Student-made products also provide the means whereby children can express a point of view on a current issue based on their own research and understanding. Too, direct experience with making cartoons is the best way for pupils to acquire a clear understanding of the different kinds of symbolism used in their preparation.

The most meaningful graphic materials for the young child are those which use situations within the realm of his experiences. The further they are removed from the child's experiential background, the more abstract and difficult to teach they become at the elementary level.

Although the elementary school provides an opportunity for pupils to grow in their ability to interpret and use graphic materials, it must be recognized that only the groundwork has been laid. Further understanding and meaning is dependent upon life experiences and continued instruction at higher-grade levels.

TEACHING TIME-CONCEPTS IN THE ELEMENTARY SCHOOL

One of the goals of social studies instruction is to help children acquire a more mature and accurate sense of time and chronology. There is considerable evidence that prior to the sixth grade most children have not developed accurate concepts of time, particularly as it relates to historical events.[8] When studying historical events, children tend to telescope time by shortening the distance between events and bringing them much closer to the present than they actually were. Children in the primary grades have much difficulty even in obtaining an accurate concept of the age of their teacher. A deep and full understanding of time and chronology is the result of a planned sequential program in teaching time concepts that begins with children's earliest school experiences and extends throughout the secondary school level. Among both children and adults there are great variations in range and depth of time sense. Although the more complex understandings of time must wait for maturation on the part of the child, the schools can do much more than they have in the past, particularly on the primary grade levels, to further the child's ability in this important area.

[8] Edgar Bruce Wesley and Mary A. Adams, *Teaching Social Studies in Elementary Schools*, revised edition (Boston: Heath, 1952), pp. 301–302.

A sense of time and chronology is indispensable to the study of history, which is the record of change through time. Of all the social science areas covered in the social studies, history makes the greatest contribution to the development of a mature time sense. If children are to understand the ideas of change or development and of continuity in human affairs—to see the relationship of history to their own lives, they must develop a sense of the past. This includes more than merely the memorization of lists of unconnected date-events. It means grasping some understanding of problems in human relations and their historical antecedents. A mature sense of time is dependent upon the learner's ability to view an event of the past as part of a development in time influencing other events. The complete process, then, is one not only of understanding how time is measured and of knowing specific date-events, but of having some comprehension of the relationships that have resulted from a blending of the past with the present.

Teaching Time and Chronology

Spieseke has identified seven elements that compose the sense of time and chronology and that are to be included in the elementary school social studies program. Listed in a sequential arrangement according to the maturation of children they are: (1) mastering the telling of time by the clock, (2) understanding the days, weeks, months, and years as expressed by the calendar, (3) establishing a framework for time relationships, (4) developing a meaningful vocabulary of definite and indefinite time expressions, (5) coping with time concepts in reading and listening situations, (6) relating dates to personal experience and to life-span, (7) placing related events in chronological order.[9]

The social studies carry the greatest burden of developing and applying the above concepts; however, mastering the telling of time may be dealt with as a part of mathematics instruction and the reading and listening to time concepts as part of the language arts program.

A brief discussion of each of the seven elements in developing time sense is in order:

Mastering the Telling of Time by the Clock **/** Most children by the time they have completed the second grade can tell time by the clock. Such words are added to the time vocabulary as midnight, noon, hour, half-hour, quarter-hour, minute, and second. Each of these concepts will have an important bearing upon the child's future ability to talk about and understand more clearly time relationships.

Understanding the Days, Weeks, Months, and Years as Expressed by the Calendar **/** Through noting birthdays and other special days of the year, pupils in the primary grades will grow in their ability to understand time as it is associated with morning and afternoon, the day of the week,

[9] Alice W. Spieseke, "Developing a Sense of Time and Chronology," reported in *Skill Development in Social Studies*, Thirty-third Yearbook, ed. Helen McCracken Carpenter (National Council for the Social Studies, 1963), p. 178.

the month of the year, the season of the year, the months associated with each season, and the present year. This will lay a good foundation for later understanding and development of terms such as "decade," "generation," and "century." By the time they reach grade 2, children are most interested in knowing the time as it relates to their personal experiences such as "What time do we go to school?" "When is morning recess?" "What time do we eat lunch?" and "When is school out for the day?"

Establishing a Framework for Time Relationships **/** Children are continually exposed to time-events related to the present, past, and future. Although an accurate understanding of time-span associated with events in the distant past and projected future is lacking in most children prior to age 11 or 12, some pinpointing of important specific date-events may be helpful. These will give children some established frames of reference in learning about other date-events, particularly those that are of high motivation and interest to the individual child. But generally speaking, we must begin to establish a framework for time relationships with events close to the experiences of children where time between happenings can be observed or understood. For example, the time involved in building a new home, school, etc. Once a child has had direct planned experiences with a number of different time measurements within his own experiences, he can bring more meaning to understanding time-span related to the distant past.

Developing a Meaningful Vocabulary of Definite and Indefinite Time Expressions **/** The social studies have a vocabulary specifically related to them that needs to be worked on and mastered by children just as in other areas of the curriculum such as science and mathematics. One would not think of teaching mathematics, for example, without having children learn its terminology. Similarly there is a special need in the social studies for specific instruction related to the vocabulary of time and other symbolic materials.

Definite time concepts such as day, week, month, year, decade, and century are gradually acquired by children through continued use and repetition. Terms related to longer time periods and indefinite terms such as "generation," "era," "old," "ancient," and "eon" are considerably more difficult to elementary pupils. Full facility in the use of these terms cannot be expected of the average child on the elementary school level.

A suggested procedure for making the term "generation," an indefinite time concept, more meaningful to students is stated by Wesley and Adams as follows:

> Ask each member of the class to find out in what year his father was born. From this date subtract the birth year of the pupil. When the average for the whole class is ascertained the difference between the two dates will be surprisingly near thirty-three years. It is then easy to see that three generations make a century.[10]

[10] Wesley and Adams, op. cit., p. 304.

The development of vague time concepts will require many specific experiences of this kind if they are to be made meaningful at all to children. Even then, building a vocabulary of meaningful general time concepts is dependent, in a measure, upon maturational factors, and therefore must extend beyond the elementary school years to be most successful.

Coping with Time Concepts in Reading and Listening Situations / Numerous occasions arise throughout the school day outside of the social studies period when the teacher can strengthen children's abilities to comprehend and use time expressions. For example, in reading and story-telling experiences one will find reference to many different kinds of expressions such as, "They journeyed many days before arriving at their destination." Through context clues the children may make deductions about the meaning intended by the author. The teacher can capitalize on these kinds of situations whenever found. Through class discussion, she can help children correct any erroneous concepts held and can help them learn how to deduce time expressions more accurately. By dealing on occasion with time concepts close to children's interests and experiences, such as those found in literature and storytelling, efforts at teaching time concepts in the social studies will be greatly strengthened.

Relating Dates to Personal Experience and Life-span and Placing Events in Chronological Order / The starting point for developing a sense of sequence begins with important events within the child's own life-span. To this can be added events related to his family, school, and community that are within his experiential background. Gradually, the child can be helped to push back the present to events and conditions in the lives of his parents and grandparents. Thus by arranging events in order of occurrence as they relate to their personal lives, children begin to develop a sense of chronology.

The use of time lines strengthens children's understandings of chronology by showing clearly the distance of time between events. There are a number of different kinds of time lines that can be used. Generally with young children pictorial time lines of events within the lives of their family are most meaningful. Typical time lines for use in the early school years are listed by Preston as follows:

> A series of pictures of children at various stages to show their progression at intervals from birth to their present age.
>
> A series of pictures to show the child's daily routine, each picture depicting an event such as eating breakfast or arriving at school.
>
> A line drawn along a lengthy stretch of chalkboard, divided to show the weeks and months of the school year and providing the opportunity to enter words or sketches to record significant school events as they occur.
>
> Rearrangement of a calendar by clipping it to make the dates of a month run in a continuous horizontal line.[11]

[11] Ralph C. Preston, *Teaching Social Studies in the Elementary School,* revised edition (New York: Holt, Rinehart & Winston, 1958), p. 237.

Another kind of time line can be made by running a light wire the length or width of the room. Events for any period of time can be depicted by clipping dates and pictures to the wire with clothespins. It is important to make the time line to scale so that events are placed according to the mathematical base used. Failure to use some scale or base in the construction of time lines will render them useless and defeat the purpose for which they were constructed.

Ragan and McAulay demonstrate the use of a time wheel (Figure 19) to show the concept of millennium as follows:

> To give time understandings concerning the explorers, a time wheel might be used. It is marked off in centuries beginning with the year 1000 and ending with the year 2000. The present year is represented by an immovable hand. The movable hand is used to illustrate the approximate date of discovery in each century. The name card of each explorer is placed outside the circle near the date shown by the movable hand.[12]

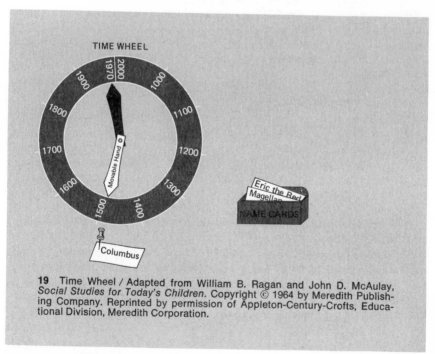

19 Time Wheel / Adapted from William B. Ragan and John D. McAulay, *Social Studies for Today's Children.* Copyright © 1964 by Meredith Publishing Company. Reprinted by permission of Appleton-Century-Crofts, Educational Division, Meredith Corporation.

Variations of the above time wheel could be used effectively for other time periods and events with children. It would also provide a valuable means of drilling children on symbolic material related to time concepts such as names, dates, places, events, etc., related to any time period desired.

---

[12] William B. Ragan and John D. McAulay, *Social Studies for Today's Children* (New York: Appleton-Century-Crofts, 1964), p. 297.

Time lines of all kinds are important tools in teaching about the past. As a general rule, at the elementary school level it is best to begin with simple time lines which develop the chronology related to one single theme at a time, for example, "The Development of Transportation" or "Important Events in My Lifetime." Once these kinds of relationships are learned, children have the foundations necessary to understand more complex time lines depicting related events.

QUESTIONS AND ACTIVITIES

1 / State at least three reasons why a wide range of learning resources are needed to effectively teach the social studies.

2 / What are some of the major weaknesses in the textbook approach to teaching the social studies? What principles might serve as a guide for the more effective use of the textbook?

3 / Make a collection of flat pictures you could use in connection with a given unit of work. List some of the advantages the use of flat pictures have for teaching.

4 / Summarize the advantages and limitations of the major categories of educational media discussed in this chapter.

5 / Discuss the place of programmed learning in the social studies program.

6 / How does the use of a wide variety of instructional materials contribute to the individualization of the social studies?

7 / Construct a cartoon that might be suitable for use in the elementary classroom. Plan how you would present it to pupils in your classroom. Have the students construct their own cartoons.

8 / List the major types of graphs that might be used in teaching the social studies in the elementary school. Give an illustration of how each type can be most effectively used.

9 / Discuss the major problems involved in teaching elementary school pupils time concepts. What steps must be taken to insure the accuracy of time lines?

SELECTED REFERENCES

Brown, James W., Lewis, Richard B., and Harcleroad, Fred F. *A-V Instruction: Media and Methods*. Third edition. New York: McGraw-Hill, 1969.

Brown, Ralph, and Brown, Marian. "How to Select a Social Studies Textbook." *Social Education* 25 (8): 391–397, December 1961.

Brown, Walter L. (ed.). *Selected Readings in Educational Media*. New York: Simon & Schuster, 1968.

Costello, Lawrence F., and Gordon, George N. *Teach with Television: A Guide to Instructional TV*. New York: Hastings House, 1965.

Dale, Edgar. *Audio-Visual Methods in Teaching.* Third edition. New York: Holt, Rinehart & Winston, 1969.

Eboch, Sidney C. *Operating Audiovisual Equipment.* San Francisco: Chandler, 1968. Distr. by International Textbook Co., Scranton, Pennsylvania 18515.

Erickson, Carlton W. H. *Fundamentals of Teaching with Audiovisual Technology.* New York: Macmillan, 1965.

Glaser, Robert (ed.). *Teaching Machines and Programmed Learning II.* Washington, D.C.: Department of Audiovisual Instruction, NEA, 1965.

Jarolimek, John. *Social Studies in Elementary Education.* New York: Macmillan, 1967. Chap. 4.

Kemp, Jerrold E. *Planning and Producing Audiovisual Materials.* San Francisco: Chandler, 1968. Distr. by International Textbook Company, Scranton, Pennsylvania 18515.

Michaelis, John U. (ed.). *Social Studies in Elementary Schools.* Thirty-second Yearbook. Washington, D.C.: National Council for the Social Studies, 1962. Chap. 7.

Preston, Ralph C. *Teaching Social Studies in the Elementary School.* Third edition. New York: Holt, Rinehart & Winston, 1968. Chap. 12.

Schultz, Morton J. *The Teacher and the Overhead Projector.* Englewood Cliffs, N.J.: Prentice-Hall, 1965.

Weisgerber, Robert A. (ed.). *Instructional Process and Media Innovation.* Skokie, Ill.: Rand McNally, 1968.

Wittich, Walter A., and Schuller, Charles F. *Audiovisual Materials: Their Nature and Use.* Fourth edition. New York: Harper & Row, 1967.

References for Media Materials and Equipment

Weber, Olga S. (ed.). *Audiovisual Market Place.* Second edition. New York: Bowker, 1970. (Directory of equipment manufacturers, software producers and distributors, professional and trade associations, film festivals and conferences, and reference books.)

Suttles, Patricia H. (ed.). *Elementary Teachers Guide to Free Curriculum Materials.* Randolph, Wisconsin: Educators Guide Series, Educators Progress Service, Inc., 1968. (Box 97, Randolph, Wisconsin 53956.)

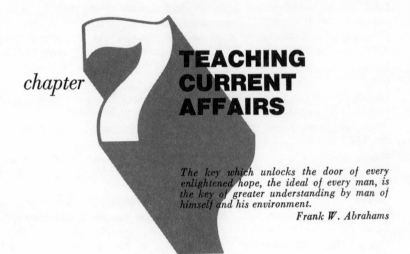

chapter

7 TEACHING CURRENT AFFAIRS

The key which unlocks the door of every enlightened hope, the ideal of every man, is the key of greater understanding by man of himself and his environment.

Frank W. Abrahams

A good current-affairs program can add greatly to the social studies learnings at every grade level. Even first-grade pupils enjoy discussing the news and should be given ample opportunity to discuss happenings that are close to them or within the range of their understandings. Because of the nature of social studies content, many of the current affairs or significant happenings in the news are directly related to the topics covered. Their utilization will greatly strengthen ongoing units of study. Of course, some current affairs or current events selected for discussion have no immediate application to topics under study. But they have value as a means of accomplishing additional social studies objectives such as helping children read more critically or helping them develop power to differentiate more clearly. They are of special value in helping children become more aware of their total relationships to the world in which they live.

Three major purposes of current-affairs instruction are identified by Jarolimek:

> The only way a citizen can keep himself up-to-date on the rapidly changing course of events is to develop and maintain a continuing interest in current affairs as reported via the various news mediums. If the nation expects its adults to have permanent interest in news, current developments, and a sincere desire to keep informed, the groundwork for these attitudes, interests, and skills must be laid in the elementary school. The first major purpose of current affairs teaching at the elementary school level is, therefore, *to promote interest in current affairs and news developments.*

Intelligent consideration of current affairs requires the use of a variety of skills and abilities: (1) to read news materials; (2) to discriminate between important and less significant news items; (3) to take a position on issues based on a knowledge and critical evaluation of facts of both sides; and (4) to predict likely consequences in terms of present developments. *Promoting the growth of these skills and abilities represents the second major purpose of current affairs instruction at the elementary school level. . . .*

The third major purpose of current affairs teaching is *to help the child relate school learning to life outside the school.*[1]

Perhaps today there is a greater need than ever before for young people who can discriminate among news items and judge their accuracy. Langer points up the importance of the school's role in this regard as follows:

Today's emphasis on current events in secondary and elementary school classrooms requires that teachers provide their students with background and guidelines for understanding what is printed or broadcast as news. The general assumption that objectivity and accuracy in reporting can be counted on should be particularly suspect in the light of recent occurrences. Teachers should provide a healthy, critical skepticism, along with a set of criteria for evaluating the media and their messages.[2]

He further suggests the following guidelines for teachers in helping students acquire accurate data on which to base judgments, draw inferences, and develop conclusions regarding the accuracy of news reports:

Provide an opportunity for students to learn the relative value of different news sources. [For example, quotes in context from persons clearly identified as authoritative are more reliable than "informed sources."]

Students should be taught to find facts in a news report. [This can be accomplished by having students compare a series of news reports on a single ongoing event, discover how so-called facts change, are left out, or are revised in different newspapers and magazines.]

Students should understand that columnists or commentators have the right to express opinions in print or on the air, but that opinion and fact differ, and opinion in print is often a substitute for facts not available.

Students should know that there is, occasionally, careless or dishonest reporting.

Students should understand that time may make more facts available; they should not expect the press to have or report them all.

[1] John Jarolimek, *Social Studies in Elementary Education,* third edition (New York: Macmillan, 1967), pp. 382–383.
[2] John H. Langer, "The News Media and Social Science Teaching," *Phi Delta Kappan* 51 (6): 318–320, February 1970.

Students should be shown how press reporting of emotional responses of public persons can stimulate others to those same emotions.

Long- and short-range effects of media news treatment, especially television, strongly affect public opinion.

Students must understand that the free press and broadcast media are profit-making enterprises.[3]

DIFFERENTIATING CURRENT AFFAIRS AND CURRENT ISSUES

A current-affairs program in the elementary school refers to a study of the more significant contemporary happenings in the news at the local state, national, and world levels. Sometimes the terms "current affairs" and "current events" are used synonymously. But "current affairs" is a much broader term that connotes significant events of more than passing interest that are worthy of considerable study and research. A current event, on the other hand, may be a less significant happening in the news that is viewed with only passing interest.

"Current issue" indicates that there is some degree of controversy concerning the contemporary problem under study. Because of the controversial elements in these problems or issues, they are more appropriate for study at the upper-grade levels of the elementary school. With younger children, more emphasis might be placed on the study of current events. But teachers must not underestimate the background that children have gained through mass media such as television and through travel. Events need not be restricted to their own local environment. For example, children can understand, in a simplified way, problems related to the ways of living of children in other lands. In simple terms, children can discuss many of the interesting national and world events.

THE IMPORTANCE OF CURRENT-AFFAIRS INSTRUCTION IN ELEMENTARY GRADES

A fundamental responsibility of every citizen is to keep himself informed on happenings that affect him and the society in which he lives. The basic attitudes, interests, and skills necessary to do so must be laid in the elementary school.

A major concern is to help young people understand propaganda. Today, children are bombarded with propaganda and mass persuasion techniques on every hand. Because of this endless flow of appeals to emotion, elementary school teachers have a responsibility to help children see clearly how propaganda is used and to recognize and understand the major propaganda devices. Major devices such as using glittering generalities and using transfer—joining a symbol or idea toward which most people have favorable attitudes with another symbol whose acceptance is less sure or less certain—are common procedures today in many kinds of advertisements or commercials. These and a large number of other similar devices are continually

[3] Langer, op. cit., p. 319.

used by all news media—newspapers, magazines, television, and radio. To cope with efforts being made to engineer thinking, children must be made aware of the emotional motivations upon which propagandists play, and be taught to think critically and to make up their minds intelligently without being "taken in."

There are a number of other values that might be attained through a good current-affairs program in the elementary school. Among them are the following:

> 1 A study of current affairs or events is necessary to the development of intelligent and inquiring minds capable of critical thinking about current problems and about the real world in which children live.
>
> 2 Good current-affairs instruction can reinforce children's positive attitudes and loyalties toward their country and can enlarge their appreciations for the accomplishments of mankind everywhere in the world.
>
> 3 Through current affairs a wide range of skills related to the social studies can be reinforced. These include using many sources of materials for collecting information, organizing data, reporting and using graphic materials and maps of various kinds.
>
> 4 Current-affairs instruction may motivate children to study the historical antecedents of some present national and world happenings.
>
> 5 Current-affairs instruction can supplement and bring up to date many topics presented in textbooks. Because textbooks are not revised each year, current materials can help close the gap between outdated topics in the text and changing developments related to them.

TEACHING CURRENT AFFAIRS IN THE ELEMENTARY GRADES

There are a wide number of approaches to the teaching of current affairs. Some teachers prefer to take a few minutes each morning at the beginning of the school day for reporting current events. Often children are required to search the newspapers and magazines at home for *important* news items. Generally, this practice results in a hurried selection of news items by children, or by their parents, that are often inappropriate or of little value for class discussion. This procedure is of dubious value and does little to motivate children's interest in current affairs. Even if children were capable in all cases of selecting the more significant items in the news, little could be gained toward accomplishing the major goals of current-affairs instruction by merely reporting events each morning. Current-event periods could be of greater value if they were related to one area of interest or to ongoing lessons rather than to a general survey and superficial coverage of all the big items covered by the various news media. Thus, it would be preferable to include current affairs as part of the social studies period. There would be some days when teachers could incorporate current affairs in the regular lessons; other times none would be used. Children would be motivated to develop a genuine interest in current happenings when they were related to topics under study in the social studies. This would also "bring to life" the social studies and help the child relate school learnings to life outside the school.

The role of the teacher would be to encourage children to be alert for news items related to ongoing units of work. The teacher would also look for means to make the discussion and sharing of news more worthwhile.

To encourage greater interest, one must help the child get below the surface of what he reads in the news. How to help children develop more depth of understanding of current events is well stated by Endres:

> To take children beneath the surface of events about which they read, the teacher must possess the art of questioning. *Probe* for responses that get beneath the surface considerations; *probe* to get the child to reflect, to relate his past experience and knowledge to the present; *probe* to get him to dig for understanding and to demand of the teacher more than surface generalities; *probe* to get out in the open the child's concerns about his world. A child between the ages of ten and fifteen sometimes shows a startling perception of the fundamental issues facing mankind today.[4]

After some maturation in the study of current events, children in the middle and upper grades of the elementary school should have the opportunity, under competent guidance and instruction and in an atmosphere free from bias and prejudice, to study special problems of a controversial nature. The social studies content fields, by their very nature, contain many areas where difference of opinion exists. Alert teachers will find a number of controversial issues, appropriate to the maturity level and needs and interests of elementary pupils, readily available for study. Complex, explosive, or highly controversial issues that may cause tension, hostility, or unkind feelings among the community, parents, or children should be avoided. More mildly controversial problems, of which there are many of significance to children, may be more appropriate for discussion with elementary pupils.

In teaching controversial issues, teachers should be aware of their role as guides, not indoctrinators, and should help children consider issues critically and openly. Because young people are highly impressionable, there is always the danger that their opinions might be unduly influenced by the opinion of the teacher who is an "authority figure" to them. Therefore, the teacher has the obligation to see that all sides of an issue are presented fairly and impartially. If his personal opinion is asked for, the teacher has the right to express it. But in doing so, he must be careful to point out that other adults may hold different points of view and that there are many honest differences of opinions on the issue under discussion. But, in all cases, the teacher's major purpose should be to teach children how to think for themselves and to develop power of critical judgment.

SPECIFIC AIDS AND LEARNING ACTIVITIES

Among the most useful aids or methods that might be used to motivate and develop a good current-affairs program are the following:

[4] Raymond J. Endres, "Criticism of Current Events: An Analysis," in *Readings for Social Studies in Elementary Education*, second edition, by John Jarolimek and Huber M. Walsh (New York: Macmillan, 1969), p. 180.

Bulletin Board

Part of the pinup space in the classroom should be utilized as an attractive news bulletin board. It should be located in a part of the room where children pass by regularly and where they can have the opportunity to examine it in their free time. If the bulletin board is to serve any useful purpose, news items need to be categorized under related headings such as world news, national news, local news, developments in science, sports, humor, and oddities in the news. The news items under the various headings should be changed often and kept up to date. A good news bulletin board, one to which pupils can contribute regularly, will help them develop an increased interest in news items of all kinds.

Weekly Newspapers

There are a number of good weekly news publications available for use in elementary classrooms. They serve a special need on the elementary level for unbiased news materials that are of significance and interest to children. They are geared to the reading ability of pupils at each grade level. The teacher, therefore, can select from a weekly publication the grade levels that best meet the reading abilities and needs of her class.

Some of the limitations of the weekly classroom periodical are: (1) Because of its wide circulation in schools throughout the country, it can of necessity deal only with items of greatest general interest and appeal to children. Local news, of course, must be slighted in favor of national and international items, and (2) some teachers might have a tendency to rely on the weekly periodical for the total current-affairs program, thus neglecting some important aspects of that program.

The weekly newspaper, however, can be a valuable aid to the current-affairs program if it is fully and effectively utilized. This demands more than merely assigning pupils to read the paper through to prepare for a class discussion that follows—all within a 20-to-30-minute period. Best use of the periodical can be made when the teacher is creative in her approach to its use. For example, she can vary the procedure of having students report the significant news items from week to week by using such special activities as panel discussions, dramatizations, special reports, and class discussions. Where possible, the news stories should be correlated with ongoing units of work. Some items can be filed for future reference as they become more pertinent to an area of study.

A study of the weekly periodical provides numerous opportunities for students to develop map and globe skills. In connection with the study of most news items, there are many opportunities to use a variety of graphic materials and specialized maps. Opportunities may also be provided for the advanced students to do further research and study on topics of their interest and choice. These kinds of activities will highly motivate students to make the best use of weekly newspapers.

The following special weekly newspapers are for boys and girls of elementary school age. There are teacher editions which go with each of these publications.

American Education Publications, Education Center, Columbus, Ohio 43216.

Kindergarten / Surprise	*Grade 6 / Senior Weekly Reader*
Grades 1–5 / My Weekly Reader	*Grades 7–8 / Current Events*

Civic Education Service, 1733 K Street, N.W., Washington, D.C. 20006.

Grades 5–6 / Young Citizen	*Grades 7–9 / The Junior Review*

George A. Pflaum, Inc., 38 West 5th Street, Dayton, Ohio 45402 (for Catholic schools).

Grades 1–3 / Our Little Messenger
Grades 4–6 / Junior Catholic Messenger
Grades 6–8 / Young Catholic Messenger

Scholastic Magazines, 50 West 44th Street, New York City, New York 10036.

Grade 1 / News Pilot	*Grades 5–6 / Young Citizen*
Grade 2 / News Ranger	(slower readers)
Grade 3 / News Trails	*Newstime*
Grade 4 / News Explorer	(faster readers)
	Grades 6–8 / Junior Scholastic

Current-events Quiz Bowl

The game technique appears to be a valuable approach with elementary school pupils in teaching current affairs. Children of this age level are highly motivated by games. When there is strong personal involvement in a learning activity, the child gains a greater degree of knowledge. For these reasons, games seem to have considerable value as a teaching tool. They are of particular value to a current-events program that has become somewhat routine and boring to pupils. The quiz-bowl game can be used regularly to create a new and increased interest in current affairs.

The current-events quiz-bowl game is played by dividing the class into teams of four. Teams are chosen on Monday. Preliminary competition between teams is held on Thursday, with the final round on Friday. It is best during a given week to limit the quiz-bowl competition to four teams only—representing sixteen pupils. The balance of the class can participate effectively in other ways, which will be explained later. During the second week, those teams who did not actively compete during the first week will be given an opportunity to take their turn. In preparation for competition, each member of a team chooses a category or an area of news in which he is to become especially well prepared. The four areas he may choose from are: local news, national news, world news, and sports. The group of four then select a name for their team, such as "Wildcats," "Tigers," etc.

The first competition between the teams is on Thursday. Current-event questions related to the four categories of news are prepared by the teacher and are taken mainly from the news items previously discussed or reported in class. But the teacher may feel free to ask questions related to any prominent happenings in the daily news that are appropriate to the understanding and the age level of her pupils. In the preliminary competition on Thursday each of the teams is matched with an opponent. After four teams compete on Thursdays, the two winners meet on Friday in the final round. As helpers, the teacher will need a time keeper and a scorer. The teacher will act as judge to determine which hands are raised first and the correctness of answers. A time limit of ten minutes is set for each round of competition between two teams. The team that is ahead in points at the close of the allotted time is declared the winner. Points are awarded for correct answers to questions given by the teacher. The first question asked by the teacher is a "toss-up" question, worth four points to either team that answers it correctly. The first person who raises his hand after the question is given by the teacher answers it for his team. He must answer the question without help or prompting from other teammates. If this question is missed, the teacher goes on to the next question. The first team to amass twelve points, or to answer three questions correctly, is given a bonus or "satellite" question worth five points if answered correctly. For the "satellite" question, the team may confer on the answer. If they miss the question, the other team is given an opportunity to answer it and win the five points. At the close of the ten-minute time period, the team that is ahead in points is declared the winner and advances to the next round of competition. The above plan is not hard and fast. The teacher should feel free to vary the game procedure to best fit the needs of her class. Its main purpose is to act as a motivational device to help students become more aware of important happenings around them.

Rules for Current-events Quiz Bowl

1 There are three rounds in the tournament.

2 A team is eliminated after one defeat.

3 Each match will last ten minutes.

4 The team with the most points at the end of the ten-minute period is declared the winner and will advance to the next round.

5 The team that wins the final round on Friday is declared the tournament winner for the week.

6 The team members of a team that wins a tournament are not permitted to combine in any way in subsequent matches during the year.

7 Teams are formed the first day of each week.

8 Tournaments are to be held the last two days of each week.

9 Quiz questions are drawn from all forms of news media reported Monday through Thursday of each week.

10 When a player is responding to a question, any coaching from the audience will nullify the answer.

11 When a question is being asked, the first member of either team to signal that he knows the answer is permitted to respond. If he responds correctly his team is credited with the proper number of points. If his answer is incorrect no points are awarded.

12 When a team acquires 12 points it is entitled to go on to the satellite group. The team may choose from one to five

questions from this set and team members may collaborate in each of their responses. If they choose only one question from this group and answer correctly, they receive 5 points; if they answer incorrectly no penalty is given. If they choose two questions and get them right they earn 10 points. If they answer incorrectly on either question, no points are awarded and no penalty is assessed. However, if they choose either three, four, or five questions the team receives 5 points for each question and a 5-point bonus for each question if each answer is correct. If a team fails to answer any question correctly they draw a penalty of 5 points for each question chosen.

13 If the ten-minute time period ends during a satellite question period, the game continues until the satellite group has been completed.

Other Activities

There are a number of different methods that can be utilized in teaching current affairs. Creative teachers prefer to approach the teaching of current affairs through a variety of means. Among those approaches that have been used profitably are the following:

Individual Reports / Through individual pupil reports, information obtained by independent research may be shared with the class. Individual reports are valuable in that they provide opportunities for the student to organize materials for a report and to express himself freely before the class. The teacher should make sure that the reports are well planned before being presented to the class, and that the pupil giving the report uses appropriate visual aids such as pictures, maps, and charts to strengthen his presentation. Otherwise, on the elementary level particularly, they can become time-consuming, boring, and of little instructional value to other students.

Panel and Round-table Discussions / A panel discussion is quite similar in nature to a round table. The fine line for distinction between the two is that panel discussions are more audience-oriented. That is, after initial statements by the panelists, the discussion is opened for audience participation. The round table is a more informal discussion of a significant topic limited generally to a small group of participants. But both kinds of procedures are appropriate for pupils in the upper grades of the elementary school. Elementary pupils are highly motivated by the challenge to participate as an "expert" in the discussion. A considerable amount of study and research on their part is required to prepare adequately for their roles as participants.

Comparative Study of Newspapers / An interesting approach to the study of newspapers is to have children make a critical study and comparison of news headlines and articles. This can be done best when the school subscribes to two or three different daily newspapers. The same news item appearing in different daily papers can be compared to determine biases in reporting. An examination of sensational headlines often reveals that they are used to sell newspapers rather than to reflect accurate facts. A careful study and comparison of a headline story reported by different newspapers may reveal many discrepancies in the account. After a series of such comparisons, children can learn to discriminate between propaganda and fact, and to detect slanted news and biases in reporting. Occasional study of the editorial page of the newspaper may also be profitable for the older and more advanced students.

Special Telecasts **/** Occasions might arise when the teacher would find it desirable to require the class to view a special news event or program on television. The special program may be viewed at school or at home depending upon the timing of the telecast. It is most desirable to have students view special newscasts that are related to an ongoing study in the classroom.

In the final analysis, a good current-events program in the elementary school depends in a great measure on how well it is organized by the teacher and on the teacher's interest and enthusiasm for the program. Also, for the greatest effectiveness, it is essential that the news be categorized into different areas. Without any organization or structure under which children collect and report news items, the whole program can become dull and ineffective.

QUESTIONS AND ACTIVITIES

1 / Review the three major purposes of current-affairs instruction as given in this chapter. Which purpose seems to be most crucial for children today? Why? List other related purposes that might be accomplished through a good current-affairs program in the elementary school.

2 / What are the crucial points that should be kept in mind when teaching controversial issues to elementary school children?

3 / List the advantages that you see in the use of a weekly periodical in the classroom. What limitations do you see in their use?

4 / How can a current-affairs bulletin board be organized so as to be most effective?

5 / How may the study of current affairs integrate geographical understandings and study?

6 / What are some of the essential elements of a good current-affairs program?

SELECTED REFERENCES

Crowder, William W. "A Good Nose for News." *Grade Teacher,* September 1965, pp. 158–160.

Fraser, Dorothy M. "Current Affairs, Special Events, and Civic Participation." *Social Studies in Elementary Schools.* Thirty-second Yearbook. Washington, D.C.: National Council for the Social Studies, 1962.

Jarolimek, John. *Social Studies in Elementary Education.* New York: Macmillan, 1963. 418 pp. Chap. 14, "Teaching of Current Affairs."

McAulay, John D. "Current Affairs and the Social Studies." *Social Education,* January 1959, pp. 21–22.

McLendon, Jonathon C. "Using Daily Newspapers More Effectively." *Social Education* 23 (6): 263–265, October 1959.

Smith, Lloyd L. "Current Events for the Elementary School." *Social Education* 25 (2): 75–78, February 1961.

TEACHING CITIZENSHIP AND INTERNATIONAL UNDERSTANDING

chapter

And as the Cock crows, those who stand before the Gates shout, "Open, then, a Door!" You know how little while we have to stay; But open One, and we will open More!

Omar Khayyám

Citizenship training is a prominent phase of the elementary study of political science or government and is directly related to the second major objective of the social studies having to do with the "affective domain" or the development of attitudes and values. Therefore, developing effective programs of citizenship education has long been a dominant concern of those planning the social studies for children in our elementary schools. The schools have been specifically charged with the responsibility to teach democratic values and to become laboratories where children can practice democracy in a meaningful way. But as yet we have not been as effective in planning and teaching values as we have the other major objectives of the social studies. In the past the school curriculum has often stressed fact-finding to the exclusion of the study and development of values. In all too many cases, it has been hoped that proper attitudes and values would emerge as a by-product of obtaining the knowledge objectives. Also, how to proceed in teaching values most effectively has not always been clear. Too, some teachers have been hesitant to accept and work toward attitudes and values because they have felt some confusion as to what values are basic, universally acceptable, and pertinent to our American society today.

It is recognized that the ways of democracy must be learned anew by each generation if we are to perpetuate our democratic way of life. Social study programs in citizenship training must provide meaningful experiences out of which children and youth can acquire the understandings and behavior essential for effective participation in a democratic society.

TEACHING CITIZENSHIP

The home as the most basic institution of our society can have the greatest influence upon the child in the development of character, of moral and spiritual values. But although the family in so doing makes an important contribution to the overall effort of developing good citizenship, parents generally look to the schools for the continued development in today's youth of fervent devotion to basic American ideals so that they may safeguard those ideals and in turn pass them on to future generations.

Events in our society raise serious questions as to the effectiveness of our citizenship-training and of our teaching of democratic values in our schools. For example, there are present signs of the crumbling of our republic that has been brought about, among other events, by anarchy, lawlessness, massive injustice and inhumanity toward minority groups, and a growing lack of morality. Nevertheless, in spite of the confusion, change, stress, and conflict under which our values are being tested, certain values central to our democratic institutions and reflected in our basic documents are acceptable to all freedom-loving people. These characteristics of the democratic way of life are well described in the *Declaration of Independence,* the *Constitution of the United States,* and the *Bill of Rights.*[1] The basic characteristics of the democratic way of life may be catalogued as follows:

1 Respect for the dignity and worth of the individual human personality

2 Open opportunity for the individual

3 Economic and social security

4 The search for truth

5 Free discussion

6 Freedom of speech

7 Freedom of the press

8 Universal education

9 Rule of the majority

10 Respect for rights of the minority

11 Justice for the common man; trial by jury; arbitration of disputes; orderly legal processes; freedom from search and seizure; right to petition

12 Freedom of religion

13 Respect for the right of private property

14 Practice of the fundamental social virtues

15 Responsibility of the individual to participate in the duties of democracy.

Recognizing that these (and other related or subordinate values) are central features of a good citizenship-education program, the question is not whether they should be taught in the elementary schools, but rather how they may be taught so as to become more vital and valid for children and youth today.

[1] See statement of Educational Policies Commission regarding values that could be considered a common denominator of our democracy. Educational Policies Commission, *Moral and Spiritual Values in the Public Schools* (Washington, D.C.: National Education Association, 1951).

1. The schools' concern with the development of good citizenship is a much more complex task, it seems, than merely teaching children a few elements of American history, having them memorize patriotic slogans, and increasing patriotic ceremonies in the schools. Few would deny that there is a place for a certain amount of symbolism in teaching patriotism toward one's country. From the time they enter school, young children participate in rituals and ceremonies that are associated with living in a democracy through such activities as flag ceremonies, Pledge of Allegiance, patriotic dramatizations, and songs. But, the critical factors in the effectiveness of these activities as a means of influencing the desired democratic behavior are the extent to which children arrive at a clear understanding of the underlying meanings of the symbols represented and the "whys" behind the ceremonies. However, mature understanding cannot be expected of young children all at once. It must be developed and deepened throughout the child's elementary school experience.

Meaning of the Pledge of Allegiance[2]

"I pledge" means I promise

"allegiance" means to be true. The flag is the sign or symbol of our country. The flag reminds us of our country.

"of the United States" means of our country. The United States is the name of the country in which we live. It is sometimes called America.

"and to the Republic for which it stands" means a Republic is the kind of government we have in America—a government in which the people make the laws.

"one nation under God" means one country (nation is another name for country) whose people believe in God.

"indivisible" means cannot be divided. "Indivisible" means we cannot be broken up into parts. We are one country. We may disagree but we cannot be divided.

"with liberty" means with freedom. In America we love freedom. We are free to help each other. We obey laws that help all people. We do not harm our friends.

"and justice for all" means fairness for all. Each person is given a chance to prove he did not do anything wrong if he is accused of wrong-doing.

The fact that schools have not always been as effective as possible in developing meanings in no way negates the importance of patriotic rituals nor should it be the sole criterion by which one judges whether or not they should be observed. They constitute an essential part of a good citizenship-education program. The error is in assuming that they can and should constitute the *complete* program of citizenship education in the schools and that through their observance all children will become patriotic Americans capable of exhibiting intelligent democratic behavior in their daily lives.

---

[2] One of the first steps in teaching the Pledge of Allegiance to young children should be to develop the meaning behind it. An interesting experiment is to have fifth- or sixth-graders write the meaning of the Pledge of Allegiance. Many faulty concepts become apparent.

Many schools of the past have erred in this direction. Regarding this practice, the Educational Policies Commission states:

> The school books of that day were replete with patriotic slogans and citations, on the assumption that those who could recite them would be patriots. . . . But, in the Twentieth Century the experience of the public school has fully demonstrated that the goals sought require considerably more than the memorization of precepts.[3]

Among other things it requires a home background where parents provide the personal security on which healthy social attitudes are based and where parents set examples for children to live by. Also, it requires that children have a true understanding of the real meaning and intent of the Constitution of the United States and that they be provided actual firsthand experiences in democratic government.

The idea that real patriotism must come from these kinds of deeper meanings is stated colorfully by Stevens as follows:

> First, if we are truly interested in building patriotism, it is least likely to happen by verbally whipping off 31 words every morning while the connections between the vocal cords and brains grow weaker by the day. True patriotism is most likely to develop from school programs and experiences that explain and illustrate the meaning of our great Constitution. . . .[4]

Currently, social study textbooks, teachers, and schools in general are being attacked by some uninformed but well-meaning individuals who do not understand fully or conceive accurately what is involved in the complex task of teaching citizenship. Generally, they view patriotism in a narrow chauvinistic sense as devotion to a given set of symbols or as the ability to recite patriotic slogans. Accordingly, the only safe, sure road to patriotism involves endless memorization of slogans and the increase of patriotic ceremonies in the schools. Little or no thought is given to the underlying meanings for the pupils. Unquestioned acceptance, not understanding, is the goal.

Claims have been made that many of the sayings of early American heroes have been taken out of our more recent social study texts. However, an examination of current supplementary elementary school social study texts does not bear this out. Today we have many elementary school history books that present a complete and detailed coverage of all early American heroes and that are better written and better illustrated than anything we have had in the past. So there is increased opportunity for children today to become better acquainted with the lives of American heroes than ever before through the use of new and improved materials and through the means of more modern methods of teaching. Many of the qualities exemplified in the lives of great Americans are sorely needed today, for example, moral responsibility of the individual and respect for human dignity. By encouraging youth to

---

[3] Educational Policies Commission, *Social Responsibility in a Free Society* (Washington, D.C.: National Education Association, 1963), p. 14.
[4] Leonard A. Stevens, "Do We Need a New Pledge of Allegiance?" *Look Magazine,* December 1970, p. 20.

identify with great Americans, past and present, we can encourage appreciations and values that seem to be basic to the preservation of our democratic ideals and institutions.

Again, the goal is to help children grasp the philosophy, understanding, and meaning in back of given patriotic actions, words, and symbols. It is not enough to have children engage in rote memorizations of high-sounding sayings and slogans for their own sake. For seldom does such an approach ever touch the minds and hearts of youngsters.

2. Another dimension of citizenship education has to do with the attitudes and values that the child brings with him to school from the home environment. Inasmuch as the child spends a far greater proportion of his waking hours during a week at home than at school, the home influence exerts a powerful effect upon his attitudes, feelings, and tolerance toward other children. Many negative and prejudiced attitudes toward others are firmly entrenched in the child before he enters school. For example, the child who hears his parents continually make prejudiced and stereotyped statements about people of other races or religions at the dinner table often is little affected by the school's attempt to teach positive feelings and attitudes toward others. The teachings of the home generally are far more impressive and permanent than those gained at school in this regard. Too, the kind of examples set by parents in social relationships has a profound influence upon the behavior of children. Values are far more influenced by example than by precept. When a child sees a parent engage in undemocratic and unlawful acts, he is prone to incorporate the same kind of behavior as part of his own daily life.

The child who comes from an underprivileged home also, in many cases, is handicapped in developing the needed social skills for good citizenship. According to Jarolimek:

> While there is yet much to be learned about the development of attitudes, there is a growing volume of evidence to indicate that one's attitudes are quite directly related to emotional well-being and balance. That is to say, a person who is unable to meet his personal-social needs satisfactorily develops inner conflicts which bear upon his ability to perceive and deal with his classmates in play situations and is not likely to be favorably disposed toward cooperative behavior and good will toward others. The child who comes from a family which suffers economic privation, rejection, fear of unemployment, victimization, discrimination, or disparagement presents a fertile field for the growth of prejudice, rebellion, hate, distrust, selfishness, and lack of concern for others.[5]

In agreement as to the influence of the home upon the development of good citizenship, the Educational Policies Commission points out that many basic attitudes have taken hold before the child enters school. They state:

[5] John Jarolimek, *Social Studies in Elementary Education,* second edition (New York: Macmillan, 1963), pp. 15–16.

> It has always seemed reasonable to look to the school as the primary instrument for shaping the citizen. . . . By the time the child reaches school age, however, many basic attitudes have taken firm hold. And, in general, he continues to spend much more time outside school than in it. The role of the community, and of the home in particular, in developing character can hardly be overstated. If parents do not provide the personal security on which healthy social attitudes are based and do not set examples for children to live by, the school's ability to develop the citizen is sharply curtailed, but its share of the responsibility for doing so rises.[6]

Accordingly, the schools have a responsibility to the child in being more sensitive to his personal-social needs and in finding more effective means of teaching values to children from minority groups and underprivileged homes.

3. Citizenship education during the social study period should be supported by practice of democratic living throughout the school day if it is to be effective. Children can learn to be good citizens not only in the classroom but in the lunchroom, on the playground, and on the school bus. As previously noted, one does not learn the ways of democracy simply by studying about them or by memorizing precepts; they are learned through daily practice. Democratic values must be acquired through democratic experiences in a climate of respect for others.

Children can become "practiced" in the ways of a democratic society through many kinds of democratic experiences, for example, participating in the processes of majority rule. Although there are some limitations to the use of majority rule in the classroom, children can have opportunities to express themselves through the voting process. They can learn that many crucial decisions in a democratic society are reached through the process of reason and majority decision. Unless children grow up in a world where there is faith in the use of reason and intelligence in solving problems, rather than the use of force, there can be little future for the preservation of our democratic society.

4. Another basic dimension of citizenship education is related to helping children acquire basic concepts about the processes and institutions of government. The intermediate and upper years provide the widest range of possibilities for increasing children's knowledge of the workings of government, both in our country and elsewhere.

One approach to helping pupils increase their abilities and tendencies to participate in governmental processes is through the organization of a student-government program in the school.[7] Participation in student-government activities provides the students with the direct experience necessary for the clarifying of values that underlie democratic government and of the ways different institutions of government function. Major emphasis is upon the purpose and role of government in society and the governing process rather than solely upon the structure of government.

[6] Educational Policies Commission, op. cit., p. 131.
[7] See *An Exemplary Student Government-Social Studies Program for the Elementary Schools*, Davis County School District, Farmington, Utah, Chapter III, pp. 90–92.

Finally, democratic citizenship is dependent upon a balanced development in youth of both cognitive and affective elements. They need to be informed and devoted; sensible, yet capable of deep feeling. Democracy can rise no higher than the judgment level of its citizens and voters. Judgment is improved by education. Students need to be well informed about the pressing problems in our society today. They need to know about the errors we have made in our own history, as well as our strengths and achievements.

Continued improvement of conditions in our society is directly dependent upon an educated populace. An illiterate populace cannot operate a democracy. According to Jefferson, "If a nation expects to be ignorant and free in a state of civilization, it expects what never was and never will be. . . . There is no safe deposit [for the functions of government] but with the people themselves; nor can they be safe with them without information."

TEACHING INTERNATIONAL UNDERSTANDING

We live in a world today where the need has never been greater for people who have the capacity to understand others—for people of goodwill who can respect differences and develop feelings of mutual trust toward peoples of other countries. In today's troubled world, the need for educating children along these lines in our schools is evident. Education in international understanding should begin with children of elementary school age if we are to be successful in accomplishing our goals in this respect. Unfortunately, however, very little experimentation has been conducted on how to develop in children understandings related to an international point of view. Many programs of the past have placed almost the entire emphasis upon the teaching of "world affairs" in connection with the traditional study of the world on the sixth-grade level. Obviously, such a limited approach is entirely inadequate in developing the international dimension in the elementary school. What is needed is a more comprehensive and cumulative approach to teaching international understanding beginning with boys and girls in the primary grades. It should be recognized that international understanding is primarily a point of view rather than a separate subject, and that it can permeate every aspect of the curriculum. However, while all subjects in the elementary school have an international dimension, the social studies field focuses most heavily upon the problems concerned with understanding other peoples of the world. The chief concerns are with the development of "world-mindedness" in children and with helping them develop increased sensitivity toward the larger "world community."

Relationships Between Education for World Understanding and Education for Democratic Citizenship

The fact that we live in a world that has become "a little neighborhood" makes it more imperative than ever before for us to understand and respect differences of people of all nations. This becomes essential if we are to live on the same planet in some measure of harmony. But it cannot be a one-sided relationship; people everywhere must use education as a means of helping children develop feelings of goodwill and trust. Unfortunately, some people of the world are evidently using education to develop a generation of young people who hate and distrust others.

Our attempts to develop world-mindedness in children should in no way be construed as a means of destroying the child's basic loyalty to and love for his own country or for the Constitution of the United States. It in no way implies or advocates any form of one-world government. Nor does it mean that children must accept the values of others. Education for world understanding and education for moral, responsible, democratic citizenship in our country are based on the same principles of respect for the individual and tolerance toward others. In fact, international understanding really begins in the classroom when children develop respect for others of different racial backgrounds, religions, and cultures. These same kinds of attitudes, too, are the essential ingredients of good citizenship education. Education for world understanding is merely an extension of these ideas to the different peoples of the world in an attempt to understand them better and to see a rational basis for their differences.

The Nature of International Understanding / International understanding is based on the following principles:

> 1 The purpose of international understanding is to provide a world order based on law so that people can pursue their own courses free from fear and the threat of war. World society complications are due to cultural differences that lead to misunderstandings, prejudices, conflicts, and war.
>
> 2 Intolerance and prejudices are learned behaviors. Personality traits are engendered by the culture. Therefore, we must understand people in their own culture.
>
> 3 International understanding is an extension of local, state, and national understanding. It is the achievement of a good community at the world level.
>
> 4 International understanding is based on mutual respect and the universal recognition of the dignity of man.
>
> 5 International understanding involves more than knowledge— it also includes attitudes and ideals. These ideals must be extended to all mankind: dignity of the individual, use of reason, brotherhood of man, cooperation, competence, and the capacity to use critical thought.

Major Problems to Overcome / The following problems are blocks to better understanding:

> 1 *Communication difficulties:* language differences increase the barriers; semantic differences lead to the development of stereotypes, use of emotionally tinged words, and propaganda.
>
> 2 *Ethnocentrism:* misuse of the feelings of group or racial superiority.
>
> 3 *Power as a barrier:* nations and leaders are motivated by power and the development of nuclear weapons. These factors lead to fear of war, distrust, hysteria, etc.
>
> 4 *Nationalism:* local welfare is placed above the welfare of others. This promotes differences rather than similarities and

fosters ethnocentrism. Wholesome nationalism built on local, state, national, and international communities is needed.

5 *Ignorance and illiteracy:* approximately half the world is illiterate, easily susceptible to propaganda, and filled with suspicion and mistrust.

Some Suggested Solutions to the Problem **/** Among others the following solutions are suggested:

1 Apply ideals and tenets of American democracy to all individuals.

2 Improve communications and flow of information.

3 Provide better economic help to underdeveloped nations, and provide for better food distribution to the poor and needy.

4 Interchange of experts in science, economics, etc.; students; teachers.

5 Work for broader realization of democracy in the United States. Work against racial prejudice, religious intolerance, etc.

6 Recognize the common humanity which underlies all differences of culture.

Concepts and Experiences Important to World Understanding in the Elementary School

In our times, learned biases and discriminations have been sources of social conflict that have engulfed the nations of the world. The schools can help counteract these negative influences through a united effort to teach some of the basic concepts and understandings related to improved relationships with other people of the world. The findings of Lambert and Klineberg support the idea that there is a relationship between "friendliness" toward foreign people and knowledge about these peoples.[8] That is, children who have a "friendly" view of different foreigners have more knowledge about these peoples than the children who have "unfriendly" views.

The Glens Falls Project, a three-year project initiated and sponsored by the National Council for the Social Studies, was designed specifically to improve the teaching of world affairs in the public school system of Glens Falls, New York. The program is known as Improving the Teaching of World Affairs (ITWA). The program has demonstrated that teaching for world understanding can occur in all subject-matter areas through carefully selected experiences. According to the ITWA advisory committee, the program is designed to have each pupil develop: (1) an increased understanding of other peoples; (2) a growing appreciation of different cultures; (3) attitudes of respect for others such as are desired for himself; (4) a sense of responsibility as to his personal role and the role of his country in a world of nations; and (5) an awareness of the realities of international problems.[9]

Programs designed to develop international understanding on the elementary level would teach concepts related to the above aims and objectives.

[8] Wallace E. Lambert and Otto Klineberg, *Children's Views of Foreign People* (New York: Appleton-Century-Crofts, 1967), 319 pp.
[9] Harold M. Long and Robert N. King, *Improving the Teaching of World Affairs: The Glens Falls Story* (Washington, D.C.: National Council for the Social Studies, 1964), p. 23.

Some suggestions as to where we might start are given by Kenworthy as follows:

> 1 There are 3½ billion people in the world. They are all neighbors of ours.
>
> 2 The people of the world are alike in many ways—and also different.
>
> 3 People everywhere live in families and in communities.
>
> 4 Large groups of people are organized into nations.
>
> 5 The people of the world are interdependent. We depend upon them and they depend on us.
>
> 6 People—and nations—have problems. They are working on their problems just as we are working on ours. We share some basic problems.
>
> 7 People everywhere enjoy and create fun and beauty.
>
> 8 People belong to different religious groups. We share some common ideals.[10]

Building readiness for teaching children friendliness toward foreign people begins, as previously stated, with the development of respect for individuals with whom the child lives in the classroom and in his out-of-school life. Two main obstacles to be overcome are stereotyping and ethnocentrism. A major finding of the study by Lambert and Klineberg is that the early views children form of themselves and their national group greatly influence their later views of foreigners.[11] Beginning elementary students often tend to hold conceptions of their own group that are unrealistic, grandiose, and overgeneralized. Such exaggeration of their own group's virtues is likely to contribute to a biased attitude toward "outgroup" people. Children ought to understand that all societies tend to think of their own way of life as the most reasonable and natural, and that our ways of doing things are not always superior to the ways of other cultures. They also need to understand that although there are many types of human behavior in the world, they all reflect social environments created by man in response to common basic needs and problems. Thus, they can come to understand that "other" ways of solving the common human problems are not necessarily unnatural or perverse.

The community of tomorrow's children is going to be the whole world. Therefore, the development of cross-cultural sensitivity, whether with regard to other national cultures or to subcultures within a nation, becomes a pressing task of the school in our time.

The exposure of elementary school pupils to concepts related to positive international understandings should be through a variety of methods:

1. Among the best ways to introduce children to accurate and authentic information about other countries is through interviews with persons from foreign lands—visitors, exchange students, or persons who are acquiring United States citizenship.

A closely related activity is to provide an opportunity for pupils to have

[10] Leonard S. Kenworthy, "The International Dimension of Elementary Schools," *Phi Delta Kappan* 49 (4): 204, December 1967.
[11] Lambert and Klineberg, op. cit., 319 pp.

direct contact by mail with children in other lands. Through this means, students can obtain much firsthand information about the customs of other children—their similarities as well as their differences. Many sources of information are available where teachers may obtain addresses of children in other lands. One of these is the Youth Pen Pal Exchange, Box 6992, Washington, D.C. 20020.

Another means of introducing children to the peoples in far-off lands is to "adopt" a school of another country.[12] Contacts can be made with schools through people who have lived abroad, through people from other countries who have lived in the United States, or by writing directly to school districts abroad.

Adopting a foreign school has many advantages such as an opportunity to exchange questions, photographs, children's work, and information about the school and the community where it is located. This is an excellent means of providing children authentic and detailed information about people in other countries. Much information may be obtained that would never be available in a school textbook. One main advantage is that exchange between children is carried on in their own words and is, therefore, likely to remain within their level of understanding.

2. In addition to direct contact with a country, there is a wide variety of learning materials now available to teachers in the way of textbooks, encyclopedias, storybooks, folklore, pictures, films, filmstrips, music, folk dances, art, and realia which can be used to good advantage to help children understand and respect other people. Textbooks and encyclopedias are good sources for factual data concerning a country—its geography and resources. But these do not give the child much insight into the everyday lives and feelings of the people. Storybook material and folktales are particularly valuable in this regard. There is an abundance today of well-written storybooks related to the life of children in far-off places. The study of literature can take children beyond the factual data surrounding a country to an understanding of the everyday life and feelings of the people in their close family relationships. It is at this level of understanding that appreciations of other people are developed which are most crucial for good world relationships.

3. Richer international understandings are made possible for children when opportunities are provided for them to participate in worthwhile service projects related to helping needy children in other lands or even disadvantaged children in deprived areas of our own country. For example, such programs may take the form of welfare campaigns, collecting money for UNICEF, sending CARE packages, participating in the Junior Red Cross program, making toys for others, and preparing exhibits highlighting efforts to help suffering people everywhere. Creative teachers who are themselves world-minded will find additional ways of helping children participate in worthwhile action programs. Maximum educational benefits and increased international understandings may be achieved by engaging in these kinds of worthwhile service projects.

[12] See Bruce R. Joyce, "The World-Widened Elementary School," *Elementary School Journal* 62: 343–345, April 1962.

4. Another approach to the teaching of world understanding is to have children learn about the United Nations Organization and its specialized agencies. The purposes of the United Nations are:

> 1 To maintain international peace and security, and to that end to take effective collective measures for the prevention and removal of threats to the peace, and for the suppression of acts of aggression or other breaches of the peace, and to bring about by peaceful means, and in conformity with the principles of justice and international law, adjustment or settlement of international disputes or situations that might lead to a breach of the peace
>
> 2 To develop friendly relations among nations based on respect for the principle of equal rights and self-determination of peoples, and to take other appropriate measures to strengthen universal peace
>
> 3 To achieve international cooperation in solving international problems of an economic, social, cultural, or humanitarian character, and in promoting and encouraging respect for human rights and for fundamental freedoms for all without distinction as to race, sex, language, or religion
>
> 4 To be a center for harmonizing the actions of nations in the attainment of these common ends.

The UN is not a world government. It has no citizens and can pass no laws. It is composed of sovereign member states and has no direct power over the citizens of those states, except through actions of their own governments. The principal importance of the UN rests in the discussions and recommendations that it makes to the member states. To give these recommendations the best possible chance of acceptance, the UN provides the opportunity for the opinions of all nations to be heard.

In the spring of 1945, representatives of fifty nations of the world met in San Francisco to establish the United Nations. The charter of the UN was approved and submitted for ratification by the governments of the nations eligible for membership. By October 24, 1945, enough nations had ratified the charter to establish the UN officially. At the present time, however, there exists some controversy in our country as to the nature of its organization and its effectiveness as a positive force in resolving world problems. Therefore, whether or not schools may teach about the United Nations is determined in some cases by the policies of the various school districts. Fortunately, most schools encourage teaching about the United Nations and its specialized agencies. The United Nations, regardless of present imperfections, may become a strong force in settling international disputes and in maintaining world peace.

There are many good materials available to assist the teacher in this area of study. The bibliography at the end of this chapter contains a list of books and references that will be helpful to the teacher in selecting specific learning activities basic to a sound program of study about the United Nations at all grade levels of the elementary school.

The various approaches to the teaching of world-mindedness and positive intercultural attitudes are geared in a large measure to helping children extend nationalistic feelings to the larger community of nations and to prepare them to be better able in the future to cope with problems that cut across national lines. Today our youth are tremendously fascinated by great technological developments such as our ability to successfully land men on the moon. These kinds of accomplishments in space, whether made by Americans, Russians, or people of other nations, are felt to be accomplishments for the whole of the human race and tend to promote feelings of respect and unity that transcend national boundaries. There are many such experiences that can develop in children a "hierarchy of loyalties" to larger communities of men. Such loyalties are not antagonistic to loyalty and affection for one's own nation, but rather complement them and make life richer for all concerned.

QUESTIONS AND ACTIVITIES

1 / Explain how effective citizenship education involves more than merely having pupils memorize patriotic slogans and increasing patriotic ceremonies in the schools.

2 / What are some of the major social problems faced by children from disadvantaged homes? Plan a strategy for meeting their needs in developing citizenship education.

3 / In what ways does the development of effective democratic citizenship contribute to the development of international understanding?

4 / How do stereotyping and ethnocentrism block the development of favorable intercultural attitudes?

5 / Why should a teacher avoid focusing instruction upon differences, the unique, or bizarre features of a foreign culture?

6 / Plan a short teaching unit on a topic of your choice related to the development of international understanding. For example, The United Nations, music around the world, folk dances, families around the world, types of shelter used by different peoples, etc.

SELECTED REFERENCES

Hamilton, Dorothy W. "Educating Citizens for World Responsibilities, 1960–1980." *Citizenship and a Free Society.* Thirtieth Yearbook. Washington, D.C.: National Council for the Social Studies, 1960.

Hill, Wilhelmina. *Teaching About the United Nations in the United States.* Bulletin No. 18. Washington, D.C.: U.S. Department of Health, Education and Welfare, 1960. Pp. 28–29.

Jarolimek, John. *Social Studies in Elementary Education.* Third edition. New York: Macmillan, 1967. Chap. 15.

Joyce, Bruce R. "The World-Widened Elementary School." *Elementary School Journal* 62: 343–345, April 1962.

Kenworthy, Leonard S. *Free and Inexpensive Materials on World Affairs.* New York: Teachers College, Columbia University, 1963.

Kenworthy, Leonard S. *Studying the World: Selected Resources.* New York: Teachers College, Columbia University, 1962.

Lambert, Wallace E., and Klineberg, Otto. *Children's Views of Foreign People.* New York: Appleton-Century-Crofts, 1967.

Long, Harold M., and King, Robert N. *Improving the Teaching of World Affairs: The Glens Falls Story.* Washington, D.C.: National Council for the Social Studies, 1964.

Massialas, Byron G. "Social Studies Instruction in World Perspective." *New Challenges in the Social Studies.* Belmont, Calif.: Wadsworth Publishing Co., 1965.

Muessig, Raymond H., and Rogers, Vincent R. "Teaching Patriotism at Higher Conceptual Levels." *Social Education* 28: 266–270, May 1964.

National Education Association, Research Division. *Teaching About Other Countries and Peoples in the Elementary School.* Washington, D.C.: The Association, Department of Elementary School Principals, June 1960.

National Education Association, Committee on International Relations. *A Selected and Annotated Bibliography of Resource Materials for Teaching About the United Nations.* Washington, D.C.: NEA, 1958.

Phi Delta Kappan, *International Education.* Vol. 49, no. 4, December 1967.

Preston, Ralph C. *Teaching World Understanding.* Englewood Cliffs, N.J.: Prentice-Hall, 1955.

Shaftel, Fannie R. "Cultural Understanding in a World Community." *Educational Leadership* 19: 535–542, May 1962.

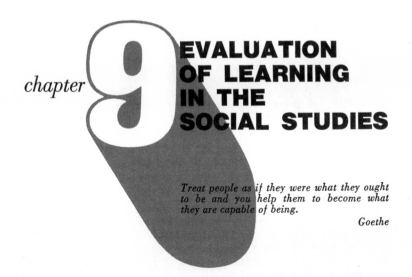

chapter **9**

EVALUATION OF LEARNING IN THE SOCIAL STUDIES

Treat people as if they were what they ought to be and you help them to become what they are capable of being.

Goethe

The true test of learning in the social studies is the extent to which previously established goals, objectives, or purposes have been achieved. This applies to short-range unit goals as well as to longer-range course objectives. Since the objectives of the social studies are broad and comprehensive, a wide variety of evaluation instruments must be used to measure learning.

Evaluation of learning must encompass more than the measurement of pupil achievement at the lowest cognitive level. It must include the measurement of higher levels of knowledge, as well as learnings in both the affective and psychomotor areas. Too, it should extend to include assessment by the instructor of his own performance. As illustrated in Individualized Units of Work, Chapter 4, preassessment or pretests might be used before launching the unit, to help the teacher plan for the incorporation of most pertinent learnings. This would require continuous examination and revision of what is taught and how it is taught to meet class needs.

Evaluation of learning in the social studies is a continuous process as a unit of work progresses, and it involves the use of appropriate instruments to measure the following kinds of learnings:

A. Extent to which there is knowledge
    1. Of the physical world as it conditions man's living
    2. Of human relationships as they modify living
    3. Of the work of the world
        a) In conserving and improving natural and human resources

b) In communicating ideas through language and art

c) In producing, processing, distributing, and consuming goods

d) In satisfying aesthetic and spiritual impulses through religion, appreciation, and creative expression

e) In extending freedom through social controls, customs, institutions of education, and new knowledges

B. Extent to which understanding has been developed toward change in customs, institutions, industries, modes of transportation, standards of living

C. Extent to which the learner uses authentic research in gathering and presenting data

D. Extent to which the learner can determine differences and likenesses in his own environment as contrasted with that of other people of today and yesterday

E. Extent to which the learner can use with facility the materials involved in the social studies: books, graphs, maps, charts, etc.

F. Extent to which the learner has an appreciation of the need of law and the desire on the part of the individual to make laws as means to ends.

Succinctly then, the major purposes of evaluation are to determine what the child knows about the world in which he lives, how well he can think, what skills and abilities he possesses, and what he feels and values.

To move toward the accomplishment of such goals, evaluation must be a continuous process employing a wide variety of evaluative devices and procedures.

USING BEHAVIORAL OBJECTIVES AS A MEANS OF EVALUATION

When it is adequately stated, the behavioral objective becomes surprisingly powerful in influencing instruction, because it provides (1) a clear objective, (2) a diagnostic preinstructional test, (3) the identity of the required content and procedures, (4) the final achievement test, and (5) very high transfer value for out-of-school life.

The four categories of objectives—the acquisition of knowledge, the development of a mode of inquiry, the development of attitudes and values, and the development of academic and social skills—comprise the general objectives of the social studies. However, these broad goals must be related to more specific behavioral outcomes if learning situations are to be evaluated effectively. Stated in behavioral or operational terms that clearly define the expected behavior, objectives become more tangible and provide a basis for accurate appraisal of student growth. For example, growth in good citizenship is more easily evaluated if it is agreed operationally just what a good citizen is—one who has a concern for others and for significant social, political, and economic problems; who recognizes that with freedom comes responsibility to others; who respects and appreciates cultural differences; who is well informed, etc. Learning situations should be provided in which desirable student behaviors, as defined in the objectives, can be developed and observed. It is only at this level that the forward growth of young people toward the objectives of social studies can be appraised with some accuracy.

Two kinds of lists of behavioral objectives are appropriate for the social studies. The first type would consist of a list of objectives applicable to a given unit of work. The combined number of units taught during the school year would thus provide a list of yearly objectives. The second type, written for each individual lesson, would designate detailed and specific daily goals to be achieved.

Mager[1] discusses the concept of terminal behavioral objectives and how to write them. Terminal behavioral objectives refer to the behavior that the teacher would like to have the learner demonstrate at the time his influence over the student ends. They are statements of intent that enable the students to know what is important and what is expected. Useful suggestions are given as to how to write them effectively on an operational level so that the statement tells explicitly what the learner will be doing when he displays his concepts, skills, or habits.

A terminal behavioral objective consists of three parts:

> 1 What the student will be doing when he illustrates his concepts, skills, etc. (construct, write, cite, etc.)
>
> 2 Definition of important conditions (restrictions and limitations)
>
> 3 Criterion of acceptable performance (five out of ten, etc.).

The following objective is illustrative:

Given a list of factors leading to significant historical events, the learner must be able to select at least five factors contributing to the depression of 1929.

A good behavioral objective identifies the specific student behavior that is sought. The specificity of the objective is of major importance. In writing behavioral objectives, vague and ambiguous terms such as "to know," "to really understand," "to comprehend," and "to appreciate" should be avoided.

A well-written behavioral objective is of special value to the teacher in selecting and evaluating learning experiences. If the behavior of the student can be observed while he demonstrates the knowledge he has acquired, or if the product of his knowledge is observable, then the objective is acceptable.

Useful as they are, lists of objectives stated in terms of behavior may become long and unwieldy. They can, however, be made to serve more useful purposes if they are arranged in meaningful categorization or classifications. That is, related objectives should be identified and grouped under the appropriate main headings of objectives so that they are more manageable. This will greatly increase their practical usefulness. Thus, they may become more valuable as a means of improving content, instruction, and evaluation.

A taxonomy of educational objectives, developed by Bloom and his associates, covering both the cognitive and affective domains, offers a valuable classification system of objectives.[2] The objectives are classified under three major headings:

---

[1] For a more detailed discussion of terminal behavioral objectives, see Robert F. Mager, *Preparing Objectives for Programmed Instruction* (San Francisco: Fearon Publishers, 1962).
[2] Benjamin S. Bloom, ed., *Taxonomy of Educational Objectives: Handbook I: Cognitive Domain* (New York: McKay, 1956); David R. Krathwohl et al., eds., *Taxonomy of Educational Objectives: Handbook II: Affective Domain* (New York: McKay, 1964).

Cognitive / Cognitive behaviors involve mental activities and are grouped into six classes of behavior arranged in a hierarchy from simple to complex in which the behaviors of each succeeding category require for their performance the abilities of the preceding categories. The cognitive objectives include the recall of specifics or simple knowledge of facts, comprehension, application, analysis, synthesis, and evaluation. For our purposes in the social studies, a dichotomy or two-way classification of cognitive objectives is sufficient: (1) lowest cognitive level—objectives whose performance requires the recall of specifics or a knowledge of simple facts and (2) higher-than-lowest cognitive level—objectives whose performance requires that the student engage in higher mental processes such as to comprehend, apply, analyze, synthesize, or evaluate information.

Affective / Affective behavior involves attitudes, interests, values, appreciations, and other feelings involving the emotional element. Because of the subjective nature of the learnings in this domain, accomplishments are often more difficult to assess than are those related to cognitive and psychomotor objectives. It is in the affective domain that informal teacher observation can be most effectively used. In many cases, especially in the self-contained classroom, where the teacher has close association with each child throughout the school day, affective behaviors may be more validly determined by teacher observation than by formal tests. Through careful observation of children in work or play situations, the teacher can observe any antisocial behaviors or socially acceptable behaviors, and can determine over a period of time whether or not a child is making progress in the development of positive social attitudes and skills.

The use of anecdotal records are valuable in this regard as a systematic means of recording over a period of time the child's pattern of behavior. Anecdotal records are objective descriptions of pupil behavior recorded by the teacher or observer following a significant incident or happening in the life of the child. Anecdotal records should be written up as soon as possible after a given incident is observed, so that all details of the actual happening can be recalled accurately. The record should contain a complete description of the incident, including the time, setting, and circumstances under which it occurred. Care must be taken to see that judgmental and emotional words and phrases are avoided. Taken over a period of time, these records can become an accurate account of an individual's characteristic behavior.

Briefly the properties of affective goals are:

1 Receiving—The child becomes aware of idea, process, or thing.

2 Responding—The child actively responds, doing something with or about phenomenon.

3 Valuing—The child exhibits a consistent attitude about the worth of some object, phenomenon, or behavior.

4 Organizing—The learner starts to establish a value system and has established a conscious basis for choice-making.

5 Characterizing—The internalization process is complete.

Psychomotor **/** This domain of learning relates directly to the teaching of motor acts and developing skills. As it relates to motor actions, improvement in skill or ability is a task of improving neuromuscular coordination, not a task of developing understanding. The skill level depends largely upon the development of muscular coordination and kinesthetic cues that guide the performance. Opportunities should be provided for the student to utilize specific skills in practical situations. Skills can degenerate quite rapidly when not used; therefore, the teacher should provide opportunities for their continued practice and reinforcement. Skills will tend to level off at whatever level of quality the student is permitted to display in his daily work. Although skill development is not as prominent in the teaching of the social studies as are the cognitive and affective learnings, it does constitute an important part of social studies teaching, for example, teaching cartographic skills and the manuscript writing used in connection with them.

The following behavioral objectives are organized into four divisions: lowest cognitive, higher-than-lowest cognitive, affective, and psychomotor. The behavioral objectives under each division are examples of what might be required of students as outcomes of unit studies. Such expectancies should provide an excellent means of evaluation in each of the major areas of learning in the social studies.

Lowest Cognitive Level

Behavioral objective: Given a list of twenty foods, the student will identify five kinds of food eaten by the early California Indians.

Behavioral objective: The student will be able to list on a chart five kinds of implements, utensils, and weapons used by early California Indians.

Behavioral objective: The student will be able to name three distinct kinds of climates found in Oregon and will point out their general geographical areas on a large map of Oregon.

Behavioral objective: The student will be able to name one county which is first in the state of Oregon in the production of any given product and will give the name of the product.

Higher-than-Lowest Cognitive Level

Behavioral objective: The student will describe orally or in writing how the climate and topography of California affected where the early Indians lived.

Behavioral objective: The student will describe in a written report the characteristics of the California Indians and explain why they dressed as they did.

Behavioral objective: The student will select one of the natural regions of Oregon and list the reasons why he would like to live there.

Behavioral objective: The student will analyze in writing the relationship between the lumber industry and banking in the state of Oregon.

Affective

Behavioral objective: The student will describe orally or in writing problems encountered in our society by a minority group such as the American Indian and will describe how he would feel if he were a member of a minority group.

Behavioral objective: The student will write a report on the topic "What I Appreciate About Oregon."

Psychomotor

Behavioral objective: The student will construct a model of the different types of Indian shelters.

Behavioral objective: The student will prepare a meal using only products produced in Oregon.

Behavioral objective: The student will find out the difference between "indoor" and "outdoor" plywood by using plywood in actual construction activities, for example, making model houses, Ping-Pong paddles, or a jigsaw-puzzle map of the state of Oregon.

Of the above objectives, the mastery of specific facts at the lowest cognitive level is the easiest to test. Traditionally, they have been considered the most important kinds of learnings in the social studies. Because of the high value that teachers have placed on the mastery of specific subject-matter content, evaluation in the social studies has often been narrow, with an overdependence upon one or two written assignments; and teacher-made objective tests have frequently dominated such evaluation programs. Therefore, there is need today for a variety of evaluation techniques designed to yield information across the broad range of objectives in the social studies. Assuming that teachers have the needed skills, evaluation must be determined largely by the nature of the objective being evaluated.

PREASSESSMENT

Ideally, preassessment or pretesting should be an important part of teaching in all content areas. Often, however, teachers feel that they lack the time, resources, or skill to preassess adequately. Nevertheless, the ideal goal would be to preassess and then instruct each learner, beginning where he is in all content material.

Preassessment is an indispensable part of the organization of individualized units of work in the social studies. Until a teacher preassesses his learners, he cannot possibly tailor instruction to meet their individual needs and abilities. Through preassessment the teacher can determine whether or not the learner (1) has the knowledge and skills necessary to begin instruction and (2) can already demonstrate the behavior for which the instruction is designed. The performance of the student on the pretest determines where he is to begin in the sequence of learning experiences. If the learner can already perform the objectives of a given lesson, he should be allowed to move to other objectives.

Preassessment may be done formally through the use of written tests or more informally through observation or oral questioning. Informal observation and questioning may be more appropriate for the early primary grades. Some form of preassessment, however, should be used with each unit of work studied throughout the school year. The teacher is then in a better position to place students where they can learn best, and the teacher can make wise decisions as to the next steps in the teaching sequence to meet individual needs.

OTHER EVALUATIVE TECHNIQUES AND DEVICES

Teacher-Pupil Evaluation

Teacher-pupil evaluation provides opportunity for the teacher to elicit views from the children regarding their progress or achievement in a large number of activities in the social studies, such as special projects, reports, study trips, committee work, or regular class assignments. This involves the children in a form of self-evaluation that is most useful. For example, the evaluation may center around committee work standards (How well did the work in the committee go today? Did everyone have an opportunity to contribute? How much more time will be needed to complete the project? Were all work materials cleaned up and put away in their proper places? What special materials will be needed for the next work session? What other special problems need to be discussed?) or in relation to a study trip just completed (How well did we observe safety standards? Did you take adequate notes? How could we have done better?).

This form of evaluation helps children become more sensitive toward others and more aware of individual standards and responsibilities. The teacher will find opportunities for similiar kinds of evaluation with individual pupils on individual assignments.

Charts of work standards, social behavior, or skills to be attained, developed cooperatively by the teacher and pupils, are valuable aids to the teacher-pupil evaluation. They establish standards against which pupils may judge their progress in each area of work. For the elementary grades, charts should be kept simple and uncluttered and should reflect many of the children's own ideas.

Sociometric Techniques

Although there seems to be some controversy regarding the value of sociometric study, particularly at the lower-grade levels, some valuable information can be gained that would be useful in both planning and evaluating social studies. The major tool of sociometric study is the sociogram, which is used to evaluate existing social relationships in the classroom and to identify any changes in social status that may take place from time to time as children engage in various kinds of group activity. The sociogram is constructed from an analysis of responses to questions asked of the pupils in a classroom. For example, the teacher might simply ask each child to write down the name of two children with whom he would most like to work on a given class project, or the names of two children he would prefer as close friends. The data collected through this means indicate a pattern of social relationships that exists at the present time. These patterns change quite often, particularly among younger children and, of course, vary with the type of questions asked by the teacher. Therefore, to be most valid, sociometric evaluations need to accompany each major activity or project in which the children are engaged. A simple diagram is then made showing the choices of each child.

Information derived from an analysis of the sociogram may be valuable in helping the teacher (1) identify the extent to which individual children are accepted by their peer groups, (2) make plans to help isolates and peripheral children improve social relationships and gain more status among the group, (3) form groupings to include new patterns of associations among the students, and (4) evaluate the progress and growth of the class in improved human relationships.

Because of the factors causing different patterns of social relationships to emerge in a class from time to time, one needs to be careful that he does not base all of his judgments on just one sociometric evaluation given at the beginning of school. Even at best, sociograms are not precise tools of evaluation.

Teacher-made Tests

A variety of teacher-made test items, both objective and subjective, have been devised to assess pupils' knowledge of the objectives of instruction in the social studies. Among them are multiple-choice items, true-false, matching, completion, short-answer, and essay-type questions. Douglass has categorized the various kinds of teacher-made tests into four basic types: "the dichotomous statement (or some variation on the true-false theme), the matching or organizing type of question, the extended response or essay question, and the multiple-choice or best answer item."[3]

Posttests

Upon completion of a unit of study, the teacher should administer a posttest to determine to what extent each pupil has acquired the major concepts and behavioral objectives outlined in the unit. Gaps in the pupil's knowledge of major understandings and in his ability to demonstrate the behaviors outlined would indicate a need for him to have additional learning experiences in the areas of deficiencies.

Inasmuch as paper-and-pencil tests are heavily dependent upon the child's ability to read and write, they may be of limited value for use with primary grade children and with many so-called culturally disadvantaged children. Their value increases as they are used with middle- and upper-grade children. With younger children and the culturally disadvantaged, other means may be utilized, such as oral testing, using discussion pictures, or having the child draw or act out his responses.

Needless to say, good test items are difficult to construct. They are of maximum value when they focus on concepts or large understandings and

[3] Malcolm P. Douglass, *Social Studies From Theory to Practice in Elementary Education* (Philadelphia: Lippincott, 1967), p. 468.

meanings rather than on trivial details. When test questions overemphasize the recall of specific facts and minutiae, they inevitably lead to an emphasis in the child's study upon isolated and inconsequential facts rather than upon principles and meaning. Experience in writing tests is one of the most important factors in the ability of the teacher to write meaningful and useful tests. It may be useful to the teacher to study examples of a variety of technically correct test items.

Many standard references on measurement, such as Buros[4] and Davis,[5] discuss the advantages and disadvantages of various kinds of tests, as well as giving suggestions for their construction and interpretation.

Standardized Tests

Standardized tests provide other means of evaluating pupil achievement in the more tangible outcomes of social science instruction. The "norms" for standardized tests are established by administering the tests to thousands of children throughout the country. Test norms are usually reflected in terms of grade-level scores and percentile rankings. Because standardized tests are developed and published for use in all parts of the country, the teacher can, if he desires, compare the growth or achievement of children in his group in the social studies with that of other children of the same age and same grade level.

However, certain precautions should be noted in interpreting the results of standardized tests. (1) Standardized tests are objective tests measuring knowledge of specific content and certain skills associated with reading maps, graphs, and charts. Few, if any, standardized tests have attempted to measure the broad range of social studies objectives including growth in creative abilities, attitudes and values, or problem-solving skills. (2) If the school district erroneously uses tests as a means of evaluating or comparing teachers, teachers often "teach for tests," which highly invalidates the results. (3) Because of local autonomy and wide variations in individual social studies programs throughout school districts in the United States, published tests often contain numerous items of information that pupils in local areas never had an opportunity to study or learn. (4) Most social studies achievement scores are based on the child's ability to read. In some cases a test may be more a test of reading ability than of social studies achievement. (5) There is a need for more and improved standardized tests in social studies for the elementary school, particularly on the primary grade level. At present, there is a general inadequacy of standardized tests for use in the social studies. (6) From among the available standardized tests appropriate for elementary school pupils, the school district should select one or more that relate most closely to the overall social studies objectives of the district. The district should then establish its own local norms for any test selected to be used over an extended period of time, against which children's progress from year to year can be plotted.

[4] O. K. Buros, *Sixth Mental Measurements Yearbook* (Highland Park, N.J.: Gryphon Press, 1965).
[5] Frederick B. Davis, *Educational Measurements and Their Interpretation* (Belmont, Calif.: Wadsworth, 1964).

An annotated list of social studies tests for use in elementary and secondary schools has been compiled by Peace.[6] Unfortunately there are few tests available for younger children. Some in the form of test batteries contain only short sections directly related to the social studies area. Subscores from test batteries can at best represent only a sampling of social studies information as compared to that obtained from separately prepared social studies tests.

The following is a partial list of sources of standardized tests, including both test batteries and separately prepared tests entirely devoted to the social studies curriculum.

Bureau of Educational Research and Service, State University of Iowa, Iowa City, Iowa 52240.

California Tests in Social and Related Sciences, California Test Bureau, Los Angeles, California.

Coordinated Scales of Attainment, Educational Test Bureau, 720 Washington Ave. S. E., Minneapolis, Minnesota.

Iowa Every-Pupil Test of Basic Skills, Houghton Mifflin Company, 2 Park St., Boston, Massachusetts 20107.

Metropolitan Achievement Tests, Harcourt Brace Jovanovich, Inc., New York, New York.

Scholastic Testing Service, 3774 W. Devon Ave., Chicago, Ill. 60645.

Sequential Tests of Educational Progress: Social Studies, Level 4, Grades 4–6, Educational Testing Service, Princeton, New Jersey 08540.

SRA Achievement Series, Science Research Associates, 259 Erie St., Chicago, Illinois 60611.

Stanford Achievement Test, Harcourt Brace Jovanovich, Inc., New York, New York.

Tests of Critical Thinking in Social Studies, J. W. Wrightstone, Bureau of Publications, Teachers College, Columbia University, 525 W. 120th St., New York, New York 10027.

Reporting to Parents

Reporting to parents is an important phase of pupil evaluation which requires that the teacher bring together in a meaningful form all the knowledge she has available on each member of her class. Because parents do not always understand the broad range of goals in the social studies, any interest they may have in their child's progress is related to his success on the acquisition of specific subject-matter content as represented by a letter grade. To this extent, the teacher has an additional responsibility to help *educate* parents so that they will gain a broader perspective of what the social studies program seeks to accomplish.

A wide variety of reporting practices can be found in elementary schools. It is quite likely, however, that the report card alone as a basic instrument for

[6] Barbara A. Peace, "Bibliography of Social Studies Tests," in *Evaluation in Social Studies,* Thirty-fifth Yearbook of the National Council for the Social Studies, ed. Harry D. Berg (Washington, D.C.: NCSS, 1965), pp. 230–247.

communicating progress to parents has outlived its usefulness. Any acceptable program must include along with the report card an opportunity for the teacher to meet face-to-face with the parents for individual discussions regarding their child's progress in school. It is only by this means that the more vital information about the child's progress in the social studies can be communicated effectively to parents. The teacher-parent conference provides an opportunity for the teacher to bring many reliable types of evidence in support of her evaluation of pupil progress.

This will require that the teacher be systematic about collecting evidence of many kinds regarding each child's progress. Perhaps a good approach would be for the teacher to keep an up-to-date individual file on each pupil. The kinds of information that might be collected for each individual folder would include samples of the pupil's daily work from time to time—particularly those samples where marked improvement was noted, copies of test results, both standardized and teacher-made, written reports, interest inventories, checklists of skill development, and anecdotal records written by the teacher that contain some indications of the child's growth in attitudes, social adjustment, and participation. Armed with this kind of information, the teacher could evaluate each child more accurately in relationship to his total growth and development.

In all phases of the evaluation program it is important for the child himself to have a knowledge of his progress. He should be made aware of how well he is doing in comparison with his own previous levels of performance. Corrective measures can then be planned cooperatively by the teacher and the pupil to remedy deficiencies.

Finally, continuous evaluation is the key to successful teaching in the social studies. Without continuous evaluation, social studies become like a ship without a rudder. But, since time is always limited in teaching, finding time for adequate and continuous evaluation in the social studies may seem overburdensome to some teachers. Nevertheless, with properly planned units of work containing the desired behavioral outcomes and with careful and systematic planning, the task of evaluation will not become too time consuming. In fact, the time spent will add greatly to the teacher's effectiveness in his major role, which is to teach.

A LOOK AT THE FUTURE IN THE SOCIAL STUDIES

For the past decade the social studies have been in a state of ferment and change. During this time, more than fifty major projects have been initiated to develop new materials and programs for the social studies. They have been financed by various agencies: the United States Office of Health, Education, and Welfare, private foundations, business, and public school systems. New proposals have been made for change in the social studies at all grade levels from kindergarten through the first two years of college. This reform movement is now having a great impact upon the social studies, touching upon the areas of instructional patterns, new materials, teaching strategies, and teacher preparation.

Current curriculum projects in the social studies have brought about considerable modification and change in the more traditional patterns of organization such as the "expanding-communities approach" and textbook-centered approaches. Some exciting new programs have been experimented with in virtually all the social science disciplines, including political science, economics, anthropology, geography, and history.

Some attempts have been made to organize the social studies around a single social science area. Two such projects are notable: Science Research Associates' "Our Working World," developed under the direction of Lawrence Senesh, is organized around economic concepts; and the Curriculum Study Project at the University of Chicago focuses on anthropological units of study. Although each project has focused on an individual social science, attempts have been made to integrate other social sciences in functional and meaningful ways. It is quite likely, however, that too heavy an emphasis has been placed upon a given discipline, to the exclusion of some vital understandings in other social science areas. Programs based upon a single discipline of the social sciences, regardless of attempts made to integrate subject matter, can never provide a complete program for the elementary school. Granted they have made a great contribution to elementary school social studies in their respective areas of specialties and have pointed new directions for study. This has enhanced greatly the total social studies program and the new knowledge from such studies should be utilized fully. It is quite likely, however, that social studies for the future on the elementary school level will of necessity be interdisciplinary in approach, utilizing more fully the learnings and contributions that all social science disciplines can make to the social studies. At the present time there is a movement toward programs that are multidisciplinary in scope, conceptually structured in organization, inductively orientated in method, and worldwide in involvement.

Throughout a child's school experience he would be exposed in some depth to all areas of the social sciences through an orchestration of the curriculum. At different points in his school experience, as he moves from grade to grade, a different social science would assume a leading role. For example, economic concepts might be dominant in the child's early school years, becoming a little less dominant during the later elementary school years as anthropological and historical ideas and concepts receive additional attention.

In new curricular patterns, also, a greater emphasis is being placed upon contemporary events in the child's life and upon "hot issues" related to national and world problems. In the new social studies there will be a place for children to come to grips, although on an elementary level, with the more pressing problems of our society. This will help prepare them to deal more adequately with such problems in the future. False assumptions have been made about the learning potential of children. We have expected too little of them. Educators have tended to protect children from such "harsh realities of life" as discrimination, unemployment, crime, and war. They are part of the children's lives whether by exposure to mass media or through their own experiences. Newer programs, then, will place more emphasis upon these kinds of problems. Some of our most pressing ones at present relate to group relations, interactions between groups and subcultures, ecological imbalance, the moral values and priorities of our society, population explosion, and war and peace. Of course, it cannot be expected that we will solve automatically all of these problems by exposing children to them in the schools. It will require the effort and cooperation of all institutions and agencies of our society: the home, the school, churches, and government. But the elementary school can and should make a small beginning—every effort is needed.

Because of the diversity of local conditions in the schools of our country, a wide variety of plans for the social studies should emerge. These plans reflect the local conditions and needs. We still need more of such programs. Any tendency toward the establishment of a national curriculum for the social studies should be avoided. It would be most helpful if a number of centers for the dissemination of social studies information and materials were established throughout the country as a means of aiding administrators and teachers in planning new programs.

The new social studies will demand better-trained teachers than ever before. If a teacher is to gain a broad liberal education and learn the new math, the new English, the new social studies, and other modern methods of teaching, five-year teacher training programs will be needed. Even a five-year program may become a minimal requirement. Finally, in the long run, a social studies program can be no better than the teacher, no matter how good it may look on paper.

QUESTIONS AND ACTIVITIES

1 / Discuss evaluation in the social studies from two points of view: (1) the traditional emphasis and (2) what you would consider to be an ideal program for today's social studies.

2 / Explain why a well-written behavioral objective is of special value to the teacher in selecting and evaluating learning experiences.

3 / Write four behavioral objectives. (Include one in each area: lowest cognitive, higher-than-lowest cognitive level, psychomotor, and affective.)

4 / Define preassessment. What kinds of essential information does preassessment give you about a student?

5 / What are some of the precautions that should be observed in the selection and use of standardized tests?

6 / Refer to a standard work on measurement and test construction. Construct a pretest and a posttest on a unit of work of your choice.

7 / Describe the kinds of evaluation instruments you would use in assessing attitudes and values.

8 / Collect sociometric data on a group of elementary school pupils. Make a sociogram and analyze the social relationships that exist. How could you use this data to the best advantage in the classroom?

SELECTED REFERENCES

Berg, Harry D. (ed.). *Evaluation in the Social Studies.* Thirty-fifth Yearbook. Washington, D.C.: National Council for the Social Studies, 1965.

Chauncey, Henry, and Dobbin, John E. *Testing: Its Place in Education Today.* New York: Harper & Row, 1963.

Davis, Frederick B. *Educational Measurements and Their Interpretation.* Belmont, Calif.: Wadsworth, 1964.

Ebel, Robert L. "The Problem of Evaluation in the Social Studies." *Social Education* 24 (1): 6–10, January 1960.

Evans, K. M. *Sociometry and Education.* London: Routledge & Kegan Paul, 1962.

Flanders, Ned A. *Teacher Influence, Pupil Attitudes and Achievement.* Washington, D.C.: Superintendent of Documents, 1965.

Fox, Robert, et al. *Diagnosing Classroom Learning Environments.* Chicago: Science Research Associates, 1966.

Green, John A. *Teacher-made Tests.* New York: Harper & Row, 1963.

Gronlund, Norman E. *Measurement and Evaluation in Teaching.* New York: Macmillan, 1965.

Hoffmann, Banesh. *Tyranny of Testing.* New York: Crowell-Collier and Macmillan, 1962.

Hunnicutt, C. W. (ed.). *Social Studies for the Middle Grades.* Washington, D.C.: National Council for the Social Studies, 1961.

Jarolimek, John. *Social Studies in Elementary Education.* Third edition. New York: Macmillan, 1967. Chap. 16.

APPENDIXES

appendix

BASIC IDEAS OR CONCEPTS FROM THE SOCIAL SCIENCES

The following lists of major generalizations in the social sciences represent a statewide effort to identify the central understandings of greatest importance to the social studies curriculum.[1] Although general in nature, they provide a base point for the selection of subject-matter content in the social studies. The California State Curriculum Commission called upon social scientists in each of the various social science disciplines represented to provide them with a suggested list of basic generalizations. Such lists are helpful to teachers and curriculum workers in that they provide a complete up-to-date outline of the important understandings in each area of concern to the social studies.

III / BASIC IDEAS OR CONCEPTS FROM THE SOCIAL SCIENCES

Each of the eight social sciences contributes certain basic ideas or concepts to the social studies program. These are broad, central generalizations that should become progressively more meaningful, even though they are not specifically introduced, through organized learning experiences at the various grade levels.

To prepare the generalizations which are presented on the following pages, groups of social scientists throughout the state were asked to review the content of their particular discipline and to assess its contributions to competent citizenship in our modern, complex society. The findings of these groups

[1] *Social Studies Framework for the Public Schools of California* (California State Department of Education, June 1962), pp. 89–109.

were then studied and analyzed by educators and other interested citizens on a statewide basis. As the generalizations were developed, "goals of understanding" were formulated. These were appropriate for application to adults rather than to a particular grade. Therefore, the curriculum planner must decide what subgeneralizations, concepts, and factual information are appropriate for youth in each of the grades that comprise the elementary and secondary school programs. These subdivisions then become reference points for planning and organizing instruction and for preparing courses of study and other classroom materials. The reference points need to be cumulative so that understanding in the social studies is moved in the direction indicated by the generalizations.

Although these goals for understanding will be invaluable in guiding school district personnel in the selection of specific units of instruction, in determining learnings to be stressed, and in appraising pupil progress, they must necessarily be supplemented by understandings applicable only to the local community.

It is also recognized that the content of the social studies does not come exclusively from eight social sciences. When children and youth study topics related to this aspect of the curriculum, they utilize information from additional fields. Such is particularly the case in the elementary school, where pupils sometimes need information about the natural and physical sciences, art, music, literature, health, and safety to comprehend the significance of what they are studying. Although a setting for the practical application of information from these fields is thus established in a way that enhances learning in the social studies, the fields also receive attention in other parts of the instructional program.

The social studies simply provide an opportunity to bring the contributions of related social disciplines into a meaningful context for children and youth. In so doing, they serve as an essential and central aspect of general education and as a background for successful living in our American society. Contributions of the eight social sciences, however, do more than indicate the basic sociocivic learnings that relate to general education. In addition, they reflect persistent contemporary problems. Influences of general trends in our society—such as population growth, increased mobility of the population, and changes in the pattern of family living—can be noted in a number of the ideas or concepts.

These social science generalizations should not be taught but should emerge as conceptualizations from what has been studied. Acquiring of new information is essentially training, but the discussion and relation of new facts to other knowledge from which generalizations may be drawn constitute education.

Curriculum specialists know that pupils can generalize only to the extent that the breadth and depth of their knowledge will permit and that limitations in this process cannot be overcome by pupils through learning to verbalize a mass of words that have little or no meaning to them. Children and youth acquire meaning only from a broad base of experience and learn to generalize at ever higher levels only through skillful guidance from informed teachers.

Generalizations from Geography

Overview

Geography deals with areal arrangement. Its principal orientation is toward the earth's surface and the varying distributional patterns created by nature and man. It seeks to define the earth's physical and cultural features, to show their distribution, to make them understandable by explaining the basic forces or factors that affect them, and to present the more fundamental of their inter-relationships. Because of its dual nature, geography is both a natural and a social science and, as such, helps to integrate both. As part of its educational responsibility, geography seeks to help pupils become earth-minded (even universe-minded) and spatially oriented, to build a useful mental image of the world and its parts, and to develop the pupils' sense of space in a manner similar to the way in which history seeks to develop their sense of time.

Physical Geography

It is the task of physical geography to describe and explain the distribution of surface features and to define natural regions that are caused by and continuously affected by forces and processes in nature.

1 Life on the earth is influenced by the earth's (global) shape, its size, and its set of motions.

2 The shape of the earth causes the unequal distribution of sunlight, or energy, from the sun, which in turn influences the circulation of the atmosphere and causes differences in climate and natural vegetation.

3 Earth movements of rotation and revolution are basic to understanding climate and time: rotation of the earth on its axis is a measure of time and causes night and day; seasons are caused by a combination of revolution, inclination, and parallelism of the earth's axis.

4 Earth movements and earth-sun-moon relationships also offer bases for the understanding of the geography of outer space.

5 Weather, climate, and earth crustal movements affect the surface of the earth and cause regional differences in landforms, minerals, drainage, soils, and natural vegetation.

6 Climate is determined by sunlight, temperature, humidity, precipitation, atmospheric pressure, winds, unequal rates of heating and cooling of land and water surfaces, irregular shape and distribution of land and sea, ocean currents, and mountain systems.

7 Because of various combinations of heat and moisture and the distributions of these two factors, the earth is divided into climatic regions, consisting of tropical, middle latitude, polar, and dry lands; each of these types has several subtypes. These classifications are a means of organizing information about the earth.

8 The crust of the earth consists of various types of rocks that

influence topography. It contains useful mineral deposits and is the parent material of soils.

9 Soil, water, solar energy, and air are the natural resources most indispensable to man. The great source of all activity and life on earth is heat from the sun.

10 Soil and vegetation may be thought of as the cover over the nonliving surface configuration. This cover provides the landscape with character and color.

11 Major climatic regions coincide approximately with major vegetation zones because vegetation is related to climatic conditions. Natural vegetation is a great resource utilized by man.

12 Soils are altered by nature and man. Nature combines the action of climate, vegetation, and animals on parent materials to produce regional variations in soils.

13 The physical elements of the earth are a unit, and no part can be understood fully except in terms of its relationship to the whole.

Cultural Geography

Cultural geography is concerned with the distribution of man and his activities on the earth's surface. Since man's occupation of an area is affected by the physical environment, cultural geography is also concerned with the adjustments that he must make to this environment. The nature of these adjustments depends upon man's stage of technology and on the controls of social behavior and nature.

Cultural geography involves not only population distribution but also settlement patterns; land-use activities; ethnic, linguistic, and religious characteristics; and features of political organization. Since cultural geographers are interested in the activities of people in relation to their spatial organization, they seek to interpret the various world, regional, and local patterns of economic, social, and political behavior.

1 Man constantly seeks to satisfy his needs for food, clothing, and shelter and his other wants; in so doing, he attempts to adapt, shape, utilize, and exploit the earth. Some aspects of the natural environment, however, are not significantly altered or utilized by man.

2 The significance of the physical features of the earth is determined by man living in his environment. The natural environment may set the broad limits of economic life within a region, but it is man who determines its specific character within the limits of his culture.

3 To exist, man must utilize natural resources. Groups develop ways of adjusting to and controlling the environment in which they exist. Human change, and even the whole structure of civilization, may depend upon the nature and extent of man's supply of energy and his ability to utilize and control it.

4 The extent of man's utilization of natural resources is related to his desires and to his level of technology.

5 The processes of production, exchange, distribution, and

consumption of goods have a geographic orientation and vary in part with geographic influences. The nature of the organization of economic processes within an area (spatial organization) results from the kinds of resources, the stage of technology, and the sociopolitical attitudes of the population.

6 The location of production is controlled by the factors of land (natural resources of the physical environment), labor, and capital. In most cases, the attainment of maximum efficiency, as motivated by competition for the factors of production, determines location of production. In some cases, the location is determined by political or other social controls rather than by economic efficiency.

7 Land is less mobile than the other basic factors of labor and capital and has a dominant role in determining the location of production. Since people, in general, prefer to live near their work, this location becomes significant in the distribution of the population.

8 The kinds of climate, soil, native vegetation and animals, and minerals influence the nature and extent of man's achievements within each region. The amount and the kind of food needed for health vary with climatic conditions and man's technology.

9 Factors of production, including technology, are subject to change. Therefore, geography is concerned with changing patterns of land use.

10 Understanding the location of political or other social institutions is contingent upon a knowledge of the economy of an area. Since understanding of this economy depends in part upon a knowledge of the natural environment, it follows that political and social institutions are related to this environment.

11 The sequence of human activities and culture patterns is related to geographic location and accessibility and to the particular time in which human beings live. People in different stages of civilization react differently to similar environments.

12 Man and animals may, by their activities, upset the balance of nature. Man is different, however, in that he may do something—such as undertake conservation—to regain the balance.

13 Competition for the acquisition of the earth's natural resources sometimes results in political strife, and even in war.

14 Political cooperation and strife between nations are related to their geographic locations.

Summary

Geography encompasses more than a description of the earth's surface. Its prime concern in the social studies is the way in which man utilizes the raw materials and resources of his natural environment. The study of geography, therefore, has a major role in the development of civic competence. The problems of mankind cannot be fully understood or successfully solved without a knowledge of the geographic factors involved. Man's geographic distribution and his utilization of the resources of nature are basic to understanding many contemporary problems that have local, regional, and international implications. Geography is also closely related to all the social, biological, and physical sciences.

Generalizations from History

Overview

History is the record of what has happened to man. It is the effort to grasp the whole of human experience within a chronological framework. History is interpretive, imaginative, and normative. It is the script of human drama and also the drama.

Because of the interpretive role of history, the principal ideas—or major generalizations relative to it—necessarily involve other social sciences. The social sciences deal with man and his experience, but history alone presents a chronology of human experience.

The past furnishes a base from which to understand the present and from which to project into the future. The maturity of men and women is built upon reflections from the past. We are thus continuously indebted to the past and to the historical record of human activities.

Chronology, Sequence, and Change in History

1 Space and time form a framework within which all events can be placed. All of man's experience has occurred within a space and time framework; however, the same relationship does not necessarily apply to events as they have occurred in various parts of the world.

2 Man's struggle for freedom and human dignity has occupied a relatively brief period of time, as compared with the total span of man's existence.

3 The past influences the present, and the present cannot be adequately understood without knowledge of the past. Life goes on against the intricate tapestry of the past. History does not repeat itself, but events tend to occur in some sort of sequence. Events in nature usually occur uniformly. Human events are predictable, but to a lesser extent.

4 History contributes much to man's preparation for his social and political life. It is possible to derive basic principles and implications for thought and action in contemporary affairs from the historical backgrounds of our society.

5 Change has been a universal condition of human society. Change and progress are, however, not necessarily synonymous. Many civilizations have risen and fallen, but only some have contributed greatly to our present civilizations. The tempo of change has increased markedly in the recent past.

Main Tendencies in the Growth of Civilizations

1 History reveals a degree of homogeneity in mankind during all periods of recorded time. Environments in many places and regions have been altered physically, but human motives or drives within them have remained nearly the same.

2 Brotherhood, in the sense of peaceful cooperation, is one of man's worthiest and earliest historical concepts. Conflict and hostility are also within man's experience. Men of all races have many basic physical similarities. Geographical variations and time variations in man's environments help explain his past actions and continue to influence his behavior in the present.

3 In the contemporary world, historical events may have a significance that reaches far beyond the limits of a state or province or the place of their origin. The worldwide implications of such events must be understood.

4 Although certain historical customs and institutions have characterized individual civilizations or nations in the past, men in every age and place have made use of basic social functions in adjusting themselves to their world.

5 Past and present civilizations represent our cultural heritage. The races, cultures, and civilizations in most areas of the world and of most historical periods, beginning with the dawn of recorded history, have made some contributions to the growth of our present civilizations.

6 Interdependence has been a constant and important factor in human relationships everywhere.

Historical Interpretation

1 Such factors as the passing of time and advances in the techniques of scholarship have brought new perspectives and understandings of history. New interests and controversies of our own day and of past centuries have also had marked effects on the interpretation of events and ideas. Use of the historical method in fact-finding and problem-solving has made possible the discovery and use of new data and perspectives.

2 Human motives, drives, and ideas of many kinds, whether correct or incorrect in terms of historical progress and human improvement, have markedly influenced local, national, and international actions. The interpretation of these motives is one of the most critical tasks of historical analysis.

3 There are various traditional and contemporary interpretations of historical processes and movements of a national and international scope that may illuminate the study of history. Such historical processes are sometimes referred to by such terms as action and reaction, rise and fall, and growth and decline as they are applied to civilizations, nations, and empires.

4 The efforts of people, great material achievements, and important ideas are delineated, assessed, interpreted, and placed in perspective by historians.

5 History demonstrates that mankind has been motivated by morals and ideals and by material wants and needs. The demand for moral standards has persisted throughout man's experience. The ideals of men in all parts of the world and in all ages have been rooted in the value systems of large and small groups.

Summary

History is especially responsible for pointing up and interpreting the similarities and differences within man's experience. It serves as a yardstick of evaluation for the actions, institutions, and events of men. History, together with other of the social sciences, should show the great basic and universal values that comprise man's efforts to reach the worthiest of human goals. The study of history thus provides contemporary man with a basis for intelligent action now and in the future.

Generalizations from Political Science

Overview

Political science is the study of government—of the theory and practice of man in organizing and controlling the power needed to formulate public policy and administer the public services. It is divided into several branches.

Political theory is that branch which seeks to formulate principles, conclusions, and valid generalizations concerning the state and man's many relationships to it. The political theorist attempts to synthesize and integrate existing knowledge about the state, utilizing data and analyses of specialists both within and outside the social sciences.

Political scientists have been concerned with such basic questions as the origin of the state; the purpose or justification of the state; the nature of law, justice, and liberty; where the authority of the state should be reposed (i.e., in a monarch, an aristocracy, the whole people, a dictator, an elite, the proletariat); and, especially in the twentieth century, how far the authority of the state should extend into the realms of business, social life, and individual conduct.

Other branches of political science are *public law,* which embraces constitutional law, international law, administrative law, and criminal law; *politics,* which encompasses the institutions, processes, and methods of governing; *public administration,* which deals with the theory and practice of the executive branch of government; *national, state, and local government,* which includes study of the Constitution and the functions and services of government; *comparative government,* which includes comparisons of institutional phenomena and of political behavior and political values of foreign political systems; and *international relations,* which encompasses diplomacy, international law, economic policies, ideological competition and propaganda, military power, and international organization.

The State or Government

1 Throughout history, the peoples of the world have experimented with a wide variety of governmental forms. While Americans are engaged with their own governmental problems, the peoples of all other countries are endeavoring to resolve their problems of government.

2 Government is but one of the institutions serving society. The state or government is essential to civilization, and yet many human needs can best be met by the home, the school, the church, the press, and private business.

3 Two essential functions of government are to serve and to regulate in the public interest. The ultimate responsibilities of government are divided into five major categories: (a) external security; (b) internal order; (c) justice; (d) services essential to the general welfare; and, under democracy, (e) freedom. Perhaps the clearest indication of the importance of the state in the twentieth century lies in the fact that, although it has exclusive responsibility in none of these fields, it has residual responsibility in all.

4 In a democracy, government is the servant of the people; people are not the servants of government. Government is by

right an institution made by man for man. The source of authority resides in the people.

5 It is the business of government to do for the people what they cannot do or what they cannot do as well for themselves. Philosophies of government range from laissez-faire, in which a minimum of services is provided, to totalitarian collectivism, in which every phase of the individual's life is dictated for him. Government is indispensable to assure internal order and external security. Since order is indispensable if freedom is to have any genuine meaning—indeed, if life itself is to be tolerable—its establishment and maintenance are prime tasks of government.

6 No one yardstick is adequate for comparing different political systems. It is particularly important for citizens in a free society to understand the ideas and techniques characteristic of authoritarian political systems and to develop attitudes that will permit them to cope objectively with problems arising from the real or potential hostility of those systems.

7 When government is organized, it is essential that leaders be authorized power with which to act and that they be held responsible for its wise use.

8 Government cannot be effective unless it has the flexibility to cope with new conditions. Adaptation, social invention, and gradual change provide the best safeguards against political revolution. To fulfill its role in a democracy, government must be adaptable. The Constitution of the United States provides for flexibility to meet changing conditions.

9 Political parties and special interest groups perform certain necessary services in the governing process. The political parties of this country and of every free nation were formed so that citizens having common beliefs and interests may seek to mold basic policies and choose government leaders. Parties and interest groups both have a check-and-balance and force-and-counterforce role, which leads to evolutionary changes and growth. The politician generates interest and musters popular or legislative support necessary for formal approval or adoption of policy.

10 All nations in the modern world are part of a global, interdependent system of economic, social, cultural, and political life. The evolution of the international law of war has been paralleled by the effort to develop an international law of peace and by the attempt to devise and build international political institutions and organizations capable of making such laws effective. Consideration for the security and welfare of the people of other nations remains the mark of the civilized man and has now become the price of national survival as well.

Democracy

1 Democracy implies a way of life as well as a form of government.

2 Democracy is based on certain fundamental assumptions. Among these are the integrity of man, the dignity of the individual, equality of opportunity, man's rationality, man's ability to govern himself and to solve his problems cooperatively.

3 Man develops his fullest potential in a climate of freedom.

Much of the progress of civilization can be traced to man's search for a larger measure of freedom. For the truly civilized man, no amount of material wealth can ever compensate for lack of freedom. A society benefits when its individual members are relatively free to develop their creative talents.

4 Human beings are creatures of self-interest. For democracy to function, however, self-interest must be curbed to a degree in favor of public interest.

5 A chief goal of democracy is the preservation and extension of human freedoms. Freedom is unworkable, however, unless it is balanced by corresponding responsibility. Freedom appears to range from legal to political freedom, and from political to genuine economic and social freedom.

6 Civil liberty—freedom of thought, speech, press, worship, petition, and association—constitutes the core of freedom. With civil liberty, all other kinds of freedom become possible; without it, none of them can have any reality.

7 Basic to democracy is belief in progress. A free society is hospitable to new ideas and to change and encourages the unfettered search for truth. Peaceful action rather than violence is one of its hallmarks.

8 Certain factors are necessary for democracy to succeed and survive. These include (a) an educated citizenry; (b) a common concern for human freedom; (c) communication and mobility; (d) a degree of economic security; (e) a spirit of compromise and mutual trust; (f) respect for the rights of minority groups and the loyal opposition; (g) moral and spiritual values; and (h) participation by the citizen in government at all levels.

9 Opportunity for the individual to choose his type of occupation voluntarily is a concept that has flourished under democratic philosophy and practice and the capitalistic system.

Citizenship

1 The well-being of the state is dependent upon the education of its citizens.

2 A citizen can do his part in making democracy work only if he is sufficiently informed to think intelligently on the issues of the day. Information can best be provided by free and responsible mass media of communication.

3 The citizen has civic responsibilities as well as rights. ·

4 A democratic society depends on citizens who are intellectually and morally fit to conduct their government. Civic responsibility and moral courage are balanced wheels in a democracy. To fulfill their obligations of citizenship, individuals must be aware of the quality of service that must be performed by the government; they must also be willing to participate actively in community affairs. The capable citizen should evaluate objectively information received through mass media of communication in making political choices.

Summary

Political science helps individuals to become more keenly aware of their opportunities and obligations as citizens. It provides perspective for the study of such current problems as recruitment of personnel for civilian and military services, costs of defense and other public services, raising of revenues to underwrite these costs, and achievement of security. To be a capable and conscientious citizen, the individual needs (1) to understand the structure and function of government; and (2) to develop citizenship skills. These include knowing how to read newspapers, speak in public, and conduct meetings; and how to be an action-minded participant in the affairs of the school, community, state, nation, and world.

Generalizations from Economics

Overview

Economics is concerned with analyzing information, issues, and public policies connected with the production, distribution, and consumption of wealth and income. This discipline begins with the study of scarcity and unlimited wants and proceeds through specialized production, interdependence, exchange, markets, prices, costs, and public policy. Emphasized are economic stability and growth; the allocation of resources to their most important uses; an equitable distribution of income; and, in our economy, a wide range of economic freedom for workers to choose their jobs, consumers to choose goods, and investors and entrepreneurs to own property and choose their investments.

All problems that may properly be termed "economic" must be considered in these categories whether they originate in capitalist, socialist, fascist, or communist countries. Economic theory has been defined as "a method rather than a doctrine, an apparatus of the mind, a technique of thinking which helps its possessor to draw correct conclusions." The study of economics is thus important to the individual and society for both the knowledge which it provides and the thinking processes which it requires. Valid information about our economy and the ability to use it effectively are indispensable to effective citizenship in assessing many of the most pressing public issues of the day.

Consideration of specialized areas in economics must be based firmly on this approach. Included in economics are the study of money and banking, business cycles, public finance and taxation, industrial organization and public policies toward business, labor-management relations, accounting, finance, statistics, consumer economics, international trade and finance, economic growth and development, and comparative economic systems.

Economic Ends and Means

1 Economic welfare is a goal in most, if not all, modern societies. It is believed that it is beneficial for people to have more rather than fewer economic goods and that poverty *per se* is not desirable. Many economists believe that economic welfare is an important quality of society, that economic progress makes the other qualities of society more readily obtainable, and that the creative arts—such as painting, music, and literature—flourish more fully in a highly productive economy.

2 Productive resources are scarce, and human wants are unlimited. Since man cannot satisfy all of his desires for material goods, he must make choices. The essence of "economy" lies

in making wise decisions with regard to such matters as saving, spending, purposes of expenditures, kinds of investments, and types of jobs to be undertaken. The "real cost" of any end product is thus the alternatives sacrificed in producing it. This is known as the "opportunity cost principle."

The Gross National Product—A Measurement of Economic Achievement

1 The size of the Gross National Product (consisting of the total value of all economic goods—products and services—produced annually) depends upon many conditions. Among these are (a) the extent and richness of natural resources; (b) the number, quality, and motivation of the working population; (c) the amount and nature of capital goods (factories, houses, bridges, roads, machines and tools of all kinds) created through saving and investment; (d) the effectiveness of investors and entrepreneurs in organizing and developing productive activity; (e) the existence of a large free-trade area, in which the free flow of goods permits each locality to specialize in the production of those goods in which it has the greatest relative advantage and to obtain other goods by trade (the "principle of comparative advantage"); and (f) the presence of political institutions that are conducive to and encourage creative and productive effort on the part of all people. To maintain the conditions upon which high productivity (and consequently our high standard of living) depend, conservation must be practiced.

2 The size of both the GNP and population greatly influences economic welfare. This welfare depends upon the balance between population growth and depletion of resources and upon improvements in production techniques and expansion of capital goods. When population growth exceeds the capacity of the land and capital goods, output per worker declines unless there are compensating improvements in technology. This principle is known as the "law of diminishing returns."

3 The full use of productive facilities directly influences economic welfare. Fluctuations tend to be more severe in industrially advanced nations than in those that are primitive. In the former, specialization and complexity are vastly greater, shifts in demand and changes in techniques are more frequent, a larger proportion of resources is devoted to the production of durable consumer and producer goods, and substantial changes in the volume of investment expenditures are dependent upon the people's desire to save a fairly stable part of their incomes.

4 Government can contribute to the maintenance of high-level production and employment, rapid economic growth and progress, and the stability of the dollar by proper use of its authority through sound fiscal and debt-management policies.

5 High per-capita income is the result of high productivity of labor. The total income of a society is its total output of goods. Therefore, if American labor is ten times as productive as foreign labor, American wages can be ten times as high without curtailing the ability of American industry to sell its products in world markets. High wages thus rest on high productivity, not on tariffs.

The Composition of Income—The Allocation of Resources

1 Basic to sound economic organization is securing effective cooperation among specialized producers. The type of economic system determines how much of each commodity and service is to be produced and how each resource unit is to be allocated to its most important use.

2 In a competitive, private-enterprise system, prices indicate the relative value of goods and services. On the one hand, these prices reflect the willingness of buyers to buy and sellers to sell; and, on the other hand, they influence the decisions of both consumers and producers. A relatively high price tends to restrict present consumption and to stimulate production of a larger supply in the future. A relatively low price has the reverse effect. Raising or lowering a competitive price by artificial means, whether by private monopoly or governmental authority, is likely to aggravate the situation that the action is designed to alleviate, unless the change in price is accompanied by the power to affect directly future demand or supply in an appropriate manner.

3 A market price system works best when both buyers and sellers are highly competitive, well informed, and able and disposed to act in accordance with the information available (competition—knowledge—mobility). Thus, a free-enterprise system is supported and strengthened by government action designed to keep markets free (antitrust policy), buyers and sellers informed (prohibition of false advertising and laws against misrepresentation), and the system mobile. At the minimum, government must maintain order and justice, protect property, enforce contracts, and provide a sound money system in some fields if free enterprise is to be effective.

4 Because of special conditions in such fields as public utilities, government has been authorized to regulate prices to assure that they are not discriminatory. The quality of service rendered by electric power, gas, and telephone companies has also been regulated. In some cases, the government has directly undertaken the provision of services such as those required in the operation of post offices and distribution of the water supply.

5 There are many ways to organize economic activity. Most national economies in the world today, though differing in fundamental respects, make considerable use of the price system to ration goods, provide incentives for productive services, and allocate resources to their best uses. A free society provides opportunity and incentives for the individual to invest what he owns in an effort to make a profit.

The Distribution of Income

1 In a competitive system, the prices paid for productive services also serve to divide the total output of goods among those responsible for their production. Thus, the wages of workers, the dividends of investors, and the rents of landlords all provide the incomes that determine the size of each individual's claim to actual goods and services.

2 In a competitive market, each productive agent tends to receive as income a sum equal to the value of his productive

contribution to society. The greater the demand of the public for the particular service or product and the smaller the supply, the larger is the income. Those possessing the greatest skills demanded by the public tend to receive the highest incomes. Inequality in the distribution of income thus is the result of unequal payments for services and of unequal ownership of property. At the same time, the opportunity to acquire a larger income furnishes an incentive to develop abilities, to save and acquire property, and to use resources most efficiently and productively.

3 Imperfections in competition creat important public problems. The power of monopoly, whether exercised by buyers or sellers, management or labor, or private groups sometimes supported by government, usually distorts the allocation of resources and distribution of income.

4 The way to improve the standard of living for all the people is to increase productivity. Such has been the tremendous economic achievement in the United States. Industrial output per man-hour has increased six times since about 1850. Half of this gain has been realized in shorter hours (and more leisure) and half in more goods. Thus, the average length of the work week has been reduced 50 percent and, at the same time, real income per capita has tripled. The grinding poverty in which a large part of the world's population lives today is caused by the sheer unproductivity of human labor, not by deficiency in purchasing power or imperfection in the distribution of income.

Summary

Since the world's resources are insufficient to satisfy all wants, the study of economics, both theoretical and applied, is essential to the general education of all people. The individual makes economic decisions throughout his life. Through voting and other types of community participation, he helps to decide problems involving the economic welfare of all people.

Generalizations from Anthropology

Overview

Anthropology is the comparative study of man. It is concerned with his evolution and present characteristics as a biological form; with his various modes of organizing group life; and with his utilization of the natural environment. Thus, anthropology is a social science with a special relationship to the biological sciences.

Specialists in the field include physical anthropologists; anthropological linguists, who study the numerous unwritten languages of the world; archaeologists who seek to understand the story of prehistoric man by unearthing and studying remains of his activities; and cultural anthropologists, who investigate the cultures and modes of organization of extant societies to reconstruct prehistoric life and formulate generalizations about the essential characteristics of human social life.

Although anthropology may be primarily identified with the study of preliterate societies, many modern anthropologists devote all or part of their research to the study of major civilizations.

Anthropology has perhaps made its greatest contribution to social science by developing the concept of culture as its central theme, which has illuminated all the disciplines concerned with the study of human group life. Research method in anthropology is notable for its emphasis on long-term intimate observation and participation in the day-to-day life of the society under study.

Development Through Biological Evolution

1 Many persons believe that man has developed to his present form through the same processes of biological evolution by which animals have developed, and that the process of man's evolution has involved approximately one and one-half billion years. During this period, it is believed that a multitude of plant and animal forms have also evolved.

2 Physical anthropologists generally believe that man's separate stem of evolution spans several million years; however, in the scale of biological time man is a relatively new phenomenon.

3 Fossil remains of early man illustrate the ultimate evolution of distinctively human characteristics. The most important include a large brain, upright posture, manipulative hands, keen vision, and mouth and throat structures that make speech possible.

4 Man attained essentially his present-day biological attributes many thousands of years ago; his development since that time has been overwhelmingly cultural. Man's survival no longer depends chiefly on further biological evolution but rather on cultural development.

Development of Culture

1 Although man is identified with other living creatures, he differs profoundly by virtue of his development of culture.

2 Culture is a product of man's exclusive capacity to comprehend and communicate by means of language. Culture is socially learned and consists of the knowledge, beliefs, and values which humans have evolved to establish rules of group life and methods of adjusting to and exploiting the natural environment.

3 The variety of cultures developed by human societies affords man more diverse ways of living than animals. At a specific time and place, every society has a culture to some degree different from that of any other society, past or present.

4 Culture can be altered rapidly to cope with new conditions, and a society can borrow ideas readily from another culture. The superiority of man's cultural adaptations is thus emphasized in contrast with the slowly developing and constrictive biological adaptations of animals. Man's superiority illustrates the desirability of encouraging the continuance of many different cultural streams and of fostering sympathetic understanding of them. Such diversity enriches all of human life.

Cultural Heritage

1 No modern society has evolved more than a small fraction of its present cultural heritage. Each is deeply indebted to the contributions of other civilizations.

2 Man has left evidences of his presence in the Old World for at least the last 500,000 years. Paleolithic ("Old Stone Age") men invented and developed languages; made crude tools of chipped stone and probably less durable materials; eventually developed primitive clothing and learned to control fire; and still later domesticated the dog.

3 Some nine or ten thousand years ago, men living near the east end of the Mediterranean Sea first domesticated food plants and animals, thus beginning the Neolithic ("New Stone") Age. Such control of the food supply constituted one of the most far-reaching revolutions in human history. Populations increased rapidly where farming developed and permanent towns sprang up. The increased density of population and the additional security and leisure made possible by the relatively assured food supply gave man his first opportunity to develop those parts of culture which are the basis of civilization: writing, mathematics, and science; specialized technologies, such as weaving, pottery-making, and metallurgy; organized philosophy and religion; and legal, political, and economic organizations. These advances and their improvement began soon after the agricultural base was established.

4 No real break exists between the cultures of the ancient Neolithic farmers and the great civilizations of today. But the rate of cultural progress and the dissemination of new knowledge have accelerated tremendously. This speed-up—particularly in science and technology—has created new opportunities and new pressing problems for man. How the great cultural advances are put to use is the most urgent problem in the modern world.

Culture as an Influence on Society

1 The culture under which a person matures exerts a powerful influence on him throughout his life.

2 Since the culture of a society has such an impact upon an individual's personality, he feels, thinks, and acts in accord with its imperatives, not only to be accepted by his fellows but also to maintain his self-respect and confidence. The world into which every individual must fit is defined by his culture.

3 Language is an essential, effective, and exclusively human tool for the invention and transmission of culture. Art, music, and other symbolic and aesthetic expressions are also effective means of transmitting culture.

4 Culture, the creation of human activities, may be altered by them. Norms of culture are derived historically but are dynamic and thus may be subjected to planned change.

5 All cultures provide for the essential needs of human group life but differ, sometimes markedly, in the means by which they fulfill these needs. Different cultures result in different modes of thought and action. People generally prefer the culture of their own society but should recognize that they would probably prefer another culture if they had been subject to its influences to the same degree.

6 Anthropologists have been unable to discover a scientific basis for evaluating cultures as absolutely inferior or superior.

7 A major problem in the modern world is to discover ways in which social groups and nations with divergent cultures can

cooperate for the welfare of mankind and yet maintain as much respect for one another's cultural patterns as possible.

Human Beings as Members of Homo Sapiens

1 Since long before the beginning of written history, all human beings have been members of a single biological species, the *Homo sapiens*. For convenience of description and classification, anthropologists divide the species into "races," each of which has distinctive, observable *physical* traits. These traits, however, merge imperceptibly into one another so that most men possess characteristics of more than one race.

2 Populations have seldom remained isolated long enough, nor have they been subjected to sufficiently intensive natural selection, to become homogeneous races. Modern, worldwide interdependencies and rapid transportation and communication make it clear that such isolation cannot be expected in the future.

3 Anthropologists distinguish three main stocks or extreme limits of human biological variability: Mongoloids, Caucasoids, and Negroids. The great bulk of humanity is intermediate between the extremes.

4 Physically, all human beings are much more alike than different. Geneticists estimate that all human beings have more than 99 percent of their genes in common and that the most extreme variation results from genetic differences in less than 1 percent of the genes. Differences between members of the same main stock are frequently greater than differences between persons of different groups.

5 A common misconception is that groups can be identified as "races" on the basis of differences in language, religion, or nationality. These differences are cultural and nonbiological. So-called "ethnic groups" are generally regarded to have one or a combination of these characteristics. Even when biological traits are considered to identify a group, wide physical variations are likely to exist within it. Such an ethnic group is, in general, a minority, either in numbers or in power, whose culture differs to some degree from the majority group of the locality. If cultural differences are to be cherished for their enrichment of human life, ethnic groups should not suffer disadvantages or discrimination merely because they vary culturally from the norm of the majority.

Cultural Participation and Contributions

1 Human beings, regardless of their racial or ethnic background, are nearly all capable of participating in and making contributions to any culture.

2 The environment in which a person lives and his opportunities for personal growth have profound effects upon the development of every individual. When these opportunities are limited by cultural poverty or repressive action, society loses as much as the individual.

3 So-called "race problems" are cultural problems arising from conflicts between ethnic groups or an ethnic group and the majority population. If the positive social value of cultural diversity is recognized, ethnic differences can add to the general richness of life.

Summary

The person who has gained some anthropological knowledge about the range of human variation, both physical and cultural, and who understands and accepts the anthropological viewpoint about the causes and positive values of such differences will understand more fully his own behavior and that of others. Study of a variety of cultures increases a person's understanding of his own culture and reactions to life situations. The study of anthropology can also increase a person's effectiveness in daily life by helping him to understand the viewpoints of others and to be more effective in adapting to, introducing, or controlling social and cultural changes. Through knowledge of anthropology, a person can learn to appreciate man's universal qualities.

Generalizations from Psychology

Overview

Psychology is the science of human behavior. Its aim is the understanding and prediction of behavior. Broadly speaking, psychology is concerned with the scientific study of all its forms, such as learning, growth and development, thinking, feeling, perceiving, social behavior, personality development, and atypical behavior; and with the physiological processes underlying behavior. Psychology is closely related to both the social studies and the biological sciences.

Individual psychology is concerned with the description and understanding of the patterns of behavior exhibited by the person. Included are the nature of growth and development, appraisal of personality characteristics, measurement of individual differences in various aspects of behavior, and the discovery of the pattern of influences producing given forms of behavior, such as aggression, withdrawal, delinquency, and creativity.

Social psychology is a bridge between sociology, which focuses attention on understanding large social settings and group structures, and psychology, which focuses attention primarily on understanding individual behavior and personality. Social psychology deals with such problems as the effects of social pressure on the behavior and personality of individuals, differences in the behavior patterns of individuals living in the same culture groups, and the processes through which the behavior of individuals is influenced by their culture groups.

Behavior

1 Behavior is caused and is not its own cause. Each form of individual behavior has a pattern of causes that are multiple, complex, and interrelated. Behavior is not capricious or random. The discovery of causes leads to an understanding of behavior.

2 Human behavior is purposive and goal-directed. The individual may not always be aware of basic purposes and underlying needs that are influencing his behavior. The study of psychology attempts to bring about a greater awareness of the underlying causes of behavior.

3 Behavior results from the interaction of genetic and environmental factors. Through genetic influences, all individuals have

a potentiality for development and learning; yet these genetic factors produce differences among individuals. The character of the physical and social environment promotes or limits the degree of realization of the individual's potentialities.

Influence of Social Groupings

1 As a biologic organism, the individual possesses at birth certain physiological needs, but the methods of satisfying these needs and their subsequent development are to a great extent socially determined by his particular cultural unit.

2 Through the interaction of genetic and social and physical environmental factors, the individual develops a pattern of personality characteristics. This pattern includes motives for action, the organization and development of self, values and standards of conduct, and relationships with other individuals.

3 Individuals differ from one another in personal values, attitudes, personalities, and roles; yet, at the same time, the members of a group must possess certain common values and characteristics.

4 Social groupings develop as a means of group cooperation in meeting the needs of the individuals. The basic unit of the family makes it possible for two individuals to cooperate in producing and training children. Similarly, other social groupings—such as communities, social organizations, and nations—enable individuals to work together toward satisfaction of common needs. The nature and structure of groupings tend to change and become more complex with the circumstances under which man lives.

5 Every individual is a member of several social groups, each of which helps to satisfy his needs. The child starts life as a member of a family but soon establishes additional memberships in school, neighborhood, church, and other groups. As he matures, he extends his membership into a greater variety of groups.

Society and the Individual

1 Each of the social groups to which an individual belongs helps shape his behavior. Members of different societies learn different ways of acting, perceiving, thinking, and feeling. Groups exert pressures on their members so that they will accept and follow group ways and mores. The behavior of any individual reflects in many ways the influences of group pressures.

2 Differences are important in the personality structure and behavior of individuals and make possible the infinite variety of work and recreation activities that characterize modern culture. Differences also furnish a basis for flexibility and creativity, which are essential to social change and development. In any social group, the range of differences among individuals is likely to be greater than the differences between any two groups.

3 Socialization processes, such as methods of child training, differ markedly in different social classes, groups, and societies. Personality structure and behavior are largely influenced by

these processes. Individuals develop standards of values that reflect these influences as they seek to relate themselves to the group and to satisfy personal needs.

4 The satisfaction of social needs is a strong motivating force in the determination of individual behavior. Values placed on learning, as well as levels of aspiration, are largely attributable to the mores of the individual's "reference groups." What sometimes appears to be nonconforming behavior may be in reality conforming behavior in terms of a particular group in which an individual seeks status. The strong human tendency to conform to social pressures often prevents individuals from seeing reality. The stereotyping of individuals because of racial or cultural backgrounds is another example. In general, non-cooperative, aggressive behavior indicates that the individual's need for social acceptance has been frustrated. The individual displaying such behavior usually has been forced, through repeated experiences of rejection, to develop an attitude of defeat and inferiority.

5 The behavior of individuals is related to the structure and organization of the group in which they are placed. A range of roles, such as leadership, fellowship, aggression, and sub-mission, may be exhibited by the same individual in different groups. The "need-satisfying" quality of a group and the member-to-member relationship influence behavior.

6 For preservation of its identity, a social group resists change through the phenomena of cultural lag and conservatism. A social group also changes in various degrees to preserve its identity when new conditions arise.

Summary

Psychology contributes to the social studies through its content and method. Both are important to those who guide learning experiences. Generalizations that deal with relationships between individual behavior and group structure illustrate important considerations in the development of content and method.

Generalizations from Sociology

Overview

Sociology is a scientific study of the social relations which men develop in their interaction with one another. Sociologists analyze the basic structures and functions of societies and of associations and groups within societies to discover how they became organized, to identify the conditions under which they become disorganized, and to predict the conditions for reorganization.

Groups, Society, and Communication

1 The work of society is performed through organized groups. Group membership requires that individuals undertake varied roles involving differing responsibilities, rights, and opportunities. Groups differ because of their purposes, their institutions, heritage, and location. Nevertheless, they are generally similar in organization, structure, and properties. Every person belongs to many groups, and, therefore, groups overlap in member-

ship. In an open-class society, an individual may move up or down in the social system and thus experience significant changes in group membership. An individual's participation in several groups may produce conflicting demands and involve him in several roles that have varying responsibilities and opportunities. Moreover, any group may change its membership and its objectives. Therefore, the individual needs to analyze his relationship to various groups to discern the conflicting demands made upon him and to recognize that he must identify himself as a person as well as a group member. There are differences in the significance or importance of membership in various groups. Many stereotypes ignore their important characteristics.

2 Communication is basic to the existence of culture and groups. Individuals and groups communicate in many ways other than language. However, every type of communication involves symbolism of varying meanings. These differ from one group to another. Basically communication takes place between individuals. Therefore, the tools of communication are vital to every individual. Stereotyping and ethnocentrism are serious distorting elements in the communication process.

Personality and the Socialization Process

1 The expression of man's biological drives is influenced by his social environment.

2 The realization of self is modified by contacts with others.

3 Socialization results from the methods of child training and the experiences of childhood. Social controls and pressures tend to lead to the child's acceptance of the folkways and mores of his culture.

4 Role is determined by the expectations of others. Nonconformity, for example, is perceived in one culture as leadership behavior. In others, it may be regarded as damaging to society. Man occupies different social roles as he moves from group to group.

5 Status within a culture is achieved by means of the prestige attached to natural and artificial differences, such as caste, vocation, class, age, sex, and individual traits.

6 Individual or group organization or disorganization reflects the presence or absence of coordinated and integrated behavior.

Social Relations and Culture

1 An established society, association, or social group gradually develops patterns of learned behavior accepted by and common to its membership. These patterns, together with their accumulated institutions and artifacts, make up the cultural "way of life" of the society and its associations and groups.

2 Social relations and their complexes are generally shaped by culturally defined rights and duties shared by members of a group.

3 Cultures vary from society to society. Any given culture changes in the course of time. Some behavior and institutions within a culture are universal while others vary widely, even during the same period.

4 Changes and variations may result from factors generated by the culture itself, such as the invention and use of machines, or contact with other societies and cultures.

5 Children growing up within a society tend to learn that its particular behavior patterns, folkways, and institutions represent the "right" values and that those of other societies are "wrong" values.

6 Within any large and complex society, subsocieties with varying cultures exist. Often, these subsocieties consist of peoples who have migrated and are regarded as minority groups in the larger society.

7 People with a common culture sometimes become grouped as social classes and think of themselves as having (a) status or position; and (b) roles or functions quite distinct from those of other classes. A society which becomes so rigidly stratified that it allows little, if any, significant interaction between classes is described by sociologists as having a social caste system.

8 Culture tends to standardize human behavior and to stabilize societies by developing many interrelated and elaborate institutions.

9 Societies that fail to evaluate continuously these institutions and modify them intelligently are subject to cultural lag. This is a maladjustment between parts of a culture that leads to social disorganization. Cultures that fail to make adjustments rapidly enough tend to be absorbed or exploited by more aggressive and rapidly developing cultures. Sometimes societies are eliminated in the process.

10 Internal cultural crises tend to provoke social revolutions. These purport to bring about sweeping changes in the old social order.

Demography and Human Ecology

1 Many individual, social, and physical problems are influenced by changes in population. These problems may involve considerations of old age, youth, migration, war, housing, famine, employment, government, transportation, recreational activities, education, vocational opportunities, sanitation, social controls, living habits, and medical facilities.

2 National migration develops cultural diversity within a group and cultural diffusion among groups.

3 The environment influences man's way of living. Man in turn modifies the environment. As he becomes more technically efficient, man is less influenced by his environment and more able to modify his environment. The spatial and temporal distribution of populations and their institutions, as well as the processes that bring about their establishing of patterns, is called human ecology. This is the study of the reciprocal relationship between the community and its physical and social environment. It involves, for example, climate, clothing and shelter, natural resources, water and food, social environment and institutions, and folkways and mores.

4 Individuals generally function as members of communities. A community has a fixed geographic location, but its essence lies in the interaction of the persons that comprise it. They are

grouped in a locality to cooperate and compete with one another for sustenance, survival, and cultural values. Communities have been increased and developed by modern inventions.

Social Processes

1 Societies develop in accordance with recurrent sequences of interaction called social processes. Social interaction and communication are the general processes through which more specialized processes evolve. These include association, dissociation, and stratification; cooperation and accommodation; competition and conflict; and assimilation.

2 In association, human beings in interaction continuously organize and join groups and "societies." Dissociation is illustrated by the fact that groups tend to dissolve in time, losing members to new groups. Stratification is the tendency of individuals, families, and groups to become ranked by society into a hierarchy of social classes based on heredity, wealth, education, occupation, group memberships, and other status factors.

3 Cooperation is illustrated by the way in which members of families and other more intimately related social groups tend to work together in performing functions of community living and in attaining common goals. Those persons who cannot fully accept other members of their intimate groups, other groups, or the way of life of these groups, often make the necessary compromises or adjustments to remain in the groups or larger community and to enjoy their high priority values. This process is known as accommodation.

4 In competition, persons become rivals of other group members or groups. They may compete as well as cooperate. Conflict occurs when a rivalry precipitates a clash or struggle because either side feels it must defend its social institutions and values or impose them on the other side.

5 Assimilation is the process through which persons and groups migrating to a new environment lose previously acquired modes of behavior and gradually accept those of the new society.

Social Control

1 Societies require a system of social control to survive. This control is based upon uncodified rules of behavior (mores and values). Infraction of the rules will bring ostracism or pressure to conform to the controls.

2 Some of the techniques of social control that are used by groups on individuals to secure conformity are shunning, ostracism, gossip, jeering, praise, approval, and acceptance. Informal social control is the strongest factor in securing conformity to group standards.

3 Social control, particularly in complex societies, is also partially secured by formal, codified rules of behavior (laws), infractions of which result in formal penalties. The formal, legal

controls are imposed upon those areas of social life which are too important to be governed by informal controls. When a "power group" seeks an objective which cannot be reached by other means, it may attempt to impose legal controls.

Summary

The study of sociology reveals and clarifies the structure of groups, group phenomena, and the role of the individual in various kinds of groups. Sociologists endeavor to predict social behavior by use of the scientific method and social research. These means of investigation and the application of what is known about group processes help to solve social problems. Thus, sociology contributes directly to the social studies.

Contributions of Philosophy

Overview

Within the past two hundred years, fields which were once considered a part of philosophy have been developed as separate social sciences. Before their emergence, philosophy and history were the disciplines within which students of human behavior inquired into the conditions and consequences of institutionalized life. Philosophy continues to be concerned with questions, concepts, and valuations related to the study of man and appraisals of his conduct. Thus, it is similar in subject matter to other social sciences. Philosophy has an essentially critical role in the analysis and valuation of concepts and generalizations contributed by these fields. It is the responsibility of philosophers to explore methodology, foundations of theorizing, and judgment criteria concerned with man's activities and values.

Although philosophy is not studied separately in elementary and secondary schools, it contributes to all social studies undertaken in the spirit of *inquiry*. If the study is to enlist pupils as effective participants, they must acquire and employ intellectual skills requisite for following arguments, clarifying ideas, and submitting claims to tests. Social studies conducted to develop the spirit of inquiry must utilize these skills.

Logic, Scientific Method, and Ethical Analysis

1 Philosophy contributes to social studies the tools of logic, scientific method, and ethical analysis. It contributes also to social philosophy, political philosophy, and the philosophy of history. These tools and areas of study equip individuals to cope critically with questions, problems, concepts, theories, and value judgments that arise in discussion of race, private property, the family, the state, human nature, obligation of others, socialism, free enterprise, civic responsibility, civil disobedience, classes and class conflict, self-government, the rights of man, and the relation of religion to morality.

2 Because of the influence of interests and emotionally charged words in discussions of human affairs, the teacher needs to make clear the "how" and "why" of requirements laid down for testing assertions on the basis of evidence and right reasoning

and to point out the pitfalls that trap discussions that do not fulfill these requirements. By utilizing the requirements and developing respect for them, pupils learn to make intelligent choices and decisions as citizens. They learn how to face up to controversial issues through objective examination of ideas and arguments.

Ability to Make Judgments

1 The study of philosophy, either as a separate discipline or in conjunction with other social sciences, helps pupils to develop the ability to make well-considered judgments.

2 The processes by which sound conclusions are reached need to be emphasized to pupils continually and utilized in their oral and written discussion. Thereby pupils engage in the work of critical analysis essential to judgment. They will not be satisfied with ready-made answers or with the omission of issues that can stimulate the spirit and practice of inquiry.

Summary

For its own well-being, a free society must keep open the path of free inquiry and develop in its future citizens those habits of study which result in responsible commitments in thought and action. Conducted as an inquiry to which philosophy contributes tools and areas of investigation, the social studies can be expected to develop the ability of pupils to make well-reasoned judgments. Concepts, generalizations, and doctrines which pupils encounter will be subjected to questioning. Reasons for their acceptance or rejection will be reviewed, their applications investigated, and their implications explored. In this way, the examined life which Socrates declared to be the life most worthy to be lived by man will be developed and encouraged in the pursuit of social studies in all grades.

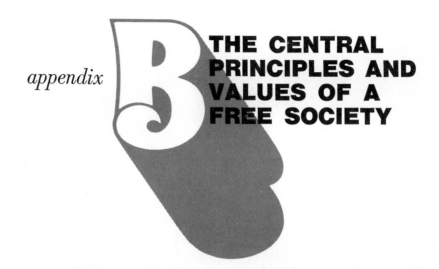

appendix **THE CENTRAL PRINCIPLES AND VALUES OF A FREE SOCIETY**

The following fifteen themes, developed by a committee of the National Council for the Social Studies, provide a guideline for the important kinds of understandings and values which should be taught through the social studies. Each theme is essential to the perpetuation of our democratic way of life and individual freedom.

THE CENTRAL PRINCIPLES AND VALUES OF A FREE SOCIETY[1]

Theme 1: Recognition of the Dignity and Worth of the Individual

The uniquely distinguishing quality of Western democracy is the insistence that the individual is the all-important unit of society. Following the philosophy of John Locke, it is the individual man who possesses inalienable rights, derived from God and Nature. This in turn springs from the Judaic-Christian and Stoic value of the preciousness of the individual human life. In this system of values, government is an implementing agency, a means to the end of protecting and guaranteeing these rights. The state is therefore not an end in itself, as totalitarianism would maintain. The rights which are inalienable and which democratic governments should sustain include life with at least a minimum standard of living, liberty compatible with the rights of others, freedom of thought and speech with their concomitant responsibilities, freedom of religion and from an established church. In his relations with other

---

[1] Dorothy McClure Fraser and Samuel P. McCutchen, eds., *Social Studies in Transition: Guidelines for Change,* Curriculum Series Number Twelve (1201 Sixteenth Street, N.W., Washington, D.C. 20036: National Council for the Social Studies, 1965), pp. 11–50. Reprinted with permission of the National Council for the Social Studies. Illustrative concepts and generalizations to be used in the development of each of these themes are suggested in this document.

men, the democratic individual should treat them as individuals, avoiding stereotyped thinking, and looking for the essential worth and dignity of each. This is not an uncritical sentimentality, for some men may have little worth and no dignity. When we try to see why persons act as they do, however, we understand them better. We need to know better the interpersonal competences, the skills of getting along with people in individual contacts and in groups. The social ideal is that each man, by his own work and his own effort, may make what he wishes of himself.

Any comprehensive analysis of American history and its society, however, does discover instances of intolerance and prejudice; they illustrate our imperfections and sins. Stereotyped preconceptions are widespread; we generalize in terms of race or religion. Society's evaluation of the individual is based in too large part on what work he does. The nature of the work is the major element in establishing social class, which while more fluid than in some other societies, is distinguishable here.

Theme 2: The Use of Intelligence to Improve Human Living

As one of its essentials, democracy assumes intelligence, actual or potential, in every man. Because of this assumption, democracy promises the freedom of the mind. It offers the free competition of the market place for ideas and values. Freedom of the mind involves the right to knowledge, the freedom to learn, and the freedom to teach. As democracy requires intelligence, so its perfecting depends upon open-mindedness and critical thinking. The processes of inquiry and investigation are involved in the right of the individual to participate in decisions on matters which affect him. If there is to be open competition of ideas and values, there must be a wide dissemination of knowledge and opportunity for independent value-judgments; communication and education become social tools. This means that the schools and the mass media of communication have a direct social responsibility both to the dissemination of knowledge and its use, and to the maintenance of the free market place for ideas and values. As our pattern of living grows more complex, experts are trained in various fields. The intelligent citizen knows how to discern and select the expert—and to avoid the demagogue—but he also comes to know how far to use the expert and at what point he must take the responsibility of making decisions which affect him and/or his democratic society.

Individuals, like institutions, have responsibilities commensurate with their freedoms. With the freedom to learn and teach goes the discipline of scholarship. Academic freedom denies itself subservience to an external and *ex officio* authority. The individual's right to decide carries a responsibility not to permit authoritarian usurpation of decision-making by default. Superstition stands as the enemy of knowledge and has not yet been routed. The mass media do not use their opportunity to teach, but instead cater to a growing appetite for thrills. Emotional bias conceptions remain rooted, though shaken by education. Where ignorance is widespread, greedy and selfish groups can organize irrational, cruel, and selfish programs. The cure may require a study of man himself—the relation of his biological make-up to his drives, desires and ambitions. If groups come naturally to be formed of like-minded folks, the study of greater intelligence in the roles of leadership and followership would be profitable.

Theme 3: Recognition and Understanding of World Interdependence

The most important influence of modern technology has been exerted through modern communication and transportation. Communities which were once isolated and self-contained have been made neighbors to distant continents. Distinctive institutions which have developed because of basic differences in cultures have been brought into contact with each other and into competition. A Moslem world of nomads must deal with complex Western economic organization. Economic activities have changed from self-sufficiency to specialization, as modern industry has come to depend on imports of scarce materials from far places, and as the reciprocal export trade has grown to be essential, markets have become global. Freedom of movement to all parts of the world has become a feasible luxury, verging upon tomorrow's necessity, and if we are not citizens of the world, we are world members. The stage upon which our nation's role is cast has already become the planet so that we are affected by Asians, Africans, Australians, Argentinians, and Austrians.

The world has shrunk but it is more complex and harder to understand. In it can be found, existing now, nearly every stage of social evolution from the savage, through barbarism and feudalism, up to the experimental patterns for day after tomorrow. The intricate machinery of modern industry clanks and roars by the side of ancient handicrafts and both must make adjustments. "Democracy" has taken on a dozen conflicting meanings. No part of the world is more than 24 hours away, no Iron Curtain can completely shut out free ideas; but neither can we quarantine successfully against communicable disease, ignorance, or intolerance. News of happenings on the other side of the globe may reach us almost instantly but our mass media do not necessarily provide us with a representative or objective view. Our best hope for physical health and a free society is to extend technology and education so that poverty and ignorance may be overcome. We greatly need an appreciation of the value of difference. We need to know and accept responsibility for the effects of our actions on other peoples and cultures.

Theme 4: The Understanding of the Major World Cultures and Culture Areas

Western culture developed historically in relative isolation from that of other parts of the world. In an area centering around the Mediterranean Sea, men developed institutions, morals, and values which became the elements of a civilization which is homogeneous in spite of rival nationalities, differing languages, and competing economics. This Western culture migrated to the American continents with the white man and found in the breadth of the Atlantic Ocean a new basis for isolation. The 20th century, however, has seen this isolation destroyed. The technology of transportation and communication has brought non-Western cultures into immediate juxtaposition with Western civilization and the two worlds face the urgent need to understand each other.

In the 20 years following the end of World War II, the number of free and independent nations has more than doubled. These new nations, in the main in Asia and Africa, were once colonial possessions of European empires and their nationalism is sharp and obvious. Proud of their independence, they tend to emphasize their distinctiveness, their equality, and their differences.

If this shrinking world is to grow in peacefulness, we must make formidable efforts to know these peoples and their cultures.

Theme 5: The Intelligent Uses of the Natural Environment

The world of nature in which man finds himself and of which he is a part has conditioned where and how men live. In the earliest phases of primitive life, the physical environment was the dominant force in determining economic activities, religious practices and beliefs, social and political institutions. Indeed, the considerable differences in these institutions which may be found throughout the world, historically and today, may be accounted for in part by differences in natural environments. Each great stride in technology of land usage and adaptation to physical environment has caused or permitted changes in basic institutions. That adaptation has ranged from complete conformity to natural mandate to developments such as irrigation, improvements in building, and modification of plants and domesticated animals so that the original needs in a habitat, the improvement in transportation may alter basically the use of that habitat by encouraging specialization for which the region is especially suited rather than by requiring self-sufficiency within regions. In many ways, men are constantly studying the natural world and are finding ways to use its forces and resources intelligently.

The physical environment still stands unconquered in many important aspects. Floods, droughts, and major storms are threats to physical and economic security; the scanty depth of soil fertility and the falling water table stand as threats to growing populations. Human ingenuity, however, has so far kept ahead in the race with the exhaustion of basic earth resources by ferreting out new deposits and by inventing substitutes. In today's world, men are looking to the stars not only for poetic inspiration, but as new horizons of the natural world which beckon to today's explorers and pioneers.

Theme 6: Vitalization of Our Democracy Through an Intelligent Use of Our Public Educational Facilities

If we would preserve and use our major freedoms, each person must recognize the cause-and-effect connection between his freedoms and the social responsibilities which they entail. In an earlier American society, both responsibilities and freedoms were easier discerned, and participation in social affairs came more naturally for the young. In our present, more complex society where social, political, and economic relationships are more impersonal, society's dependence upon formal education has become greater, and its assignment to the public school has also become more complex.

The role of education in training for vocations, or of providing the knowledges and skills which vocations require, is generally accepted and relatively easy to implement. The task of education to make persons more intelligent and skillful in taking their places in society, and in improving that society, is less generally accepted or understood. Democracy demands a higher level of self-discipline and social morality than does an authoritarian government; a responsible social role is harder to perceive and fulfill in a complex urban society than in the simpler groups of the past century. Modern production, distribution, research, and utilization of services are largely group rather than individual functions; today's politics are impersonal, social groups are large, and it is difficult for the individual to find his place in them. The American public school system is unique in providing our society with a major instrument for bringing together all of its people in an attempt to teach individual members how to carry out satisfactorily their responsibilities.

With a rising birth rate and a rapidly increasing population, with an expanding curriculum in the schools as our society wants more subject fields taught, and as modern education learns to use more specialized facilities in the better accomplishment of its assignments, public education grows more expensive. One of our serious lags has been a failure to find appropriate ways of financing these added costs. School taxes still fall predominantly on real property, and wide variations in educational services exist between rich and poor communities and between sections of the nation. Discrimination still curtails the quality of education of segments of the population. We need to recognize that ignorance and other effects of inadequate education in any part of the country can threaten the whole nation as surely as an infectious disease.

Theme 7: The Intelligent Acceptance, by Individuals and Groups, of Responsibility for Achieving Democratic Social Action

If, as Theme 1 asserts, the individual is the central value of Western democracy, and his rights and their defense are the basic justification of government, certain central responsibilities devolve upon him. The individualism of the 18th and 19th centuries insisted that the welfare of the individual was his own direct responsibility, hence failure was due to lack of ability or effort. The 20th century has become aware of a social responsibility to provide equality of opportunity—hence universal education—and to accept some of the blame for failure—as governmental relief agencies attest. But the 20th century, at its "mid-stride," has not absolved the individual from his concern for his own destiny. He is still the master of his own fate. Indeed, his responsibility has broadened, for we have begun to make explicit his concern for the general welfare. More, perhaps, than ever before, man is becoming his brother's keeper; the competent citizen has an active and positive desire to contribute to the common good. A greater national and global population has complicated this assignment, and there are several levels of government in which intelligent participation is required of the citizen, but greater skills are required for him to relate to the several groups of which he is a part and the effectiveness of his social participation is increasing. Not only is this true for persons, but groups are becoming more alert to their social responsibilities. Political parties, corporations, trade unions, trade associations —all furnish examples of such group acceptances.

As with other goals, our grasp has not always attained our reach. Individualism is too often merely acquisitive and selfish. Conserving and planning for the future are set aside for self-gratification and aggrandizement in the present. People who fail rationalize their lack of success and blame everything but themselves. Institutions provide an anonymity for their members so that both the individuals and the group can evade the demands of social conscience. The general welfare becomes formalized and the provision of it institutionalized, and as society undertakes to see that no one starves, the defeated pauperize themselves and accept a parasitic existence. While men's sense of realism leads them to expect and tolerate some inevitable failure, faith leads them to expect a measure of success for themselves and for the majority of their fellow men.

Theme 8: Increasing the Effectiveness of the Family as a Basic Social Institution

Institutions are social inventions designed to implement ideals or to bridge the gap between a less than satisfactory situation and the desired result. In this sense the family achieves the perpetuation of the species, induction of the young into it. Western culture has deemed the monogamous family its most effective unit. Originally patriarchal in structure, the Western family has been exposed to many dynamic factors. The growing importance of women in industry has given them the basis of economic independence. The disappearance of the artisan crafts has sharply decreased the number of sons who learned their trade from their fathers, and technology's impact on urban living has tended to make chores obsolete. As children have lost the economic value they once represented as wage earners in the early industrial revolution, the size of the family has diminished, and the social value of children, of childhood and youth, has changed. Such changes have not all been for the best, and today young people tend to behave like overvalued but displaced persons, since they may no longer learn the skills of participation in primary groups. Medical advances have extended the span of responsibility. The family is more than a means of biological reproduction, and more than an economic unit of producing or spending: It is the basic means of giving the security of belonging to persons.

The problems of today's families may not be new but they may require new solutions. Housing is one of these persistent problem areas, as the growth of slums keeps up with new building. Broken homes caused in part by a high divorce rate create new problems in child training and juvenile delinquency, and those problems are accentuated by family popular understanding of the newer principles of child psychology.

Theme 9: The Effective Development of Moral and Spiritual Values

Democracy, in the long run, will rise or fall according to the extent that individual citizens live by accepted ethical, moral, and spiritual values. In our interdependent society the individual rights guaranteed in our Constitution become meaningless unless they are exercised in a manner harmonious with the moral and ethical principles that are the foundation of Western democracy. The greater the freedom enjoyed by the individual, the more urgent it is from society's point of view that he hold to these principles. The reverse is equally true: The more fully that all individuals accept and implement these principles, the greater the freedom they may enjoy in society. These principles —such as moral responsibility, devotion to truth, and the brotherhood of man—grow out of the one that is basic to them all: recognition of the dignity and worth of the individual (Theme 1). Inextricably bound up with these ethical concepts are spiritual values which mankind has ever sought to realize, both as a means of self-development and as an anchor in an uncertain world. Responsibility for helping young people develop moral and spiritual values is shared by the three great institutions of home, church, and school. Working within the context of freedom of religion and separation of church and state, our public schools cannot become involved in theological teachings. However, the school can and must carry its share of responsibility for developing moral and spiritual values. It can focus directly on problems of social ethics. And by teaching about the institution of religion, the school can help young people appreciate the great part that organized religion has played and does play in the growth of an individual's moral and spiritual values.

The need for more effective development of moral and spiritual values is dramatically demonstrated in many of our current problems. These include delinquent acts by juveniles and such things as adult crime, unethical behavior, immorality, and bigoted behavior by adults. The need is tragically demonstrated by the rising tide of mental illness, attributable at least in part to the tensions of our times. By helping young people develop moral and spiritual values, we can help them find security in an insecure, changing world.

Theme 10: The Intelligent and Responsible Sharing of Power in Order to Attain Justice

Governments are instituted among men in order to guarantee inalienable natural rights but men have to surrender some alienable freedom in order to have a society. Social order requires law, and laws must be made, interpreted, and enforced, so the legislative, judicial, and executive functions are defined. The concept of justice implies a government of law, not of man, and its ideal is an equal justice for all. Pure democracy, as practiced in the Greek city-states and in New England town meetings, permitted the citizen to take part directly in government, but the increasing size of political units and their populations has developed the machinery of representation and of federalism. In the latter, the balancing of local and central control has been a varying equation depending upon the efficiency of communication and transportation available at any given time. The ability of the central government to extend its powers to the borders of its realm has varied over the centuries and has seen many machineries of empire, none so effective as that established by the Northwest Ordinance of 1787.

The government of any society at any period has represented some balance of freedom and security for its people, ranging from the Jeffersonian ideal of little government and much freedom, to the dictatorships with some security sometimes; privilege, not equal justice for all, has at times been rampant. Economic specialization and competition have produced elements of hidden government through lobbies and other pressure-tactics on legislation. In the making of laws today, 51 grist mills, dominated by lawyers, grind out laws which often conflict and overlap bewilderingly, to the confusion of the citizen. Every generation relearns anew the hard tasks of democracy.

Theme 11: The Intelligent Utilization of Scarce Resources to Attain the Widest General Well-Being

From earliest times men have confronted a scarcity of material resources, and systems have been established to economize these resources. In the system of private enterprise, economic value is determined by scarcity, utility, and desirability; prices of goods and services vary with these factors. The price mechanism, operating in the marketplace, has served as the regulator of both supply and demand. By another basis of analysis, the consumer by means of dollars as ballots, has become the regulator of the market, determining what shall be produced, the quantity, and how it shall be distributed. Other societies have delegated work to one social class, leaving an upper class whose only social services were governing and fighting, to live upon the efforts of the workers. Industrial technology has both proliferated the specializations of labor and has made work a necessity for all except those few who live upon inherited wealth. As a regulator of the market, the consumer is also the allocator of manpower.

In any system permitting private property, the concentration of wealth and power will be a recurrent problem. In our system today the mammoth corporation and mammoth union, and their normative tendency toward monopoly, become the most serious manifestation of the problem. Growing from the central stem is the phenomenon of the business cycle with its phases of boom and bust. Wealth or power concentrated in private hands can lead to the rapid exploitation of irreplaceable natural resources which from a social point of view should be conserved. The government, representing the people, has a role to play in regulating monopoly, in controlling the extreme results of the business cycle, and in the preservation of natural resources.

Theme 12: Achievement of Adequate Horizons of Loyalty

In simple agrarian societies, in the depths of the Dark Ages, the allegiance of men reached no further than the valley in which they lived. A widening sense of belonging extended the concept of allegiance to the country, then to the duchy, and at last to the kingdom. In the American picture within the past century, men forced to choose between the Nation and State decided: "I am first a Virginian." The concept of loyalty to the national sovereign state is one of the important understandings in today's world. Sovereignty may be simply defined as the power to make the final decision, and it resides where there is no higher authority which can coerce. The past century has seen the extension and intensification of nationalism all over the world. It has witnessed the unification of important nation-states in Europe, the intensification of nationalistic awareness in Europe, Asia, and Africa, and rivalry among nations everywhere.

Nationalism has given its meaning to citizenship, and the functional analysis of that term would define the areas of civic activities and responsibilities at local, state, and national levels. Some pioneering efforts have been made to catalogue the skills of effective social participation in the various groups of which we are members; more work in that direction would be profitable. Nationalism has expressed itself at times in a glorifying, uncritical patriotism which has resulted too often in isolationism and has been used too much as a cloak to cover reactionary movements and to gild private greed. The social objective becomes a sane and reasoned patriotism, and an understanding, appreciation, and identification with the various groups of people with whom we interact, beginning with the family and extending through the local community, state, and nation to all mankind. However, loyalty to wider groups requires a kind of knowledge and of intellectual grasp which is not needed for loyalty to the small face-to-face group. It becomes important for the educator to think through the problem of teaching for an intelligent loyalty to groups which cuts across national boundaries, and a part of this teaching should consist of a thorough exploration of the question of conflicting loyalties as between nations and interest groups which cut across national boundaries.

Theme 13: Cooperation in the Interest of Peace and Welfare

The achievement of nuclear fission may have removed the cork and released the genie of total destruction. At best it has clarified the alternatives in international relations so that nations must endeavor earnestly to resolve differences or run the risk of human annihilation. Cooperation is the corollary of such interdependence. At an earlier and perhaps simpler time, aggressors could expect that initiative and their superior strength would bring them gains greater than their losses. Balance of power diplomacy developed to oppose these aggressors. Its techniques were the discovery of common dangers, of common interests, and the need for common action. The cooperation they achieved was partial and short-lived but the precedent is important. In other instances of danger or crisis, whether of war or disasters of naure, people have shown that they can subordinate selfish interests and act for the common good.

Machinery of cooperation has developed in labor-management relations and instead of strike and lock-out, riot and police rule, there has been an increase in conference and conciliation, mediation and arbitration, seeking a consensus. Unfortunately we stand today far from the goal. The bargaining table, whether diplomatic or industrial, finds the pride and prestige of the individuals who are bargaining too often the operating values, instead of the greatest good for the greatest number. The earlier polite language of conciliation, insincere though it may have been, is discarded for the language of conflict. The race for superiority in atomic weapons continues, and when the gun of final destruction is loaded, some fool may pull the trigger.

Theme 14: Achieving a Balance Between Social Stability and Social Change

The bicameral legislature has often been justified because it balanced the rashness and urge to change of the popular house with conservatism and power to delay of the Senate or Lords. Those two basic factors, progress and stability, exist and operate in many social institutions. The dynamics of modern society proposes and urges change; social conservatism resists and controls the degree of modification. When both forces operate together within an institution, orderly progress can result; when conservative forces are dominant, the institution or the society may become static or stagnant. At times the critics of the existing order and the innovators take control and fundamental and revolutionary changes come about.

The rate of modification among institutions in a society may vary markedly. Technological developments have made basic and rapid changes in our economic institutions, but conservative forces have slowed the rate of change of the political and social institutions. The resultant "cultural lag" has caused strains and maladjustments. For example, governmental machinery to control the new situations created by changes in transportation has not kept pace with crime or big business or congestion. However, in spite of sensational and visible changes in some phases of living, basic institutions stay on; tradition holds things in place. Our society reaches its decisions, either frontally or obliquely, about values which at one time were sharply controversial, and the problems then change to those of implementation. Perhaps the most important function of history is to record the conserving and maintaining, not merely the changing.

Theme 15: Widening and Deepening the Ability To Live More Richly

While man is a social being with obligations to and rewards from the groups of which he is a part, he is also an individual. A goal of living and of education, then, should be the multiplication of his sources of enrichment and the enhancement of his powers of enjoyment. Generally the arts, both fine and practical, are the avenues by which perceptions and sensitivities are increased, and the improvement of both appreciation and creative powers should be sought. But in the humanistic scheme of values, any learning, any discipline, can contribute to personal enrichment. The humanist climbs a mountain because it is there; he learns for the joy of learning and for the sense of victory over ignorance; he is not restricted to the horizons of the useful and the applicable. Most persons, of course, combine the humanist and the utilitarian and are potentially both the scientist and the engineer. Esthetics and emotions, therefore, can be used to make both the humanist and the humanitarian. In our dominant values, work becomes both a means and the end of personal enrichment.

Much still needs to be done to improve the constructive use of leisure and to improve mass tastes. In an earlier day, leisure and good taste belonged exclusively to the aristocratic leisure classes. In an age of mass media, the patron of the arts is the common man. The quality of culture in a democratic society depends upon how the great mass of the people use their leisure time. Mass media without education may lead to vulgarity and cultural mediocrity; with education the common man may build a culture equal in taste to the historical aristocracies and more varied in its patterns, because of the new contributions of many people from many lands.

A challenge for any democratic society is to find some means for preserving individual choice in an age of mass media which could lead to cultural conformity. One aspect of this problem is to help each person develop individual tastes and preferences, and to encourage like-minded groups of individuals to insist upon their share of the time and services of the mass-oriented cultural institutions.

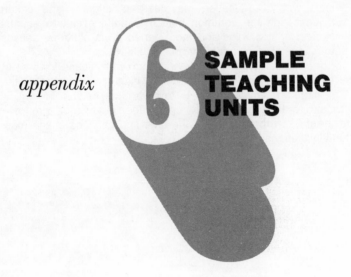

appendix **6 SAMPLE TEACHING UNITS**

The following social studies units, "Early California Indian Life" and "Oregon: Not 33rd but 1st," are organized according to the accepted format recommended in Chapter 4, "Developing Teaching Units in the Social Studies." The unit on Oregon demonstrates the traditional organization of a unit for teaching to the whole class (Roman numerals I through VII). This same unit has then been individualized (Roman numerals VIII through XI) showing how a regular unit of work can be changed to allow students to progress through it on an individualized basis according to their own rate of speed and progress.

EARLY CALIFORNIA INDIAN LIFE

Initiation of Unit

Arouse Interest by Display

1 A large outline map of California is to be displayed on the wall. It is to be filled in as study of California Indians evolves.

2 Display jackets of books dealing with California Indian life.

3 Display pictures of Indian life, focusing attention on the four basic needs: homes; clothing; food; weapons, implements, and utensils.

4 Display such things as rabbit skins, bow and arrow, arrowheads, forked stick, etc. . . .

Arouse Interest Through Discussion

1 What did you see as you looked about the room that especially interested you? (Give students a chance to share their general knowledge.)

2 From looking about at the different pictures of California Indians, how do these Indians seem to be any different from those you may already know about?

3 Teacher reads story about some children who played they were California Indians. Follow up the story by asking if the students in your class could play California Indians. (Their response would probably be no.) Bring the class to an understanding that before they play California Indians they will first have to know more about the California Indian life.

4 What are some of the things we will have to learn about the California Indians before we can play California Indians as the children in the story did? Draw out such answers as: We will have to know where they lived, where they came from, what they looked like, what they ate, how they prepared their food, etc. . . .

Arouse Interest Through Pretest

1 This gives the child an opportunity to discover that which he does not know and exposes him to all that he must learn.

Arouse Interest by Explaining Folders

1 All written reports, stories, charts, maps, pictures, etc. done by the student in this unit will be kept in his own special folder on California Indian life.

First Major Concept

California geography and climate affected where the California Indian chose to settle.

Behavioral Objective

The student will understand the climate and topography of California, and why it affected where the Indians lived. The student will be able to locate and fill in his own outline map showing the topography features and the natural resources of California.

Supporting Concepts

1 Many different kinds of climates are found within the borders of California.

2 California possesses many natural resources.

3 Topography influences the location of settlements.

4 There is no written record of when, how, or why the Indians came to California.

Learning Experiences

1 Look at the maps in the room to locate the coastal areas, deserts, mountains, valleys, rivers, lakes, bays, and islands of California.

2. Know the meaning of the following: bay, island, valley, lake, desert, river, mountain, coastal range. Be able to give the definition in an oral or written explanation.

3 Fill in on your outline map of California the different features of topography.

4 From what you have discovered from investigating the maps in the room and from having filled in your own map, can you give an explanation as to why the climate of these different regions is so varied?

5 From your study of the various types of climate, can you conclude which areas would be the best for crops, big trees, forest lands, gold, petroleum, abundant water, natural harbors and seaports?

6 Label, and with the use of symbols, show these natural resources on your own map.

7 Locate and label the various tribes on your own map.

8 Use the scale on the map and find out how far apart these early Indian settlements were.

9 Look at the maps in the room and discover the different possible routes the Indians may have taken to get to California.

10 Make a map of your own showing the possible routes the Indians may have taken.

11 Would you expect to find more Indians living in northern, southern, eastern, or the western sections of California? Give a written explanation for your answer.

12 Show, by making pictures to represent the different Indian tribes, in which section of California each tribe was located. Fill this in on the big outline map on the wall of the classroom.

13 Read *California Yesterdays*, "Maps of Tribes," page 40.

14 Look at study prints, "Native Tribes of North America."

Vocabulary

1 coastal	4 river	7 island	10 Asia
2 desert	5 lake	8 climate	11 tribe
3 valley	6 bay	9 topography	

Second Major Concept

People of a different culture often look different from people of our own culture.

Behavioral Objective

The student will be able to show in a drawing what California Indians look like. The student will be able to describe in a written paragraph the characteristics that differentiate the Indian from people of his own culture.

Supporting Concepts

1 California Indians are of a short stature, stocky, and strong.

2 California Indians are flat-nosed and broad-faced.

3 California Indians have black hair that is very straight and eyes that are very dark.

4 California Indians' skin coloring varies from light brown to dark.

Learning Experiences

1 Discuss how California Indians look different from people in our own culture.

2 Draw a picture showing what you think a California Indian might look like.

3 Examine a filmstrip. Write a paragraph explaining what you learned.

Vocabulary

1 stature   2 structure   3 stocky

Third Major Concept

1 California Indians' environment determined their manner of dress.

Behavioral Objective

The student will be able to describe in a written report the characteristics of the California Indian's dress and explain why he dressed as he did. The student will be able to show, in pictures that he has drawn, how men, women, and children dressed and be able to report orally the reasons. The student will be able to explain from which plants and animals the different types of Indian clothing were made.

Supporting Concepts

1 The clothing of the California Indian was very scanty.

2 Plants and animals provided the materials used to make clothing.

3 California Indians wore feathers, headdresses, and robes only for ceremonial occasions.

4 Shell beads were their favorite article of ornament.

Learning Experiences

1 Be able to explain orally what the climate and environment of the California Indian had to do with the way he dressed.

2 In a written report describe the kind of clothing the California Indians wore and why. Include pictures illustrating the clothing of the men, women, and children.

3 Write a story explaining why you would, or would not, like to dress like the California Indians.

4 Find as many pictures as you can of the different animals and plants the Indians could have used to make their clothing.

5 Make a chart showing the animal or plant used for making clothing and beside it show the article of clothing.

6 Make a puppet of an Indian man, woman, or child. Make sure you have dressed it appropriately.

7 View the filmstrip *Early California Indians.*

8 Read from the book, *California Yesterdays,* and *A Child's History of California.*

Vocabulary

1 ornament	3 loin cloth	5 tules
2 apron	4 scanty	6 implement

Fourth Major Concept

Food and how it was prepared. (Nature helps to satisfy man's basic needs.)

Behavioral Objective

The student will be able to chart out the types of food the Indians ate and illustrate the sources from which they came. The student will be able to demonstrate, by acting them out, the different methods of preparing food.

Supporting Concepts

1 Plants were the Indians' main food.

2 Meat and fish were important foods.

3 Indians built storehouses for food.

4 Indian foods required little preserving.

5 Baskets were used for cooking utensils.

6 Indians cooked out of doors.

Learning Experiences

1 From your study of topography, can you conclude the different kinds of food that would have been available to the Indians?

2 From your reading be able to explain how plants provide food for people.

3 Arrange a display of foods that are seeds, roots, stems, and leaves.

4 List, classify, and make illustrated charts of foods of animal origin.

5 Compare modern and early Californian methods of food preservation.

6 Make a chart showing the most important Indian foods in the different sections of California where they would be most common.

7 Find as much information as you can about one of the following questions: (1) What kind of fish were most commonly used to eat? (2) What different methods did Indians use to cook food? (3) What are the two different kinds of storehouses used by the Indians? (4) How did the Indian women prepare acorns for food? (5) How did the Indian men organize a rabbit

drive? (6) How did the Indian women prepare deerskin for clothing? (7) How did the Indian men catch fish?

8 Make a chart showing the implements, utensils, and weapons the early Indians had and give a brief explanation of what each was used for.

9 View film, *Indians of California, Part 11, Food.*

10 Read from books, *The Indians' Garden* and *California's Beginnings.*

Vocabulary

1 preserve	3 acorn	5 utensil
2 storehouse	4 Chia	6 granary

Fifth Major Concept

The climate and materials available in a region influenced the types of Indian homes built by the California Indians.

Behavioral Objective

The student will be able to make a model of the different types of Indian homes. He will be able to illustrate in drawing the different utensils and materials used in building each of these homes.

Supporting Concepts

1 The wickiup was common to most sections.

2 A village of wickiups was called a "rancheria."

3 Plank houses built of redwood were used by the northern Indians.

4 Grass houses were built by the southern Indians.

5 All villages had a sweat house and village assembly house.

6 Different tools and utensils were used to build houses.

Learning Experiences

1 What does the climate of a region have to do with the type of home that is built?

2 Make a mural showing Indian life in each of the different regions.

3 Draw a picture showing the different types of homes built by the Indians.

4 Make a model of one of the following kinds of houses: plank, grass, wickiup.

5 Make a display of the different materials used to make each type of home.

6 Write a paragraph explaining the different materials used for each home and why they were used.

7 Choose one of the following and write a brief explanation: (1) What is a village assembly house used for? (2) What is a sweat house?

Vocabulary

1 implement   3 settlement   5 plank   7 sweat house
2 fertile   4 wickiup   6 assembly house   8 rancheria

Sixth Major Concept

California Indians used tools, weapons, and utensils for their survival.

Behavioral Objective

The student will be able to illustrate on a chart the implements and utensils and weapons used by the Indians and will be able to explain and illustrate what each is used for.

Supporting Concepts

1 Implements were primarily made of stone, bone, and shell. No metal was used.
2 Implements and utensils were used primarily to make houses, boats, rafts, baskets, bowls, ornaments, and in cooking.

Learning Experiences

1 Make a chart listing the different Indian implements, weapons, and utensils, together with their uses.
2 Show in a drawing the weapons the men used for hunting and for fishing.
3 Show in a drawing the utensils the women used for cooking.
4 Read and discover how the Indians lighted fires. Be able to demonstrate.
5 Choose one of the following questions to answer: (1) What were traps and nets used for? (2) What was a rabbit drive?

Vocabulary

1 weapon   6 bone awls   11 mortar-pestle
2 hatchet   7 scraping stones 12 atlate
3 flaked knives   8 firestick   13 forked hunting stick
4 wedge   9 fire stone   14 forked fishing stick
5 mussel-shell adz 10 metate-mano

Seventh Major Concept

Indian men, women, and children participate in many activities.

Behavioral Objective

The student will be able to play an Indian game, sing an Indian song, and make either a basket, a piece of pottery, or a piece of jewelry. The student will be able to write an Indian legend.

Supporting Concepts

1 The Indians govern themselves.
2 The Indians amuse themselves with many games.

3 Storytelling was a favorite entertainment.

4 The Indian men, women, and children work hard for their survival (e.g., cooking, hunting . . .).

Learning Experiences

1 On a chart list the activities of the Indian men, women, and children.

2 Draw pictures of the activities of the Indians.

3 Make an Indian pot out of clay.

4 Weave an Indian basket.

5 Read and find out about the government of the Indians.

6 Learn an Indian song.

7 What kinds of musical instruments did they use? Illustrate.

8 Learn an Indian dance.

9 Listen to an Indian legend on the tape recorder.

10 Make up your own Indian legend.

11 Write an Indian legend and act it out for the class.

12 Write a story about yourself. Pretend you are an Indian boy or girl living in an Indian village for a day. Explain what your day would be like and what things you would do.

13 View film, *Indian Dances.*

14 Read pages 42–43, *California Yesterdays,* "How the Coyote Stole Fire for His Friends."

Vocabulary

1 amusement	3 chant	5 legend	7 pottery
2 entertainment	4 government	6 ceremonial	

Culmination of Unit

1 Plan a California Feast Day. Invite other classes to attend.

2 Make a mural showing all the different phases of a California Indian's life.

3 Complete folder or scrapbook on Indian life.

4 Write a play in a committee and present it to the class.

5 Summarize in a story the life of the California Indians.

6 Complete the outline map on the classroom wall. Included should be: natural resources, Indian tribes, types of food raised in each area, houses, etc.

7 Posttest.

Related Materials:

Books

1 Richards, *California Yesterdays*

2 Flower, *A Child's History of California*

3 Buell, *California Stepping Stones*

4 Marcy, *The Indians' Garden*

5 Hoffman, *California's Beginnings*

6 Sneddon, *Docas, Indian of Santa Clara*

Study Prints

1 Native Tribes of North America

2 Indians of California—food

3 Indians of California—village life

4 Fruits and berries of California trees

Films and Filmstrips

1 *Early California Indians*—filmstrip

2 *Indians of California, Part 11, Food*

3 *Indian Dances*

Maps

1 Political physical map of California

2 California relief map

3 Large outline wall map used for locating major Indian tribes

4 World globe

OREGON: NOT 33rd BUT 1st

I. Initiation of the unit (suggestions)

A. Arranged environment

1. A display featuring such items as: myrtle wood bowl, candle-holders, plaque; Pendleton jacket or blanket; Tillamook cheese; Bumble Bee Tuna can; a piece of plywood or particle board; souvenir sack of grass seed, etc. Use inductive questions such as: Where did this come from? What is it used for? What do all these items have in common? (They are all Oregon products.)

2. Bulletin board featuring postcards of the state. Use questions and discussion: Have you been here? What did you see?

B. Pretests. Use maps showing only county outlines and ask for names to be filled in. Use outline maps of state and ask for natural regions to be filled in. Various other items could be asked for, such as major rivers, mountain ranges, etc. After students are shown the correct answers or locations, the usual consensus is, "We don't know much about our state." This opens the way for the suggestion that we need to know more.

C. Imaginary trip

1. Give the following directions:

a) Today we are going on a trip in our state.

b) We will begin in _____ county and travel into a county which borders it.

c) We must travel into a third county before we reenter any county we have been in.

d) All travelers will have a turn deciding on which county our trip will go on next.

e) To keep traveling with our group, you must name a county which borders the one we are in when your turn comes. If you miss, you may be seated. The best traveler will be the one who remains standing the longest.

f) All travelers please stand.

2. Use a wall map to illustrate how to travel. Then cover it.

3. Play several rounds of the game, giving each student several chances to respond.

4. Ask: Were we able to travel very far? Do we need to know more to complete our trip around the state? What do we need to know?

D. Be the expert—A week or two in advance of this unit begin building the idea that anyone in class can know more than anyone else. This can be developed so that each student feels that he can be the expert for one county. (Since there are 36 counties, usually this can be arranged. With more than 36 students some kind of pairing or teams could be suggested.) At this point teacher-student planning could be used to decide what questions the expert should be responsible for. Suggested possibilities are: How did the county get its name? How do its people make a living? What are its scenic, historical, or unusual places? What does it produce?

E. Ongoing study—Fit the study of the state into the larger topic of westward movement in the United States.

F. Possibly use one of the free films.

II. Major concepts

A. Each Oregon place-name has a history.

1. Oregon counties were named for Presidents of the United States.

2. Oregon counties were named for other important people.

3. Oregon counties were given Indian words for names.

4. Oregon counties were named in miscellaneous ways.

Behavioral Objective

1. Given the four categories—named for Presidents, named for other people, given Indian names, given miscellaneous names—and a map or list of the counties, the student will categorize 32 of the 36 counties properly.

B. Oregon is divided into different geographical areas.

1. Oregon has three climates.

2. Oregon has eight natural regions.

3. Mountains help determine natural regions or geographical areas.

4. Regions have varying scenery.

Behavioral Objectives

1. The student will be able to name or describe orally the three climates and point out their general areas on a large map of Oregon.

2. The student will be able to name the eight natural regions on a map of Oregon showing regional outlines.

3. The student will be able to select one of the natural regions, name it, and list three reasons why he would like to live there.

C. Oregon acquires income by being productive.

1. Timber is Oregon's major crop.

2. Farming is Oregon's second industry.

3. Manufacturing is gaining in importance.

4. Some work is unusual: fern and brush industry, counting fish, collecting ponderosa pine cones.

Behavioral Objective

1. Using an 18-by-24-inch outline map which he has drawn, and symbols of his own design, the student will place in appropriate areas two major ways and four minor ways of making a living for one natural region of Oregon. (County boundaries should be shown in dotted lines to facilitate the locating.)

D. Oregon counties compete in productivity.

1. Some counties produce more goods and services than others.

2. Some items are produced in every county.

3. Some counties produce unusual or even rare items.

Behavioral Objectives

1. The student will be able to name one county which is first in the state in any particular product and give the name of the product.

2. The student will be able to name one county which produces a comparatively rare or unusual product in the state and give the name of the product.

III. Learning activities

A. Concept: Each Oregon place-name has a history.

1. Oregon counties were named for Presidents of the United States.

2. Oregon counties were named for other important people.

3. Oregon counties were given Indian words for names.

4. Oregon counties were named in miscellaneous ways.

B. Behavioral objective

1. Given the four categories—named for Presidents, named for other people, given Indian names, given miscellaneous names—and a map or list of the counties, the student will categorize 32 of the 36 counties properly.

C. Activities

1. Use an 8½-by-11-inch duplicated map of the counties and have students put the names of the counties in the proper places.

2. Use a large map (similar to no. 1) and have students name counties as they are pointed to.

3. Play the imaginary-trip game (see Initiation, I-C).

4. Use a double-spaced duplicated list of the counties. Have the students guess where the name may have come from in one column but put correct placement in a second column as it is discovered.

5. Research *Oregon Blue Book* for information.

6. Individual reports, oral, on "How _____ county got its name," "What historical or unusual places would be worth visiting?"

7. Reports, oral or written, on people for whom counties were named.

8. Class discussion on "How do people choose names for places?" "Why do places need to have names?" "Why are we still naming places on the moon?" "How are we deciding on these names?"

9. Practice placement and spelling tests using map as in no. 1 above.

10. Research the county envelopes for information.

11. Check the road maps for possible clues.

12. Have students attempt classification of counties as they are looking at their lists or maps.

13. Have students make up a color key and color the counties according to the classifications they have made.

A. Concept: Oregon is divided into different geographical areas.

1. Oregon has three climates.

2. Oregon has eight natural regions.

3. Mountains help determine natural regions or geographical areas.

4. Regions have varying scenery.

B. Behavioral objectives

1. The student will be able to name or describe orally the three climates and point out their general areas on a large map of Oregon.

2. The student will be able to name the eight natural regions on a map of Oregon showing regional outlines.

3. The student will be able to select one of the natural regions, name it, and list three reasons why he would like to live there.

C. Activities

1. Use a 48-inch to 54-inch-physical-features map of Oregon (for example, Denoyer-Geppert or other) as a basis for discussion of the following:

a) How are these areas different? (Point to mountain and valley, lake and river, etc.)

b) How do these mountains affect us? (Point to local ones.)

c) How do these mountains affect us? (Point to the Cascade Mountains.)

d) What do we call the effects we have been naming?

2. Read as a class—Parrish, Philip H. *Historic Oregon,* pages 4, 5, 6.

3. Use notebook-sized outline maps of Oregon. Have students put in climate outlines. Label and color them.

4. Check the county envelopes for any unusual weather conditions or claims. Treasure hunt basis, possibly. Also for unusual scenery.

5. Jigsaw-puzzle game: Divide an outline map of Oregon into eight pieces. Put a name on each piece. Be able to defend your choices. Students show examples and tell why they made the cuts where they did. See if there is any consensus on the naming of the parts.

6. Students read *Geography of Oregon* to find names and boundaries of natural regions. Students draw and label these on an outline map for their notebooks.

7. Discussion: (Using no. 1 and no. 6 above) What advantages does this region have? What might people do there for recreation? What might be an important occupation in this region?

8. Map-making: Make a larger (18-by-24-inch) map of one region showing its main geographical features.

9. Rental films, free films, filmstrips.

10. Reading: Brogan, *East of the Cascades;* Decker, *The Weather of Oregon;* Steel, *The Mountains of Oregon.*

A. Concept: Oregon acquires income by being productive.

1. Timber is Oregon's major crop.

2. Farming is Oregon's second industry.

3. Manufacturing is gaining in importance.

4. Some work is unusual: fern and brush industry, counting fish, collecting ponderosa pine cones.

B. Behavioral objective

1. Using an 18-by-24-inch outline map which he has drawn, and symbols of his own design, the student will place in appropriate areas two major ways and four minor ways of making a living for one natural region of Oregon. (County boundaries should be shown in light dotted lines to facilitate the locating).

C. Activities

1. Resource persons: representatives from the lumber industry, farming (possibly a school-board member), or manufacturing.

2. Field trip to a lumber mill, plywood plant, particle-board plant, or paper mill.

3. Resource persons: a carpenter—how does plywood help me in building; a banker—how are lumber and banking connected?

4. Discussion: What happens when Oregon cannot sell its lumber products?

5. Use plywood in some construction activities. Find out the difference between indoor and outdoor grades.

   a) Jigsaw-puzzle maps of the state.

   b) Doll houses, using plywood where it is used in home construction.

   c) Ping-Pong paddles.

6. Reports: Use material from county envelopes. What are the two or three main ways the people of this county make a living? Do they produce any unusual crops or products? If so, what?

7. Take notes on reports (no. 6).

8. Plan a meal using only products produced in Oregon. The main ingredient of each dish could be named and its place of production given as it is served.

9. Plant and raise some samples of Oregon's main crops. The cans or bedding boxes should be labeled with the name of the crop and the county where it is produced.

10. Field trip to a flour mill, a grass seed processing plant, a cannery.

11. Writing: The Job I'd Like To Have.

12. Films on maps, films on Northwestern States.

A. Concept: Oregon counties compete in productivity.

1. Some counties produce more goods and services than others.

2. Some items are produced in every county.

3. Some counties produce unusual or even rare items.

B. Behavioral objectives

1. The student will be able to name one county which is first in the state in any particular product and give the name of the product.

2. The student will be able to name one county which produces a comparatively rare or unusual product in the state and give the name of the product.

C. Activities

1. Use the county folders. Reports on most important crops or products (two or three per county) and unusual items.

2. Check the *Oregon Blue Book* for possible additional information.

3. Check John W. Reith, editor, *The West* (Grand Rapids: The Fideler Company, 1969), for its section on the state.

IV. Culminating activities (suggestions)

A. Tests

1. Map

a) Labelling the counties—72 points—1 point for spelling, 1 point for placing properly; spelled correctly in wrong place = no credit.

b) Drawing in and labeling the eight natural regions.

2. Objective

a) Based on content from reading, reports, discussions done by class. (Follow Gronlund's recommendation and make a table of specifications.)

b) Have students prepare the final test as a part of the work each day.

3. Clue test on the counties: This is prepared by making up three sets of clues for each county used in the test. The clue worth 5 points should be hard. The clue worth 3 points should be about average difficulty. The clue worth 2 points should be easy. All students taking the test are given the hard clues first. When these are corrected, they are given the 3-point page to do for answers missed on the first page. If they miss any on the 3-point page, they are then given the 2-point page for missed items. For example: On the first page the clue might be "land of horizontal rain." The second page clue might be "westernmost point of land in Oregon." The third clue might be "has the mouth of the Rogue River." (The answer is Curry County.) For this test the students should be allowed to use their notebooks and maps which they have made. A test of this type demands good listening and good note-taking.

B. Have the student plan a trip in Oregon. Give him $100, $200, or $300 to spend, or allow him one, two, or three weeks travel time, or a combination of these. Using road maps, his maps, and notes, he plans a trip. He will list where he would go, what he would see or do, and itemize how he spent his money. The trip should be possible of performance, based on his choice of vehicle for transportation, and take him to from five to ten places.

C. Writing

1. Write an essay on "What I Appreciate About Oregon."

2. Write an original poem or story about a job or product of Oregon.

D. Design a cover for your maps, notes, reports, etc.: Make a table of contents of your organization. Make the cover and fix the contents within it to be handed in.

V. Bibliography for teachers

A. Parrish, Philip H. *Historic Oregon.* New York: Macmillan, 1955.

B. *Geography of Oregon* (a source probably not available generally).

C. Reith, John W. (ed.). *The West.* Grand Rapids: Fideler, 1969.

D. Road maps of Oregon secured from service-station sources.

E. Brochures secured from Chambers of Commerce, resorts, industries.

F. Contact Oregon Travel Information Division, Room 101 Highway Building, Salem, Oregon, for free publications and two of the films.

VI. Bibliographical possibilities for additional reading

A. Recent printings

Brogan, Phil F. *East of the Cascades.* 1964.

Chase, Don M. *Pack Saddles and Rolling Wheels.* 1959.

Decker, Charles H. *The Weather of Oregon.* 1961.

Irving, Washington. *Astoria.* Reprint 1961.

Nelson, Marshall. *Shadows of Yesterday.* 1954.

Ogden, Peter Skene. *Snake Country Journals.* 1950.

Oregon Archaeological Society. *Wakeup Mound and Nearby Sites on the Long Narrows of the Columbia River.* 1959.

Palmer, Joel. *Journal of the Travels over the Rocky Mountains.* 1966.

Payette, B. *The Oregon Country under the Union Jack.* 1962.

Ross, Alexander. *Adventures of the First Settlers on the Columbia River.* 1960.

Throckmorton, Arthur L. *Oregon Argonauts: Merchant Adventures on the Western Frontier.* 1961.

Writers' Program. *Oregon, End of the Trail.* 1951.

Wyeth, John B. *Oregon.* 1966.

B. Older printings

Allen, A. *Ten Years in Oregon. Travels and Adventures of Dr. E. White and Lady West of Rocky Mountains.* 1848.

Bullfinch, Thomas. *Oregon and Eldorado; or Romance of the Rivers.* 1866.

Carey, Charles H. *History of Oregon.* 1922.

Chapman, Charles H. *The Story of Oregon and Its People.* 1909.

Cressman, Luther S. *Early Man in Oregon.* 1940.

Freemont, John Charles. *The Life of John Charles Freemont and His Narrative of Exploration.* 1856.

Hines, Gustavus. *Oregon: Its History.* 1859.

Hines, Gustavus. *Wild Life in Oregon.* 1887.

Horner, John B. *Oregon History and Early Literature.* 1931.

Kelley, Hall J. *Hall J. Kelley on Oregon.* 1932.

Lee, Daniel. *Ten Years in Oregon.* 1844.

Meeker, Ezra. *Ox-team Days on the Oregon Trail.* 1922.

Montgomery, Richard G. *The White-headed Eagle.* 1934.

Pollard, Lancaster. *Oregon and the Pacific Northwest.* 1946.

Smet, Pierre Jean de. *Oregon Missions and Travels over Rocky Mountains in 1845–46.*

Smith, Wallace. *Oregon Sketches.* 1925.

Steel, William Gladstone. *The Mountains of Oregon.* 1890.

Thornton, Jessy Quinn. *Oregon and California in 1848.* 1849.

Wyeth, Nathaniel J. *The Correspondence and Journals of Captain Nathaniel J. Wyeth, 1831–6.* 1899.

Not all of the above sources will be found in the usual school library. It is suggested that the local public library be contacted to arrange for borrowing through them from the state library.

VII. Films and filmstrips

A. Free films

1. *Northwest Empire* / sound / 40 minutes / U.P. Railroad

2. *Oregon and Its Natural Resources* / sound / 30 minutes / Bureau of Mines

3. *Parks Are for People* / sound / 27 minutes / Oregon Travel Information Division

4. *Reel Fun in Oregon* / sound / 24 minutes / (same source as no. 3 above)

The above items are listed by Educators Progress Service, Randolph, Wisconsin.

B. Rental films

1. *Maps and Their Meaning* / 14 minutes / color / rental 1–3 days / $5.00

2. *Maps and Their Uses* / 11 minutes / color / rental 1–3 days / $2.50

3. *Maps Are Fun* / 11 minutes / color / rental 1–3 days / $2.50

4. *Maps for a Changing World* / 11 minutes / color / rental 1–3 days / $2.50

5. *Reading Maps* / 11 minutes / color / rental 1–3 days / $2.50

6. *Using Maps—Measuring Distances* / 11 minutes / color / rental 1–3 days / $2.50

7. *Oregon Trail* / 25 minutes / b&w / rental 1–3 days / $5.00

8. *Pacific Coast* / 18 minutes / b&w / rental 1–3 days / $3.75

9. *Pacific—Discovery and Development* / 11 minutes / color / rental 1–3 days / $2.50

The above items are listed by Mountain Plains Film Library Association.

1. *Oregon Trail* / 25 minutes / b&w / rental / $3.20

2. *North American Regions: The Pacific Coast* / 15 minutes / color / rental / $4.60

3. *Northwest Wonderland* (Richfield Oil) / 28 minutes / color / rental / $1.25

4. *United States Expansion: Settling the West* / 12 minutes / b&w / rental / $2.30

5. *United States Expansion: The Oregon Country* / 13 minutes / b&w / rental / $2.30

6. *Geography of the Pacific States* / 10 minutes / b&w / rental / $2.10

The above items are listed in *Films for Teaching* from the A-V Center, Washington State University, Pullman, Washington.

1. *Lincoln County: Land of Contrasts* / 19 minutes / cost $125.00 / McGraw-Hill, New York

C. Filmstrips and slides

    1. *Northwestern Empire—The Pacific Northwest* / 50 frames / 2 x 2 / 35mm slides / cost $6.98

    2. *Oregon Territory* / rental $1.00

    3. *Northwestern States*

        a) *The Geographic Background* / with TG / cost $4.00

        b) *Lumbering and Fishing* / with TG / cost $4.00

        c) *Mining and Grazing* / with TG / cost $4.00

        d) *Power and Petroleum* / with TG / cost $4.00

    4. *The Oregon Coast* / 26 / 2 x 2 / 35mm / cost $2.60

    5. Scenic Coast of Oregon / 8 / 2 x 2 / 35mm / cost $.99

The above items are listed by McGraw-Hill in their *Education Media Index Geography and History* (330 West 42nd Street, New York City).

VIII. Individualizing the unit

  A. Knowledge sessions

    1. Required (10 points)

      a) Map work

        1) Climates of Oregon

        2) Natural regions of Oregon

        3) Placing names on 36 counties

      b) Class discussions (initiation and culmination plus others)

        c) Reading of Parrish, *Historic Oregon*

        d) Listening to resource persons

    2. Optional

        a) All 10-minute films

        b) All filmstrips

        c) Map instructions in how to use a grid system

        d) Play the imaginary-trip game with five other people (see I-C)

        e) Present an oral report to five other people as a knowledge session

        f) Attend and listen to the previous item

B. Reports

    1. Required (40–60 points)

        a) County expert to answer four questions:

            1) How did the county get its name?

            2) What are the two or three main ways people make a living?

            3) What places would you visit—scenic, historic, or unusual?

            4) What are the two or three most important crops or products?

    2. Oral or written (10–40 points)

        a) Dams in the Columbia River

        b) Three famous fishing rivers of Oregon

        c) Bumble Bee Tuna

        d) Santiam or Blue Lake beans

        e) Freezing or canning plants

        f) Pendleton Round-up

        g) Albany World Championship Timber Carnival

        h) Any important geographical feature, such as Abert Rim or Crater Lake

        i) History of a county

        j) Life of an Oregon author

        k) Zoomsi

        l) An Oregon Indian tribe

        m) Where is Chief Joseph really buried?

        n) Our ski resorts

        o) Why is water so important to the people of Oregon?

        p) Wildlife refuge in Harney County

        q) Uranium in Oregon

        r) Fern and brush industry

        s) Chinook jargon

        t) Cayuse pony

        u) Any one of the fur traders or mountain men of Oregon

        v) Why the beaver was trapped

        w) Jason Lee

        x) Douglas Fir

        y) The Oregon Caves

        z) Varieties of trout in Oregon

C. Special projects (35–50 points)

    1. Various maps

        a) Draw an 18-by-24-inch map including the geographical features such as lakes, mountains, rivers. Use proper colors for each.

        b) Construct a map showing the historical markers of the state.

        c) Make a relief map of the state, a county, or a region. (Use salt dough, sawdust-glue, papier-mâché)

        d) A map showing the various classifications of Oregon county names with a color for each group.

        e) Map of one region showing its products with symbols of your own design for each product shown.

        f) Jigsaw-puzzle map with hardback or wooden backing of the counties or natural regions. Use different colors.

    2. Construction

        a) Using plywood, build a doll house. The plywood must be used in the areas where plywood may be used in a normal house.

        b) Make a set of Ping-Pong paddles from Oregon plywood.

        c) Make a chart showing that Oregon is a land of geographical contrasts. Make or find pictures for two columns. Pictures opposite each other should be contrasts, such as mountains vs. valleys, lake vs. desert, etc.

        d) Design and make a cover for your maps, notes, reports, etc. Make a table of contents of your organization. Make the cover you have designed and fix your contents inside it to hand in.

    3. Activities

        a) Take a field trip with the class or with your parents and write it up.

        b) Plant and raise a sample of one of Oregon's main crops. Label the can or pot with the name of the crop and the county where it is produced.

        c) Plan and serve a meal using only Oregon products as the foods. (This could be done by a committee of four or five.)

        d) Organize a postcard collection of scenes in Oregon. Mount and explain each item.

e) Photograph album: take pictures of various geographical, historical, scenic places. Mount and identify each.

f) Learn to sing the Oregon state song ("Oregon, My Oregon"). Sing it for the class or for a smaller group.

D. Creative writing (25–50 points)

1. The Job I'd Like to Have.

2. Make up multiple-choice questions on 3-by-5-inch cards over material from required knowledge sessions, map work, reports. (1 point each)

3. Essay: What I Appreciate About Oregon. (2 pages in ink)

4. Original poem or story about a job or product or place in Oregon.

5. Creative story: A Trip to Crater Lake: Oregon's Only National Park.

E. Group work (15 to 25 points for participators, 5 points for observers)

1. A small committee reinact an incident of some pioneer family coming to the Willamette Valley or other place in Oregon. Present this to the class.

2. A small group make a mural of a highway, air route, or railroad across Oregon.

3. Pick a product and follow it along its travels to market. Make a large chart or diorama to show what happens.

4. Keep track of how far you travel to and from your home (in miles) for one week. List transportation methods used. Several members of a committee could put their individual results together for comparison. Make a large chart to show your findings.

5. Group discussion, panels, debates. Check your topic with the teacher before beginning to work on this.

F. Independent study

1. Reading of any chapter in sources in bibliography (up to 10 points by oral interview with teacher).

2. Reading of any chapter in sources in bibliography (up to 10 points for a short outline of chapter).

3. Questions answered (up to 5 points each)

a) Why is Oregon called the Beaver State?

b) What are Oregon's state bird, flower, and tree?

c) How is our community being helped by the freeway?

d) What is the highest mountain in our county?

e) How big does an evergreen tree need to be in order to be usable for lumber?

f) What is the most scenic spot in our county? Why do you think so?

g) Where does the ＿＿＿＿＿ raised in our county go?
(This list should be expanded to approximately 50 questions before beginning the unit.)

G. Vocabulary words (2 points each)

1. A challenge matching test. If the test is taken, whatever score is obtained will be all the points possible on this section.

2. Students could select 25 to 50 words which they feel they need to know and write definitions for these.

H. Motion pictures (20 minutes or longer) (10 points)

I. Quizzes or tests

1. Spelling and labelling counties: county map test (0–72 points)

2. Drawing and labelling the natural regions (32 points)

3. Clue tests (with notes) (0–150 points)

IX. Breakdown of learning experiences and point system

A. Knowledge session (10 points each)

1. Required—6

2. Optional

B. Reports

1. Required (40–60 points) 1 only

2. Oral or written (10–50 points each)

C. Special projects (35–50 points)

D. Creative writing (25–50 points)

E. Group work (15–25 points for participants, 5 points for observers)

F. Independent study

1. Readings (1–10 points each)

2. Questions answered (1–5 points each)

G. Vocabulary words (2 points each) (50–100 point total)

H. 20-minute films (or longer) (10 points)

I. Quizzes or tests

1. Spelling and labelling counties (0–72 points)

2. Natural-regions test (0–32 points)

3. County-clue test (0–150 points)

To have all the students work in all the areas above during the unit would likely be too much. If time is limited, perhaps A and B plus two or three of the other areas would be sufficient. Perhaps some student-teacher planning could be used to determine how many areas should be attempted. This could also include the total minimum number of points which should be accumulated to be considered satisfactory. If areas A and B are used as suggested, and two other areas are attempted, this unit will require three to four weeks of class periods at least forty-eight minutes daily.

X. Tally sheet   Name _____

  A. Knowledge sessions

Date	*Required* Number	Points	Date	*Optional* Number	Points
____	____	____	____	____	____
____	____	____	____	____	____
____	____	____	____	____	____
____	____	____	____	____	____
____	____	____	____	____	____
			____	____	____
			____	____	____

  B. Reports

Date	*Required* County	Points	Date	*Optional* Topic	Points
____	____	____	____	____	____
			____	____	____
			____	____	____
			____	____	____

  C. Special projects

Date	Number	Points
____	____	____
____	____	____
____	____	____
____	____	____
____	____	____

  D. Creative writing

Date	Points
____	____
____	____
____	____

  E. Group work

Date	Number	Points
____	____	____
____	____	____
____	____	____
____	____	____

  F. Independent study

Date	*Readings* Number	Points	Date	*Questions* Number	Points
____	____	____	____	____	____
____	____	____	____	____	____
____	____	____	____	____	____
____	____	____	____	____	____

G. Vocabulary words

Challenge	Single words
Date Points	Date Points
_____ _____	_____ _____
	_____ _____

H. Films

Date   Titles   Points
_____   _____   _____

I. Tests or quizzes

	Date	Points
1. Counties	_____	_____
2. Regions	_____	_____
3. Clue test	_____	_____

XI. Pretest suggestions

A. Actual testing

Use maps showing only the county outlines and ask students to fill in the names properly. Use various other items such as important rivers, mountains, lakes, etc.

B. Use class discussion

1. A question-type asking, "Where in Oregon would you go to see _____?"

2. Combine the questions with a political-physical map and ask, "How would people make a living here?" (Since some ways of making a living are common to the state, it would be necessary to watch for the ways which might not be common, or the common ways which might not be mentioned.)

3. Another possible question approach, "What's unique about _____?"

C. Give a county-clue pretest. (See Culminating activities.)

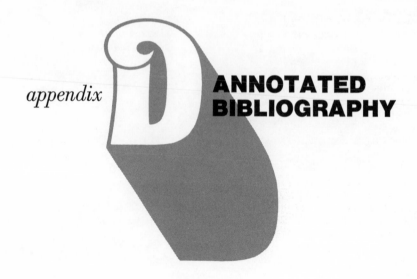

appendix **D ANNOTATED BIBLIOGRAPHY**

BOOKS ABOUT CHILDREN OF OTHER CULTURES

Africa

Mirsky, Reba Paeff. *Seven Grandmothers.* Chicago: Follett, 1955. Nomusa, a young girl in Africa, decides that being a witch doctor is not so good a profession as being a nurse. 191 pages (4–6 grade girls).

Mirsky, Reba Paeff. *Thirty-One Brothers and Sisters.* Chicago: Follett, 1952. The story of a South African girl who feels girls' work is dull and wants to do boys' work. 190 pages (5–6 grade girls).

Australia

Phipson, Joan. *Birkin.* New York: Harcourt Brace Jovanovich, 1965. Some children in Australia have many problems raising a young calf, Birkin. 224 pages (5–6 grade girls).

Bohemia

Jones, Elizabeth Orton. *Maminka's Children.* New York: Macmillan, 1940. The story of a Bohemian family who have come to live in America. 107 pages (4–5 grade girls).

Bulgaria

Shannon, Monica. *Dobry.* New York: Viking, 1934. The story of Dobry, a young Bulgarian boy who wanted to be an artist. 176 pages (5–6 grade).

Canada

Carlson, Natalie Savage. *Chalou.* New York: Harper & Row, 1967. 110 pages (4–5 grade boys).

Carlson, Natalie Savage. *The Letter on the Tree.* New York: Harper & Row, 1964. A French-Canadian boy wants an accordion very much, but is unable to afford it. 116 pages (4–6 grade boys).

China

Bro, Margueritte Harmon. *Su-Mei's Golden Year.* Garden City, N.Y.: Doubleday, 1950. The story of a young Chinese girl whose father has gone to the university to learn more than the primitive ways of farming of their people. 246 pages (5–6 grade girls).

Handforth, Thomas. *Mei Li.* Garden City, N.Y.: Doubleday, 1938. A little Chinese girl who went to the city for the New Year's Day celebrations. Picture book (2–3 grade girls).

Lattimore, Eleanor Frances. *Bells for a Chinese Donkey.* New York: Morrow, 1951. The story of a small Chinese girl who wanted to have bells to put on her donkey. 126 pages (3–4 grade girls).

Lattimore, Eleanor Frances. *Little Pear.* New York: Harcourt Brace Jovanovich, 1931. Little Pear is a little Chinese boy who frequently gets lost and gets into trouble. 144 pages (2–4 grade).

Lattimore, Eleanor Frances. *The Little Tumbler.* New York: Morrow, 1963. The story of a little Chinese boy in a touring company. 128 pages (3–4 grade boys).

Lattimore, Eleanor Frances. *Peachblossom.* New York: Harcourt Brace Jovanovich, 1943. The story of a little girl in China who has to leave her home because of the war. 96 pages (2–4 grade girls).

Lattimore, Eleanor Frances. *Three Little Chinese Girls.* New York: Morrow, 1948. Three little Chinese sisters make friends with the boy next door. 128 pages (2–3 grade girls).

Lewis, Elizabeth Foreman. *Young Fu of the Upper Yangtze.* Philadelphia: Winston, 1942. The story of a young Chinese boy who moves to the city with his mother and learns to be a man. 257 pages (6 grade boys).

Liu, Beatrice. *Little Wu and the Watermelons.* Chicago: Follett Publishing Company, 1954. Little Wu, a member of an old tribe in southwest China, grows watermelons as a secret way to buy a gift for his mother. 96 pages (3–4 grade boys).

Denmark

Sorensen, Virginia. *Lotte's Locket.* New York: Harcourt Brace Jovanovich, 1964. Lotte is a young girl in Denmark who is torn with the idea of leaving and going to America with her mother who has just remarried. 253 pages (5–6 grade girls).

Ecuador

Clark, Ann Nolan. *Looking for Something.* Eau Claire, Wisconsin: E. M. Hale, 1961. A burro travels through Ecuador looking for something, but he knows not what. 55 pages (2–3 grade).

Egypt

Jones, Ruth Fosdick. *Boy of the Pyramids.* New York: Random House, 1951. Kaffe, a young Egyptian boy, solves the story of the missing jewels of the pyramid. 140 pages (4–6 grade boys).

England

Clarke, Pauline. *The Return of the Twelves.* New York: Coward-McCann,

1963. The story of the boy Max, in England, who had 12 living wooden soldiers which had belonged to the Bronte children. 253 pages (5–6 grade).

Clewes, Dorothy. *The Holiday.* New York: Coward-McCann, 1964. An English boy and girl go to visit his grandparents at an English seaport and are taken to France by accident. 64 pages (2–3 grade).

de Angeli, Marguerite. *The Door in the Wall.* Garden City, N.Y.: Doubleday, 1949. The story of a boy in thirteenth-century England who is crippled, but proves his courage. 121 pages (5–6 grade boys).

Godden, Rumer. *Little Plum* and *Miss Happiness and Miss Flower. See under* Japan.

France

Bemelmans, Ludwig. *Madeline.* New York: Viking, 1939. The story of 12 little girls in a French school. Picture book (1–2 grade girls).

Bishop, Claire Huchet. *Twenty and Ten.* New York: Viking, 1952. The story of twenty French children who hide refugee children from the Nazis. 76 pages (4–6 grade).

Carlson, Natalie Savage. *Luigi of the Streets.* New York: Harper & Row, 1967. The story of an Italian boy living in Marseilles who is convinced that a gypsy has put a curse on his family. 141 pages (4–6 grade boys).

Carlson, Natalie Savage. *The Letter on the Tree. See under* Canada.

Carlson, Natalie Savage. *The Happy Orpheline.* New York: Harper & Row, 1957. Brigette, a little girl in an orphanage in France, does not want to be adopted. 96 pages (3–4 grade girls).

Germany

Bemelmans, Ludwig. *Hansi.* A German boy spends his vacation with an uncle in the mountains. Picture book (3–4 grade boys).

Haiti

Ness, Evaline. *Josefina February.* New York: Scribner's, 1963. The story of how Josefina acquired a wobbly little donkey for a pet. Picture book (2–3 grade).

Hawaii

Brown, Marcia. *Backbone of the King.* New York: Scribner's, 1966. The story of a man and his son who are the "backbone" for the King of Hawaii. 160 pages (5–6 grade boys).

Holland

de Jong, Meindert. *The Wheel on the School.* New York: Harper & Row, 1954. Children in Holland rush to get a wheel put up before the storks come. 298 pages (5–6 grade).

Dodge, Mary Mapes. *Hans Brinker.* New York: Grosset & Dunlap, 1945. The story of two Dutch children who long for the prize of silver skates to be given away in a skating contest. 314 pages (6 grade).

Hungary

Seredy, Kate. *The Good Master.* New York: Viking, 1935. Kate, a headstrong tomboy from Budapest, goes to live on her uncle's farm, where she learns to love and respect others. 196 pages (5–6 grade girls).

Seredy, Kate. *The Singing Tree.* New York: Viking, 1939. When the men go to the war, the family take in Russians and then German children, and learn that all people are the same. 250 pages (5–6 grade).

India

Rankin, Louise. *Daughter of the Mountains. See under* Tibet.

Slobodkin, Louis. *The Polka Dot Goat.* New York: Macmillan, 1964. Sham Babu and his father go to the capitol and sell goats, and find that one can dance. Picture book (3 grade boys).

Italy

Angelo, Valenti. *Nino.* New York: Viking, 1938. Nino, a young boy in Italy, lives with his mother and grandfather until his father in America sends for him. 244 pages (5–6 grade boys).

Miles, Betty. *Feast on Sullivan Street. See under* United States.

Japan

Bannon, Laura. *The Other Side of the World.* Boston: Houghton Mifflin, 1960. Tommy liked the stories about Jun, a Japanese boy on the other side of the world, and Jun liked to find out about Tommy's culture. 48 pages (2–3 grade).

Godden, Rumer. *Little Plum.* New York: Viking, 1962. Two girls living next door have a fight, and the Japanese dolls end up in the middle of it. 98 pages (4–5 grade girls).

Godden, Rumer. *Miss Happiness and Miss Flower.* New York: Viking. 1960. Nona, who comes to live with cousins in England, finds herself as she acquires two Japanese dolls and learns the customs to go with them. 73 pages (4–6 grade girls).

Hayes, Florence. *The Boy in the 49th Seat.* New York: Random House, 1963. Taro is lonesome in his new school until he is finally able to make some friends. 56 pages. (3–4 grade boys).

Hodges, Margaret. *The Wave.* Boston: Houghton Mifflin, 1964. An old Japanese grandfather saves his people from a tidal wave. Picture book (2–3 grade).

Slobodkin, Louis. *Yasu and the Strangers.* New York: Macmillan, 1965. Yasu in Japan went on a bus tour with his brother's school class and got lost with some American tourists. Picture book (2–3 grade).

Yashima, Taro. *Crow Boy.* New York: Viking, 1955. Chibi was afraid of people and stayed by himself, but finally a teacher understood him and helped him find friends. Picture book (3 grade).

Yashima, Matsu Taro. *Plenty to Watch.* New York: Viking, 1954. Tells of some of the different crafts and people who make them in Japan. 39 pages. Picture book (2–3 grade).

Yashima, Taro. *The Village Tree.* New York: Viking, 1953. The author tells of various games and fun things he did as a child in Japan. Picture book (2 grade).

Korea

Buck, Pearl S. *Matthew, Mark, Luke and John.* New York: John Day Company, 1966. The story of a little Korean boy whose father was an American and how he fathers three other children. 80 pages (3–4 grade boys).

Eisenberg, Philip. *Won Kim's Ox.* Chicago: Follett, 1956. The story of a young boy and his family in Korea who think their ox is bewitched. 160 pages (3–4 grade boys).

Mexico

Behn, Harry. *Two Uncles of Pablo.* New York: Harcourt Brace Jovanovich, 1959. Pablo has to choose between his uncle with no sense of value and no money and his uncle of great wealth with no pleasure in his life. 96 pages. (4–6 grade boys).

Phillips, Eula Mark. *Chucho.* Chicago: Follett, 1957. The story of two young Mexican boys who travel alone to a distant town. 141 pages (3–4 grade boys).

Politi, Leo. *Lito and the Clown.* New York: Scribner, 1964. Lito, who lived in Mexico, lost his kitten, and with the help of the clown on stilts, was finally able to get her back. Picture book (3 grade).

Schweizer, Byrd Baylor. *Amigo.* New York: Macmillan, 1963. Francisco wanted a dog for a pet, but they couldn't afford it, so he tamed a prairie dog named Amigo. Picture book (2–3 grade).

Self, Margaret Cabell. *The Shaggy Little Burro of San Miguel.* New York: Duell, Sloan & Pearce, 1965. The story of a shaggy donkey in Mexico who wanted to go to the city, but was afraid people would laugh at him. 46 pages (3–4 grade).

Newfoundland

Carlson, Natalie Savage. *Sailor's Choice.* New York: Harper & Row, 1966. The captain of a sea ship is not able to keep his dog in the community where he lives, so he moves his home. 136 pages (4–6 grade boys).

Pacific Islands

Lipkind, William. *Boy of the Islands.* New York: Harcourt Brace Jovanovich, 1945. The story of a fun-loving boy who realizes he is to be the next ruler of his people. 55 pages (3–4 grade boys).

O'Dell, Scott. *Island of the Blue Dolphin.* Boston: Houghton Mifflin, 1960. The story of a girl who spent 18 years alone on an island, surviving many problems, and then is finally rescued. 181 pages (5–6 grade girls).

Russia

Clark, Margery. *The Poppy Seed Cakes.* Garden City, N.Y.: Doubleday, 1924. Andrewshek, a little Russian boy, finds he is often in trouble. (2–3 grade).

Reyher, Becky. *My Mother Is the Most Beautiful Woman in the World.* New York: Lothrop, 1966. A Little Russian girl becomes lost and describes her mother as the most beautiful woman in the world. (3–6 grade).

Spain

Wojciechowska, Maia. *Shadow of a Bull.* New York: Atheneum, 1965. Manlo's father was a great bull fighter, and he is expected to be the same. 155 pages (3–5 grade boys).

Sweden

Beskow, Elsa. *Pelle's New Suit.* New York: Harper & Row, 1929. Picture book of a young Swedish boy who worked to get a new suit made from raw wool. (2–3 grade).

Unnerstad, Edith. *Little O.* New York: Macmillan, 1957. The story of a little Swedish girl. 150 pages (3–4 grade girls).

Switzerland

Buff, Mary Marsh, and Buff, Conrad. *Kobi.* Eau Claire, Wisconsin: E. M. Hale, 1939. Kobi, a Swiss boy, spends the summer in the Alps helping his uncle herd goats and cows. 128 pages (3–4 grade boys).

Spri, Johanna. *Heidi*. New York: Grosset & Dunlap, 1954. The story of a young girl who goes to live with her grandfather in the Swiss Alps. 321 pages (5–6 grade girls).

Ullman, James Ramsey. *Banner in the Sky*. Philadelphia: Lippincott, 1954. The story of a boy who was determined to climb the citadel even though his father had died in the attempt. (5–6 grade boys).

Tasmania

Chauncy, Nan. *Devils' Hill*. New York: Franklin Watts, 1958. Sam, who comes to visit in the bush country of Tasmania, learns to enjoy rural life. 153 pages (4–6 grade boys).

Thailand

Ayer, Jacqueline. *The Paper-Flower Tree*. New York: Harcourt Brace Jovanovich, 1962. Miss Moon was so pleased with a tree of paper flowers that she planted a bead from one flower and waited and waited for it to grow. Picture book (2–3 grade).

Tibet

Rankin, Louise. *Daughter of the Mountains*. New York: Viking, 1948. A Tibetan girl goes to Calcutta, India in search of her stolen dog. 191 pages (5–6 grade girls).

Ukrainia

Bloch, Marie Halun. *Aunt America*. New York: Atheneum, 1965. Lesya feels a resentment toward her father because he has trouble with the government, but when her aunt from America comes, she realizes he has a great deal of courage and is happier than those who do not. 149 pages (5–6 grade girls).

Wales

Fry, Rosalie. *The Echo Song*. New York: Dutton, 1962. The story of some children in Wales, who faithfully guard the nest of a rare bird. 159 pages (3–5 grade).

Cultures in the United States

Amish

Sorensen, Virginia. *Plain Girl*. New York: Harcourt Brace Jovanovich, 1955. The story of Esther, a young Amish girl who had to make the decision about what her life would be and whether or not she would follow traditions. 151 pages (4–5 grade girls).

Indian

Armer, Laura Adams. *Waterless Mountain*. New York: McKay, 1931. The story of a young Navajo boy who wants to be a medicine man. 212 pages (5–6 grade boys).

Bulla, Clyde Robert. *Eagle Feather*. New York: Thomas Y. Crowell, 1953. The story of a young Indian boy who wants to go to school. 87 pages (2–3 grade boys).

Clark, Ann Nolan. *Little Navajo Bluebird*. New York: Viking, 1943. The story of a little Navajo girl who learned that school and the ways of white people could be helpful. 143 pages (4–5 grade girls).

French

Lenski, Lois. *Bayou Suzette*. New York, Philadelphia: Frederick A. Stakes Co., 1943. A young girl in the French communities of Louisiana adopts a little Indian girl as her sister. 208 pages (5–6 grade girls).

Miles, Betty. *Feast on Sullivan Street*. New York: Knopf, 1963. Michael wanted very much to be a part of the New York Italian Festival, but his father thought he was too young to help. 48 pages (2–3 grade boys).

Book Series

Perkins, Lucy Fitch. Boston: Houghton Mifflin.

The Dutch Twins. Grade 1	*The Irish Twins*. Grade 5
The Eskimo Twins. Grade 2	*The Italian Twins*. Grade 5
The Dutch Twins. Grade 3	*The Mexican Twins*. Grade 5
The Chinese Twins. Grades 3–4	*The Scotch Twins*. Grade 5
The Japanese Twins. Grade 4	*The Scotch Twins*. Grade 6
The Swiss Twins. Grade 4	*The Spanish Twins*. Grades 6–7
The Norwegian Twins. Grades 4–5	*The Belgian Twins*. Grade 7
The Filipino Twins. Grade 5	*The French Twins*. Grade 7

The twins in this series are boy and girl. They have a variety of experiences.
Sasek, Miroslav. New York: Macmillan.

This Is Paris. 1959	*This Is Venice*. 1961
This Is London. 1959	*This Is Israel*. 1962
This Is Rome. 1960	*This Is Ireland*. 1964
This Is Edinburgh. 1961	*This Is Hong Kong*. 1965
This Is Munich. 1961	*This Is Greece*. 1966

Picture books for fourth- through sixth-grade level. About 60 pages.

BOOKS RELATED TO THE TEACHING OF BROTHERHOOD[1]

Younger Children

Beim, Lorraine, and Beim, Jerrold. *Two Is a Team*. Two little boys have fun together. Only the illustrations reveal that Paul is white and Ted is a Negro.

Bonsall, Crosby N. *The Case of the Hungry Stranger*. Four private detectives solve the case of the disappearance of a blueberry pie. (See other books by the same author.)

Fife, Dale. *Who's in Charge of Lincoln?* Nobody believes Lincoln's tall tales. An amusing story of a self-reliant Negro boy and his family.

Grifalconi, Ann. *City Rhythms*. Jimmy becomes aware of the fascinating sounds of the city. In a lyrical combination of text and pictures, the reader follows Jimmy.

Hall, Natalie. *The World in a City Block*. Nine-year old Nick discovers that the peoples of the world are his nearby neighbors.

Justus, May. *New Boy in School*. This story of a Negro boy in a public school, told without sentimentality or dramatics, reveals that integration really does work.

[1] This list was developed by the San Bernardino YWCA Public Affairs Committee. Particular credit is due to the *Books for Friendship* booklets published by the American Friends Service Committee and the B'nai B'rith Anti-Defamation League.

Keats, Ezra J. *The Snowy Day.* Quiet fun in deep snow creates a feeling of contentment. Pictures reveal the contrast between the snow's whiteness and the golden brownness of Peter's skin. (*Also Whistle for Willie,* and *My Dog Is Lost.*)

Lexau, Joan M. *Jose's Christmas Secret.* A Puerto Rican boy wants to get a job. (See other books by same author, especially *Benjie.*)

Martin, Patricia M. *Rice Bowl Pet.* The beauty of San Francisco is reflected in this story about a Chinese-American boy named Ah Jim.

Politi, Leo. *Juanita.* On Olvera Street, Los Angeles, the observance of Easter includes the blessing of the pets. (See other books by same author, especially *Pedro, The Angel of Olvera Street.*)

Randall, Blossom. *Fun for Chris.* Chris, a preschooler, makes friends with a new neighbor, a Negro boy named Toby. Mother explains about skin color.

Showers, Paul. *Look at Your Eyes.* Race makes no difference in this excellent introduction to a study of the eyes for young children.

Showers, Paul. *Your Skin and Mine.* An explanation of what skin is and what it does which reveals differences in skin color. Humorous and informative pictures.

The Middle Years

Baum, Betty. *Patricia Crosses Town.* When Pat, a fifth-grade girl, enrolls in an all-white school, she faces the frightening problems of integration in a Northern city.

Bontemps, Anna W. *Frederick Douglass.* Born a slave, he escapes and educates himself. As writer and speaker, he fights slavery's injustices. (See other books by same author.)

Bulla, Clyde R. *Indian Hill.* A Navajo Indian boy and his family's difficult problems of adjustment to life in a city.

Carlson, Natalie S. *The Empty Schoolhouse.* Readers will identify with the characters in a small Louisiana town.

Clark, Ann Nolan. *The Desert People.* Flowing prose and superb pictures tell this story of an Indian boy. (See other books by same author.)

Clayton, Ed. *Martin Luther King.* This "official children's biography" is sensitively written by a long-time associate.

de Angeli, Marguerite. *Bright April.* The reader identifies with April and her family—Negroes who live in Philadelphia. Interracial relationships as they affect children are sensitively treated.

Estes, Eleanor. *The Hundred Dresses.* A little Polish girl in an American school finally wins acceptance by her classmates.

Fitch, Florence Mary. *One God.* Catholic, Protestant, and Jewish beliefs and rites are presented accurately and reverently through text and pictures.

Gruenberg, Sidonie. *All Kinds of Courage.* Selected stories about boys and girls of yesterday and today.

Hunt, Mabel L. *Ladycake Farm.* A Negro family moves to a country community where they and their white neighbors learn the meaning of "interracial goodwill."

Lenski, Lois. *Judy's Journey.* Judy and her family are migrants who follow the crops. A vivid story.

Lerner, Marguerite R. *Red Man, White Man, African Chief.* A dermatologist gives scientific reasons for variation in the color of human skin.

Lewiton, Mina. *Faces Looking Up.* "The differences are many, but so are the 'alikenesses.' " Stories meant to bridge distances between us and children of faraway places. (See other books by same author.)

Shotwell, Louisa. *Roosevelt Grady.* A nine-year-old Negro boy and his family are seasonal farm laborers who long for and finally secure the benefits of a "stay-put-place." (Available in paperback.)

Taylor, Sidney. *All of a Kind Family.* Jewish family life on New York's Lower East Side during the early part of the 20th century. Jewish holiday customs are well described.

Older Boys and Girls

Bishop, Claire H. *Twenty and Ten.* Ten Jewish children find themselves in a desperate situation during the Hitler regime. A story of love and courage as a nun and 20 French Catholic children risk their lives to save them. (See other books by same author.)

Clark, Ann Nolan. *World Song.* In spite of the language barrier, an American and a Costa Rican boy come to an understanding through their mutual love of birds. (See other books by same author.)

Colman, Hila. *Classmates by Request.* Carla, who is white, becomes the friend of Ella, who is Negro. Both are daughters of civil rights leaders.

Graham, Lorenz. *North Town.* A southern Negro boy's adjustment to a northern school and city.

Graham, Lorenz. *South Town.*

Holt, Rackham. *Mary McLeod Bethune.* Life of a great woman dedicated to the education of her fellow Negroes.

Jackson, Jesse. *Charley Starts from Scratch.* A realistic story about a young Negro boy in today's America.

Marshall, Catherine. *Julie's Heritage.* A Negro teen-ager faces discrimination for the first time.

Neville, Emily C. *Berries Goodman.* A dynamic narrative of a city boy transplanted to a suburban community where a friendship with a Jewish boy is almost destroyed by adult prejudice.

Riwkin-Brick, Anna. *Eva Visits Noriko San.* A Swedish girl visits a Japanese girl. Lovely pictures.

Robinson, Jackie, and Duckett, Alfred. *Breakthrough to the Big League.* The athlete's experiences and the courage with which he met them are dramatically recounted.

Sterne, Emma G. *Mary McLeod Bethune.*

NDEX

72 73 74 75 76 9 8 7 6 5 4 3 2 1